The Litigious Society

THE
LITIGIOUS
SOCIETY

Jethro K. Lieberman

BASIC BOOKS, INC., PUBLISHERS

New York

TO

Sandor Frankel

Amico, Collegae, et meo Litigatori

Library of Congress Cataloging in Publication Data

Lieberman, Jethro Koller.
  The litigious society.

  Includes bibliographical references and index.
  1. Justice, Administration of—United States.
2. Damages—United States.   3.   Actions and
defenses—United States.   I.   Title.
KF380.L53   346.7303   80-68161
ISBN 0–465–04134–5 (cloth)   347.3063   AACR2
ISBN 0–465–04135–3 (paper)

Contents

Every wrong has a remedy.

—Ancient legal maxim

The courts, as perhaps the last institutions with authority intact, became the instruments for displacing blame, some real and some imagined, onto third parties. The staggering increase in malpractice suits, most notably against physicians but also against parents, individual teachers and school systems, was a major indication that people wanted somebody to pay when things did not work out evenly or fairly in their lives. Many social critics have noted with alarm the tendency to use the courts excessively, with judges now running prisons, hospitals and school systems; their decisions replace those of physicians in assaying diagnosis and treatment, they signal if the ball game may be played, if the strike can be held, if the child may receive a certain medical treatment. Then, hundreds of other issues became the courts' business as the nation lost faith in other forms of negotiation and gave the courts power they did not seek, without any guarantee that they could exercise it prudently or effectively over a long period of time. The 70's were the setting for bringing down on the nation the old Mexican curse, "May your life be filled with lawyers."

—Eugene Kennedy
"The Looming 80's,"
New York Times Magazine,
December 2, 1979

Foreword

OURS is a law-drenched age. Because we are constantly inventing new and better ways of bumping into one another, we seek an orderly means of dulling the blows and repairing the damage. Of all the known methods of redressing grievances and settling disputes—pitched battle, rioting, dueling, mediating, flipping a coin, suing—only the latter has steadily won the day in these United States. Though litigation has not routed all other forms of fight, it is gaining public favor as the legitimate and most effective means of seeking and winning one's just deserts. So widespread is the impulse to sue that "litigation has become the nation's secular religion,"* and a growing array of procedural rules and substantive provisions is daily gaining it adherents. These days one hears a crescendo of concern that America has become a litigious society, posing dangers to individuals and to the commonweal. That claim is the focus of the book.

This book is for the general reader. It is emphatically not a lawyer's treatise or a self-help manual. It is not an attempt to summarize discrete fields of law. It is, rather, an attempt to see whole a problem growing in the public consciousness. It is, also, inevitably a preliminary inquiry, for there is not yet a great deal known about litigiousness as a social phenomenon. Indeed, even so rudimentary a statistic as the total number of lawsuits filed in court each year is unknown.

Some people have long been concerned about the swelling of court dockets and the increasing burdens on judges and litigants. Though these are real problems, they are not central to the inquiry here. The chief concern of this book is neither the distress of judges nor technical problems in the arcane specialty of litigation but the underlying right of redress, its exercise, and its consequences.

---

* "The Chilling Impact of Litigation," *Business Week*, June 6, 1977, p. 58.

Introduction to the Paperback Edition

The author fortunate enough to see his book published in a paperback edition probably should forswear all temptation to add, amend, or justify. I subscribe to that oath—and will cheat only a little, just enough to present some new data, describe the first signs of a trend toward alternatives to litigation, and respond to a few criticisms made on first publication.

The Data

During the three years since the text was written, the rate of litigation has continued to climb. Civil suits filed in the federal district courts rose from 168,789 (for the year ending June 30, 1980) to 206,193 (for the year ending June 30, 1982), an increase of more than 22 percent. Nearly one-third of the increase stemmed from suits filed by the federal government to recover overpayments in federal programs (student loans, for example) and to enforce judgments. Few of the 206,789 cases went to trial—only 6.1 percent, in fact. Nearly 149,000 cases were terminated without any court action or before formal pretrial activity.

In the state courts, the picture is more complex. Data now available from the National Center for State Courts show that in 1976 (the last year for which complete figures have been computed) total cases filed in state trial courts ranged from 70 to 108 million. These staggering figures become explicable when divided by nature of suit: between 50 and 79 million of these cases were misdemeanor prosecutions for traffic offenses. In the major trial courts of the states (the courts of general jurisdiction) litigants filed about 11.7 million civil cases. In virtually every state, more than half the incoming civil cases are divorce actions or concern child custody or other family matters. Preliminary data from a study of 1981 state litigation rates indicate that in that year more than 82 million cases (civil and criminal) were filed in the courts of the fifty states and the District of Columbia—an increase of 22 percent over 1977 for civil suits and 31 percent for criminal prosecutions. The greatest increase occurred in Virginia, where the rate jumped 64 percent during the four-year period.*

How litigious does all that make us?

The American people obviously sue each other extensively, but the data continue to suggest that we do not litigate any more so than several other nations. Although the statisticians have headaches attempting to make the figures comparable, it looks as though (according to Professor Galanter's compilation of various studies) that we are *less* litigious per capita than Australia and Canada, and only a little bit more so than Denmark, England, New Zealand, and West Germany.

Alternatives to Litigation

Less than five pages of this book consider directly the possibility of alternatives to litigation (pp. 171–75), leading a reviewer writing in *The Washington Monthly* to dismiss the book because it failed to recognize mediation as the solution to what the *Washington Monthly*'s editors saw as a surfeit of suing. I think they are mistaken to believe that mediation will ever replace any sizable proportion of our litigation, but they may have been correct to imply that more should have been said about alternatives. Yet the time was not right in 1980—when the manuscript was finished—to say much more. The faint stirrings were not yet a movement (indeed, some of my cautiously optimistic statements were, as it turned out, too optimistic; for example, Congress never appropriated funds for the Neighborhood Justice Act, and it will soon expire without ever having been tried).

Nevertheless, in three years much has changed. *Alternative dispute resolution* (or ADR as it is familiarly termed within legal circles) has become a movement. The popular press has treated its various manifestations, from the growing use of mediators in divorce cases to the development of alternative mechanisms for resolving complex business disputes. Lawyers have been quick to recognize their vulnerability and have responded by incorporating much of the rhetoric of ADR, at least,

*Data for 1981 are not expected to be published before 1984; for the preliminary data, see Victor E. Flango and Mary E. Elsner, "The Latest State Court Caseload Data: An Advance Report," 7 *State Court Journal* 16 (Winter 1983). Additional data and interpretation of various court statistical studies can be found in the Final Report of the Council on the Role of Courts, to be published in 1984, and in Marc Galanter, "Reading the Landscape of Disputes: What We Know and Don't Know (and Think We Know) About Our Allegedly Contentious and Litigious Society," Working Paper 1983-1 of the Disputes Processing Research Program of the University of Wisconsin Law School.

in their practice. By late 1982 at least one major law firm, Jenner & Block in Chicago, had established a "dispute resolution department" distinct from its litigating department. Prodded by a rising number of sophisticated and fiercely professional corporate general counsel, other lawyers will probably begin to offer similar services. It seems safe to predict that by the end of 1984, most major bar associations will have created ADR committees. At a conference sponsored by the Association of American Law Schools held at Harvard Law School in October 1982, teachers from more than 100 law schools across the country gathered to share information about new courses in dispute resolution. By the time Harvard University President Derek Bok (himself a one-time dean of Harvard Law School) issued his blast at the legal profession and the law schools in his widely-circulated report to the Harvard Board of Overseers in April 1983, a reexamination of the profession had already been launched at many institutions. How fundamental or long-lasting potential reform might be remains, however, an open question. Still, some of the impetus for resolving disputes through more pacific and less costly means than litigation will doubtless stay implanted in the legal system.*

The Criticism

In some ways, the hardcover edition of *The Litigious Society* had a curious reception. On the whole, lawyers welcomed it because it seemed to defend them against the common accusation that they are beneficiaries of a hopelessly corrupt system. Others, mostly non-lawyer reviewers, applauded because it seemed to them to warn litigious lawyers to watch out lest a wrathful society move to curb their adversary instincts. A few lawyers also took this line, one even arguing (contrary to the *Washington Monthly*) that the book advocates resolving all disputes outside the courtroom.

A few criticisms were more telling. Yale Law School Professor Joseph W. Bishop, Jr., took me to task for declaring that "the common law itself developed through the antics of the tiny class of aristocrats" (p. 13). Writing in *The American Spectator* (September 1981, p. 32), he cites a

---

*A volume of papers presented at the National Conference on the Lawyer's Changing Role in America, held at Harvard Law School in October 1983, summarizes much of the thinking to date; it is due to be published in late 1983 or early 1984, and will contain the Galanter paper cited previously.

series of cases going back to the seventeenth century that laid down
basic principles of common law in which the protagonists were chim-
ney sweeps, trainbands armed with loaded muskets, and topers who
were brawling in a tavern. I am happy to set the record straight.

Nathan Glazer, writing in the *Wall Street Journal* (October 1, 1981, p.
26), and Herman Belz in *Commentary* (November 1981, p. 106) object
to how the book deals with the question of judicial legitimacy. They
both argue that I defend "government by judiciary," the willingness of
courts to entertain suits against prisons, mental hospitals, and schools
(chapter 5), and am "much too complacent in accepting the costs of
litigation." Whether I rightly make the defense or am too complacent
is for the reader to judge, but these criticisms seem to me to miss the
mark. The fundamental purpose of this book is to describe why and how
we have become a litigious society, to underscore what is too easily and
too frequently ignored—that the reasons are complex, that simple pronouncements pro and con do not help, and that the "cures" that follow
from these pronouncements will not work.

Belz asserts that I see "no alternative to judicial rule." This is an
overstatement, on several grounds. Though they have important things
to say about our law, and though they often make policy, judges are
scarcely our "rulers" in the sense that seems to be intended. Most
important court rulings are reactions to legislative or executive actions
that cry out for clarification, not policy initiatives that they have come
to on their own. Although my personal preferences are irrelevant, I
state for the record that I would be delighted to discover legislatures
writing clearer laws and giving sharper directions to administrative
agencies. I just don't think they can or will. Finally, complaints that
courts are running America are vastly inflated. Citing, among others,
the thousands of federal suits by prisoners—29,303 in 1982—but ignoring the summary dismissal of most of them, Glazer says "there is reason
to doubt . . . whether our institutions will be able to function with any
creativity or vitality in a 'fiduciary society' of 'total redress' for all
harms." I agree. But the book makes no such claim. The difficulty is how
to construct a principled rationale for limiting litigation, as long as that
is the only means we have of determining whether redressable wrongs
have been committed.

I believe there is a way, but it entails a sea change of consciousness:
it requires that we refuse to provide redress for some acknowledged
injuries. Why we should do this and how we could do it I must leave
for another book.

The Litigious Society

Chapter 1

Right of Redress: Toward a Fiduciary Ethic

The Impulse to Sue

IN one form or another, litigation is as old as civilization. It was known in ancient Rome and decried in much the same terms one hears directed toward our own times.

From the reign of one emperor to another, litigation was a rising tide which nothing could stem, throwing on the public courts more work than men could muster. To mitigate the congestion of the courts Augustus, as early as the year 2 B.C., was obliged to resign to their use the forum he had built and which bears his name. Seventy-five years later congestion had recurred and Vespasian wondered how to struggle with the flood of suits so numerous that "the life of the advocates could scarce suffice" to deal with them.[1]

Those days may be at hand again. Not so long ago it was necessary to have strong proof that the defendant directly injured the plaintiff in a palpably physical or financial way. Injuries to class, race, or feelings were not redressable in court. Citizens were then dependent solely on political action, economic boycott, or moral suasion to achieve most reforms. Or they could suffer in silence. The opening to the courts was through a narrow door. Today, however, people have gained the means individually to seek redress for an increasingly wide category of complaints. Judicial decrees have changed the face of the social order, and Americans seemingly take to the courtroom at the merest whisper of an insult.

By anyone's measure, the range of controversies brought to court is astonishing. Consider:

• In 1976 the Italian Historical Society of America asked a federal court to
prohibit the United States Postal Service from issuing a stamp commemorat-
ing Alexander Graham Bell on the ground that one Antonio Meucci invented
the telephone.[2]

• In 1978 a twenty-four-year-old Boulder, Colorado, man sued his parents
for $350,000, alleging that in neglecting his needs for food, shelter, clothing,
and psychological support, they were guilty of "malpractice of parenting."[3]

• A New Jersey woman sued her doctors in 1975 for "wrongful birth"
when her child was born a mongoloid. She sought monetary damages on the
ground that the physicians negligently failed to advise her of a medical procedure that might have given her advance warning and thus a chance to abort
the fetus.[4]

• Enraged at the decision of referees in a St. Louis Cardinals-Washington
Redskins football game that a Cardinal receiver held a pass long enough in
the end zone before dropping it to score the winning touchdown, a group of
Redskin fans went to federal court to try to have the disputed call
overturned.[5]

• In the early 1970s General Motors was hit with a class action on behalf
of "all persons everywhere now alive and all future unborn generations" seeking $6 trillion in damages for alleged pollution.[6]

• A man confined to a wheelchair sued the New York City Road Runners
Club for discrimination when it refused to permit him to participate in the
1977 New York City Marathon.[7]

• When she was dismissed from the law school of Gonzaga University for
failure to maintain the requisite gradepoint average, a Washington State
woman sued the school demanding either a law degree or $110,000. She ar-
gued that given her college grades and law board scores, the school authorities
should have told her at matriculation that she had only a slim chance of
graduating.[8]

• The International Association of Machinists and Aerospace Workers
sued the Organization of Petroleum Exporting Countries (OPEC) for treble
damages totalling more than $1 billion, charging that OPEC's decision to hike
oil prices on the world market was a violation of United States antitrust law.
Among other things, the union wanted the court to tell the United States government what to do to reduce American dependence on foreign oil.[9]

• Though he could show no physical injury, a man who had worked for
thirty years at the Los Alamos Scientific Laboratory sued for occupational disability benefits on the ground that he had become mentally disabled "by a
neurotic fear that radiation would kill him."[10]

- A Bristol, Connecticut, high school girl sued her gym teacher and the city after she broke a finger trying to catch a pop fly in a school softball game. She alleged that her teacher not only failed to instruct her in the art of catching but also failed to warn her of the inherent dangers in playing the outfield.[11]

- Senator Barry Goldwater sued President Carter in 1979 over his handling of American policy toward Taiwan. Goldwater sought a judicial declaration that the President could not lawfully terminate our recognition of the Republic of China without congressional assent.[12]

The plaintiffs lost most of these cases; some were blatantly frivolous. But that is not the salient point. Most—perhaps all—would have been impossible to conceive only a quarter century ago or less, and many worked their way through the court system before being dismissed. Taken together, critics charge, these lawsuits and the millions of others that are filed every year in the 17,000 courthouses that dot the landscape amount to a "legal explosion," a "society bent on waging total law," a litigious storm of hurricane proportions.[13]

By 1980 lawsuits were being filed in the fifty state court systems and the local courts of the District of Columbia and Puerto Rico at the rate of 5 million a year. And according to the National Center for State Courts in Williamsburg, Virginia, the number could be as high as 12 million a year.[14] Federal courts, a much smaller, though far more noticeable, judicial operation, were receiving nearly 170,000 suits annually.° According to one widely quoted estimate, if the rate of lawsuits filed in federal courts alone during the decade 1965–75 continues to increase as it has, by early in the next century federal *appellate* courts will hear more than 1 million cases annually—and the appellate branch typically gets only a tiny fraction of the cases decided by the trial courts each year. During this same period, the number of lawsuits brought to these courts has increased by 84 percent, and though statistics of state dockets are not nationally maintained, the experience in individual states that do keep statistics suggests a similar rise (for example, California's judicial dockets, in courts of general jurisdiction, had swelled by 90 percent from 1968 to 1976).[15]

These figures should be put in perspective. According to University of

°From July 1, 1979, to June 30, 1980, a total of 168,789 civil suits were filed in the federal district (trial) courts. Of these, the United States government filed 39,810. This was a 28 percent increase over the 1979 total. Included in this figure were 2,138 tax suits, 3,029 real estate foreclosure cases, 4,433 land condemnation suits, and 15, 423 suits for the recovery of overpayments and enforcement of judgments (this last up from 1,856 in 1978; most of the increase is accounted for by suits to recover defaulted student loans). Additionally, there were some 49,000 contract suits, 22,000 personal injury suits, 9,000 Social Security cases, 23,000 prisoner petitions, and 13,000 civil rights cases. There were also 7,755 product liability cases (up from 6,132 in 1979); many of these cases are included in the personal injury figure. In 1980, 1,568 class actions were filed (representing 0.9 percent of total filings); this was a drop of 24.8 percent over 1979. (1980 Annual Report of the Director, Administrative Office of the United States Courts, table 18, p. 60; table 19, p. 61; table 23, p. 64; p. 72, table C2, pp. A16–17.)

Southern California Law School Professor Earl W. Johnson, one of the few to collect and analyze statistics on civil litigation, the United States is "roughly comparable" in litigiousness to England, based on the rate of civil filings per capita. By this measure, however, the United States is 25 percent more litigious than West Germany, and some 30 to 40 percent more so than Sweden. "We may be the most litigious society," he says, "but if so our rate is only marginally higher. In some years, England is higher."[16]

Moreover, until comprehensive statistics are developed, the sense of litigiousness can only be measured subjectively. Professor Johnson reports that the traveler to England, West Germany, and Sweden hears the same bemoaning of the litigious impulse that is heard in the United States. At least for this country, the anguish is somewhat mysterious, since the rate of civil filings to the population remained nearly constant from 1960 to at least the mid-1970s. The lament can be explained, however, by the relatively dramatic swelling of federal court dockets. The tide of federal cases has been out of all proportion to any growth in population and reflects the outpouring of congressional enactments from the mid-1960s on that reach to the roots of private activity. Because it keeps better statistics, because it is national in scope, and because it has far more prestige than the state courts, the federal system generates media attention. When he speaks about a "court crisis," Chief Justice of the United States Warren E. Burger, who can command better press coverage than anyone else concerned with judicial matters, is taken as the spokesman for all courts, though he speaks with authority only of the federal courts. We are also more aware of litigiousness because the voice of litigants is louder: Corporate and other institutional defendants hauled into federal courts can make more noise, and public interest lawyers often file cases precisely in order to catch headlines,[17] focus public attention, and stir things up. Much of the concern thus expressed comes from a new class of losers.

But these figures and brief observations do not tell the whole story. Over the years, as anyone even mildly alert to the headlines knows, the courts have altered American society by their rulings in racial discrimination, legislative reapportionment, and abortion cases, and, equally important, in suits in dozens of other policy areas. At the private law level, recent years have seen a vast profusion of specialized areas of litigation, revealed in the titles of lawyers' newsletters and related services that have sprung up like ice cream vendors on a hot day: for example, weeklies devoted to reporting court decisions in the areas of family law, media law, occupational safety and health, housing and community development programs, federal contracts, product safety, environmental law, and fair employment practices.

The impulse to sue is commonly attributed to greed. According to the well-worn joke, the surest road to fortune is to be hit from behind by a wealthy driver. But if greed is the only cause then we are unlikely to find a "cure" for a locustlike plague of lawsuits. Mankind's rich historical experience with greed must make even the most avid social reformer quail at the assignment to eliminate it or even materially to reduce it.

The litigious impulse lies deeper than greed. A lawsuit is a signal that something has gone wrong. It may be a little thing—like the refusal of a person to abide by a promise. Or it may be a major failure: the impotence of political institutions, the disequilibrium of an economy, the decay of social organizations, the collapse of corporate competence, the decline of communal feeling.

From this perspective, litigiousness may be viewed not only as a signal of failure but also as a clarion of social health. For the willingness to go to court is a sign that we are not going to the streets—the court of last resort.

Assessing litigiousness, therefore, is an undertaking of profound difficulty fraught with ambivalence. Characteristically, many Americans think we ought to "do something about it." But unlike crime or foul weather, litigiousness is something that cannot even be sensibly deplored in the abstract. Nor is our ambivalence akin to the beloved tradition in the American political economy of condemning governmental subsidies as illegitimate when the beneficiary is the other fellow and welcoming them as essential to national security when we are the ones who benefit. Our uncertainty stems, rather, from our inability to define excessiveness. In a diet-conscious nation, no one claims that food is evil, only that there is too much of it. An excess of food can be measured by obesity. Not so with an excess of litigiousness.

Here a simple tale is instructive. It concerns a twelve-year-old Alexandria, Virginia, boy who lent his bicycle to a teacher. The bicycle was returned with a flat tire, and the teacher refused to pay the $14 repair bill, though he did refund $5 under pressure from his headmaster. Being $9 out of pocket, the boy sued the teacher in small claims court for $16 ($9 in damages, $1 in interest, and $6 in court costs). The teacher hired a lawyer, who persuaded his client to pay in full.

What can we make of this case? Should we worry that suing will become a major preoccupation of preteenagers? That, evidently, was the concern of the teacher's lawyer, Charles Geschickter of Alexandria, who commented afterward: "I hope the boy hasn't learned that the way to get action is to file a complaint. There are too many litigious people already." But that is not the only reading of the case. Geschickter himself was the first to admit that the suit was filed because "the teacher didn't think the boy was serious."[18] This puts the case in a different light. That a sixth-grade teacher would pay a just debt only when convinced that a former student would go to court is an indictment not of litigiousness but of moral standards that force ordinary citizens to take their claims to court. Thus our ambivalence toward litigation: if it is an evil, it is indubitably a necessary one.

The Critique of Litigiousness

The statistics and the continuing encroachment of the legal model seem to signify popular approval of litigation. But this view is not unanimous. Some critics, numbering among them many leading citizens, have sharply and bitterly attacked the manifestations of our litigiousness. Thus the Chief Justice of the United States has declared that "we may well be on our way to a society overrun by hordes of lawyers, hungry as locusts, and brigades of judges in numbers never before contemplated."[19] These are not the simple musings of a judge who would prefer a less crowded docket (though they are also that). Others with no, or at least different, axes to grind have come to similar conclusions. Laurence H. Silberman, former deputy attorney general of the United States, concurs. "The legal process, because of its unbridled growth, has become a cancer which threatens the vitality of our forms of capitalism and democracy."[20] In a 1977 address entitled "Litigation-Prone Society," William J. McGill, then president of Columbia University, and a director of three major business corporations, complained that by virtue of his various positions he was a defendant in thirty-five different lawsuits, and he bemoaned "the adversary morass into which we have drifted."[21] And that melancholy genius Alexander Solzhenitsyn declared in an admonitory address at the 1978 Harvard Commencement, "The defense of individual rights has reached such extremes as to make society as a whole defenseless against certain individuals."[22]

Solzhenitsyn's remarks can be understood as coming from one disaffected by most of what passes for modernity. The conclusions of the others, partisans of democratic capitalism, may appear unjustified and disingenuous. The spirit of political liberty and the notion that the economic freedom to compete will culminate in social good necessarily implies what Lionel Trilling calls an "adversary culture." But it is not inherently inconsistent to decry an excess of something while accepting, or even welcoming, the thing itself. And that is what the critics of our growing litigiousness may be interpreted as saying, though the point is often lost in the articulation. They are challenging the optimistic belief that it is legitimate for the courts to be so grandly involved in every aspect of our public life.

To reject excessive litigation is, however, no guide to policy or reform. How much is excessive? Which claims ought to be rejected? Those of disadvantaged children, minorities, women? Who ought to be thrown out of court? Those discriminated against because of race, religion, or national origin? Those injured in automobile accidents or by a defective chain saw or by a purportedly unnecessary hysterectomy? Prisoners abused beyond endurance? Those made ill by drugs with adverse side effects or by chemicals pumped into the air and water? The list is endless. And the idea is delusive that litigation can be choked off in the abstract. Some method is required to sort out the good claims from the spurious—and that method is litigation itself. No King Canute can stem the tide of litigation by decreeing an end to the unwanted portion of it.

However, the criticism of litigiousness is not merely that the courts are flooded with spurious lawsuits, delaying the meritorious ones and damaging those who are wrongly sued. The complaint against the floodtide of lawsuits is also, and far more importantly, that the courts, to the public detriment, are actually siding with new kinds of plaintiffs and, in some cases, with lawyers suing on their own. In Nathan Glazer's phrase, the courts are becoming an "imperial judiciary,"[23] usurping the role of elected government.

But that proposition cannot be tested without essaying something more than the quantity of lawsuits filed and their effect on the courts. For litigation is a process, a means toward an end, and no assessment of the place of litigiousness in modern life would ultimately be meaningful unless we consider the object sought. Plaintiffs sue to redress their injuries, not to burden judges with pieces of paper or to enrich their lawyers (though lawyers may find clients for that purpose). Judges decide cases to achieve results, not in the expectation of earning a profit. We cannot evaluate litigiousness outside the context of rights claimed, adjudicated, and enforced. To attempt to do so would be like pronouncing the act of sweating an evil to be somehow eliminated because it is unaesthetic.

This may seem, at the outset, an uncomfortable conclusion or at least an unhappy complication. It would be relatively easy to tot up the number of lawsuits filed in court each year, show how the paper multiplies and how the judges are burdened, and prescribe practical solutions to the perceived problem. It is much more difficult to evaluate someone's grievances and to mesh his complaints and claims against those of competing millions. The trouble with the statistical approach is that it may lead us to perceive at best only the fringes of the real issue—namely, the quality of our lives and the power of our institutions to enhance or erode it. People sue because they are unhappy, and we must inquire whether they have reason to be unhappy as well as whether the means they seek to alleviate their sadness will be fruitful or cause larger unhappiness in turn.

Emergence of the Right of Redress

Redress is a fundamental concern of human beings. But its present form is a late development. We owe the modern concept of redress to a historic but un-completed transformation: the fitful substitution of human systems for natu-ral systems in the daily life of our species.

Conflicts in nature are "resolved" by force—terror, mayhem, death, ex-tinction. What matters it that one or a few or even many die, if the species lasts? And what difference does it make that even the species dies if some bet-ter, more well-endowed species conquers the ground?

It is not surprising that early man, first coming to self-knowledge, equated society itself with heartless nature. When people devoted their time to activi-ties closely related to animal survival, only the most obvious—and prevent-able—injuries would be recognized as coming from the hands of their fellows. By far the larger share of harms was naturally caused—storms, fires, disease, famine—for which remedies were excruciatingly difficult to find. Survival depended on a social system that knit the community together. The commu-nity, not the individual, was all. As Lewis Mumford puts it:

Wherever we find archaic man, we find no lawless creature, free to do what he pleases, when he pleases, how he pleases: we find rather one who at every moment of his life must walk warily and circumspectly, guided by the customs of his own kind, doing reverence to superhuman powers, be they the creator Gods of all being, the ghosts and demons associated with his remembered ancestors, or the sacred beasts, plants, insects, or stones of his totem.[24]

Tradition, not considerations of fairness or individual equity, was the con-trolling principle. It made no more sense to inquire whether a rule of the community was just than to inquire whether gravitation is moral. Social in-equality was simply a rule of nature, like storms and wild beasts that kill. In-deed, many things that cry out to us today as grievous wrongs, such as blood feuds and serfdom, were essential to the community fabric.

The use of law to create and channel social policy, as we today conceive the process, would not merely have been foolish in traditional society; it was unthinkable. Traditional society worked because people adhered to the past. Custom governed. It could change, but not by the conscious hand of man.

Of course, there came a time when people began to understand that they, not some force apart from them, were the agents of society and history. Custom, society, community, it came to be seen, are human constructs.

This understanding was one of the great revolutions in history. Like the evolution of the custom it replaced, the idea that man is responsible for himself and the society in which he lives came slowly. In many ways the revolution is still ongoing: We do not all believe it yet. But in Europe the notion has been about for at least half a millennium.

The democratic understanding, the idea that the people themselves can direct their own affairs, was much slower to emerge. Down into the mid-nineteenth century, economists were one with David Ricardo that the laws of economics prohibited attempts at ameliorating the suffering of the poor (as the laws of physics prevented the moon from crashing into the earth). In this attitude, economists were merely exhibiting that peculiar intellectual lethargy they shared with most members of the bar—common law lawyers who believed that law was found, not made; that the decisions of judges, like those of Jimmy Carter, were guided by a "brooding omnipresence in the sky."[25]

But Ricardo's was the last-ditch stand of the timorous. A century earlier the stirrings of Enlightenment belief had gathered force. Unlike in the weather, the time and effort invested in complaining about social institutions came to be viewed as worthwhile. Nor was it historical accident that the idea of the mutability of society was bruited about in those days. For the nascent industrial society exploded forever the power of traditional society to mediate change and regulate itself. Too much happened too fast for the process of custom to adapt human behavior and belief to the necessities of the age.

The problem was twofold: Scientific and technological developments created circumstances for which traditionalism was helpful to neither the agents of change nor those whom change injured. On the one hand, change in customary societies is measured in generations; the process of unconscious adaptation to small changes could no longer suffice to protect the mass of individuals uprooted from and shorn of their traditional place in the community. A society that could release people from the dark side of traditionalism, from the suffocating group order in which most of humanity had always lived, needed, at the same time, recourse to some institution that would function in place of the bright side of traditionalism, the security that in theory the social classes owed and often in practice they paid each other. Individuals truly alone in the world were no better off than those smothered in traditional conformity. But custom as man's means of brokering change was not only too slow in providing remedies for those injured by the destructive engine of industrialism. It was also too parsimonious to allow much play to the creative capacity of that same industrialism. Custom enslaved both servants and masters. It was time for law.

Not surprisingly, the masters were the first to found the law. "Finding" law was a literal claim, because monopolizing the legal process in order to direct social change could be justified only if the law was assimilated into the custom it replaced. Although for hundreds of years the common law (we are speaking here of the British tradition, though in general terms the concept does not vary elsewhere) was based on custom, it was always assumed to be plucked by judges from some juristic ether. Judges did not make law, according to the accepted canon of belief: They articulated God's natural law.

But for those who cared to listen, Jeremy Bentham had exploded the myth of judge-found law, beginning with his *Fragment on Government, A Criticism of Blackstone,* published in that annus mirabile, 1776. Law, he showed, was not some impersonal, preexisting architectural edifice of human ethics, but a means by which people could direct their lives. Too rashly Bentham wrote that the common law should be chucked into historical oblivion because men had not consciously participated in its making; too brashly he took on the impossible project of codifying all law. But his message was unmistakable and convincing: Law was a human enterprise to be made by and used for the people. Therefore, the law was available not merely to masters, who can direct the law to oppress, but also to the oppressed, who can shape it through a democratic political system to prevent and redress their injuries.

The industrial and philosophical revolutions had a far-reaching, though not immediately realized, consequence. In a world in which nature dominates, effective redress for injury through a legal system cannot, even theoretically, be more than halting. Though superstitious people have tried, there is no meaningful sense in which one can "sue" nature. Only people are subject to judicial writs. Industrial society promoted the interdependence that would put more and more people at the receiving end of the legal summons.

To conquer the natural world and direct it to his advantage, to reduce natural harms, man has learned to substitute himself, through social institutions, for nature. Today large numbers of people in the industrial nations devote little time to mere survival. Now, not nature but social institutions that manage immensely powerful technologies are dominant. The specialization that allows us as a species to accomplish more and more permits us to do less and less for ourselves individually and thereby draws us closer together. Time, knowledge, and other resources are limited. We desire things we cannot do for ourselves, so we turn to others to provide them.

But even as these institutions shield us from the vagaries of the elements, they subject us to harms that arise out of their own operations. If I as an individual can my own food and contract botulism, I have only myself to fault. But when contaminated food comes to me through a technological and human chain then there are others against whom I can assess blame for my illness and seek remedy. As human systems spread and interdependence grows, our present predicament is clearly foreshadowed. Things that happen *to* people are seen to be caused *by* people. It is a rare person in distress who cannot trace his suffering back, no matter how indirectly, to some human agency.

The Great Revolution of a Contentious People

These abstractions took on concrete reality in a nation peculiarly suited to redress through litigation. To express amazement at American litigiousness is akin to professing astonishment at learning that the roots of most Americans lie in other lands. We have been a litigious nation as we have been an immigrant one. Indeed, the two are related.

If law is, in some sense, a substitute for bonds of community, it was a substitute whose necessity would be especially apparent in a land that provided refuge to scores of dissident groups who only wanted to live according to their own customs but found themselves drawn almost willy-nilly into a larger political community. And if the yearning for religious freedom was the wellspring, those who came three thousand miles across the ocean felt a dedication to freedom in a general sense as well. Unlike those they left behind in Europe, the daring colonists possessed a hardy notion that there was great virtue in beginning a new life. This pioneering spirit would suffuse a common law tradition that, by the time of the Revolution, dominated the colonial legal system. The authority of England may have been overthrown, but the "rights of Englishmen" held their appeal.[26]

Moreover, in a democratic country these rights were democratized. The common law itself had developed largely through the antics of the tiny class of aristocrats. As one of our leading legal historians has suggested:

Leaf through the pages of Lord Coke's reports, compiled in the late 16th and early 17th century; here one will find a colorful set of litigants, all drawn from the very top of British society—lords and ladies, landed gentry, high-ranking clergymen, wealthy merchants. Common law was an aristocratic law, for and of the gentry and nobility. The masses were hardly touched by this system and only indirectly under its rule.[27]

In America where there was no aristocracy, the common law could be made to serve all.

Whether well or ill is another question. Listen to Timothy Dwight, president of Yale, talking candidly to the 1776 graduating seniors about law practice:

That meanness, that infernal knavery, which multiplies endless litigations, which retards the operations of justice, which from court to court, upon the most trifling pretences, postpones trial to glean the last emptyings of a client's pocket, for unjust fees of everlasting attendance, which artfully twists the meaning of law to the side we espouse, which seized unwarrantable advantages from the prepossessions, ignorance, interests and prejudices of a jury, you will shun rather than death or infamy.[28]

This piece of moral advice came just three weeks after a distinguished group of rebels, half of whom were lawyers, had signed the Declaration of Independence. After the Revolution the popular feeling for lawyers did not improve. Older and eminent members of the bar had remained royalists and fled, leaving the practice of law "very largely in the hands of lawyers of a lower grade and inferior ability." To them fell the responsibility—or opportunity—to guide a disrupted society out of its legal confusion. High taxes, inflation, and public debts led to an escalation of litigation. "The chief law business," wrote Charles Warren, chronicler of the colonial and postrevolutionary bar, "was the collection of debts and the enforcement of contracts; and the jails were filled to overflowing with men imprisoned for debt under the rigorous laws of the times."[29] In Worcester, Massachusetts, then a rural county with a population fewer than five thousand, more than two thousand separate lawsuits were on the docket of the court of common pleas.

The people were literally in arms over what they perceived as excess litigiousness. Shays and his followers directed their rebellion largely at the courts and the lawyers who contributed to the crowded dockets. The people of Dedham told their state representative that if some way could not be found to temper the actions of attorneys, "you are to endeavor that the order of Lawyers be totally abolished; an alternative preferable to their continuing in their present mode."[30] Nor were cries that the legal profession be abolished isolated to Massachusetts. Courthouses were burned in Vermont, nailed shut in New Jersey. In Pennsylvania, "our state rulers threaten to lop away that excrescence on civilization, the Bar; and Counsellor Ingersoll declares he'll go to New York. All the eminent lawyers have their eyes on one city or another, to remove to in case of extremes."[31] Summing up in the year the Constitution was written, H. St. John Crevecoeur in his *Letters of an American Farmer* declared:

Lawyers are plants that will grow in any soil that is cultivated by the hands of others, and when once they have taken root they will extinguish every vegetable that grows around them. . . . The most ignorant, the most bungling member of that profession will, if placed in the most obscure part of the country, promote litigiousness and amass more wealth than the most opulent farmer with all his toil. . . . The value of our laws and the spirit of freedom which often tends to make us litigious must necessarily throw the greatest part of the property of the Colonies into the hands of these gentle-men. In another century, the law will possess in the North what now the church pos-sesses in Peru and Mexico.[32]

By the standards of that time, our rhetoric against litigiousness is tepid and flat.

But even Crevecoeur recognized that the fault lay as much in the people themselves as in the members of the bar. Different ways of handling disputes are imaginable, but "a middle-class public, cherishing the ideals of competi-tion, utilitarianism, and self-advancement, found itself unwilling to forgo the advantages of an individualistic legal system in favor of some more equitable communitarian experiment."[33]

There could hardly have been another choice. The United States was not founded on revelation or ancient custom or noble conquest. It was founded on law and on a legal system that centered on litigation. The Revolution itself was cast in terms of law: a Declaration of Independence that made a legal, as well as a moral, case for separation. The words of the Constitution—and espe-cially of the Bill of Rights—were not intended as empty flourishes; double-speak was not an American invention. Alexis de Tocqueville's classic observa-tion, penned in 1835, that "there is hardly a political question in the United States which does not sooner or later turn into a judicial one,"[34] was not a pre-diction but a reflection of fact. Already at that comparatively primitive time in our history, the Supreme Court had been in the thick of the most intensely political questions, and how and why is easy to understand. From at least 1801, when an obscure lawyer named William Marbury had the audacity to file a lawsuit against Secretary of State James Madison to win a judgeship Marbury thought he had been unlawfully denied, the people have supposed they are governed by law, not by whim.[35]

Americans take literally the language in their organic charters and statute books. What good is a right that cannot be enforced or pleaded in court? If a right is observed there is no need to turn to judges; but if it is disregarded, to whom else ought one turn? "In the midst of the Civil War," Henry Steele Commager has noted,

the right of the president to resist disunion and treason was submitted to the judiciary and sustained by only five votes to four; in the midst of one depression, the right to impose income taxes—a right enjoyed by every other sovereign nation—was denied, and in the midst of another, authority to fix minimum wages, to bring order out of the chaos of the coal industry, and to establish a system of social security, all hinged on the outcome of a private suit.[36]

Any major change in governmental policy has produced its test case, the term itself an old one in American history. In 1933, after the dollar was devalued, Congress outlawed "gold clauses" in private contracts, under which payments were to be made in gold. The effect of such repayments would have been disastrous. A railroad bondholder claiming coupon interest of $38.10 due at the prevailing gold rate sued to have the act declared unconstitutional when the railroad offered only the face amount of $22.50. Two other bondholders made similar claims against the United States Treasury. "Thus in the guise of private lawsuits involving a few dollars, the whole American economy was haled before the Supreme Court."[37] The Court sustained the law on that occasion, but in the same year, the Court rejected the entire rationale of the National Industrial Recovery Act and killed the Blue Eagle because a small-time poultry dealer in Brooklyn, the funding of whose lawsuit remains obscure, complained.[38] Even those who might be thought most averse to seeking aid from the secular courts, those who have attempted to drop out of society altogether, became, if not quite habitues, at least regular visitors to the courthouse: during the nineteenth century such religious communities as the Shakers, the Harmony Society, Oneida, and Zoar were frequently squabbling with disgruntled communitarians over the division of property.[39] Commager, for one, does not like this penchant for staking so much on ostensibly so little ("nowhere else except in Alice's Wonderland could a comparable situation be found"[40]). Suffice it to say that the current litigiousness springs from a rich tradition.

Nor should there be any puzzlement that such is the case. In a market society it is inescapable that most lawsuits, brought for intensely private ends, will have public ramifications. Indeed, it is not too much to say, as the modern legal histories written during the 1970s show, that capitalism itself was brought to legal life through a succession of judicial decisions, prompted by private lawsuits, that overthrew an agrarian legal order hostile to economic development.

During the period of this development, the "underlying conviction held by all orthodox nineteenth-century legal thinkers [was] that the course of American legal change should, if possible, be developed by courts and not legislators."[41] The struggle for legislative supremacy lasted nearly half a century. But even before the legislatures triumphed in the late 1930s, in economic policy at least, the range of cases that could be brought to court was still relatively narrow. Matters of great historical moment could be thrust before judges with the proper constitutional incantation, but not every suitor was a proper litigant and not every constitutional incantation was warmly regarded by the judges. It has only been since World War II, in fact, that the courts have begun to open their doors to all. The great revolution of the contentious American people has been the democratizing and deprofessionalizing of the judicial avenue of redress.

For most of its history, the law was ringed with impediments that kept large classes of people from the courts and hence from any hope of redress. Defects in the language of pleading, for example, could lead to a suit's permanent dismissal. Charles Rembar in his curmudgeonly popular history of the law recounts the reminiscence of a nineteenth-century lawyer who

came near losing a case on a Policy of Insurance by declaring in Assumpsit [the name for a type of suit to recover damages for the failure to perform an oral or other simple contract].

When the Policy was produced at Trial, the defendant's counsel insisted that it had a Seal and so the Action should have been Covenant [for sealed contracts]. There was, indeed, a mark on the paper as if it had been stamped with a Seal or something like it, but the impression was faint, and the Judge, looking at it without his glasses, said he could see no Seal, and denied the Motion for Nonsuit.[42]

In the federal system, the absurdities of common law pleading continued into the late 1940s when the radical simplifications of new procedural rules adopted in 1938 finally began to take hold. The changes ushered in a new era of litigation because the courts were instructed to overlook putative defects in form and consider the substance, and the procedures such as pretrial discovery formally ended the days of trial as a game of chance and surprise.

From then until now, access to the courts has steadily increased. Old and often obscure legal doctrines that prevented plaintiffs from pleading their cases were greatly liberalized or overthrown altogether—"standing" to sue has been read less rigidly, mootness of certain classes of cases (like abortion) overlooked, abstention over political questions narrowed, sovereign and charitable immunities whittled away. The courts began to infer from the language of statutes that ostensibly conferred power to sue only on the government a "right of action" in private individuals to go to court on their own. Many statutes provided that, contrary to the normal rule, a successful plaintiff can recover the cost of his attorney's fees from the losing defendant. Class actions spread widely after a major liberalization of the federal rules in 1966; the change provided a hefty financial inducement to plaintiffs' lawyers because their recovery could come out of the total pool of damages assessed for all members of the class and not just for the lawyers' personal clients.

Substantively, the courts found ways of doing justice by evading or repealing old restrictive rules that insulated harm doers. The rule of "privity," for example, had required parties to have a direct relationship, so that a manufacturer could not be sued by a customer who had bought a product through a retailer. By the 1960s, privity was dead. Federal courts threw open their doors to a variety of claims against states, local governments, and officials, and the civil rights dockets of the federal courts mushroomed. The chain of causation lengthened in some cases, so that persons only tangentially or remotely involved could be sued; defendants are said to be "vicariously" liable for acts actually undertaken by others. (This in turn would lead to many lawsuits that we may still comfortably perceive outlandish: the attempt to charge the National Broadcasting Company with liability for a girl's rape because it showed a film before the incident depicting a similar assault from which the actual assailant may have gotten ideas.[43])

Lawyers themselves grew far more sophisticated in their approach to litigation, and a series of constitutional decisions underscored the growing social sense that "stirring up" litigation was neither criminal nor immoral, as it had once been thought, but a positive good.[44] Now, in this age of statistical probabilities, a lawsuit may be founded on mere suspicion, the extent of the injury may remain unknown, and plaintiff's counsel may trust to discovery procedures that will force the defendant in effect to prove the case against himself. In the right case a court may even impose liability on an entire industry because the specific wrongdoer cannot be identified.[45]

None of this was once legally permissible; now all of it, and more, has remade the law. These changes have been packed into the years following World War II, so that the law in our time has become more than ever before, and more suddenly than could have been imagined, the common possession of the whole citizenry. This democratization of our legal system, at least in theory, permits everyone to sue for anything—and bodes a revolution, still in the making and still largely unchronicled, in the concept of justice.

From Rules to Standards

To prevail in a lawsuit, the plaintiff must prove both that the defendant committed an act that caused injury and that the act was a legal wrong. One who is easily affronted cannot win a lawsuit merely because he can prove that a passerby on a public thoroughfare wore an unsavory tee shirt that in fact caused him anguish. There must be some legal policy against the wearing of loathsome shirts in public for the lawsuit to succeed.

Much of the litigation that currently clogs the courts revolves around the factual issues. Was the plaintiff injured? Did the defendant do it? In a world more densely populated with people more capable of causing injury to others beyond arm's reach, it should not be remarkable that the incidence of lawsuits has risen and that means would be found to make it easier to prove the factual issues. But that does not explain the other category of cases: those that turn on whether the act constituted a legal wrong.

New conditions have created new kinds of harms. Much of the current agitation about litigation turns on the transformation of once lawful acts into legal wrongs. There is substantive content to the right of redress as well as a mechanism for assuring that the right is realized. Through a steady stream of legislative enactments and judicial pronouncements, the citizen's right to redress has grown apace, but the enhancement of this right has come at a price. Increasingly, litigation must concern itself with the precise limits of the right to redress.

The problem of limits has become particularly acute because of a fundamental change at the core of redress: the standards of conduct by which we are governed. Where once a social philosophy extolled individual self-reliance, today there is a communitarian concern for the welfare of all. The response of the legal system to the movement toward a welfare state has been to repudiate the classical liberal doctrine caveat emptor (let the buyer beware) and related rules. In their place, the law is imposing ever more stringent duties of care on those who act.

This change in the law does not repudiate individualism nor does it embrace wholesale a welfare state as that term is often employed. Most of what we litigate over has to do, in the broadest sense, with standards of care that we owe one another and not with the establishment of general claims against the community such as are implicit in social security or the progressive income tax. That individuals have a duty to see that their actions do not harm others is recognized in all legal theories, and all but the most anarchic political philosophies permit the state to enforce that duty. In one of the most thoroughgoing philosophical defenses of libertarianism in recent years, Robert Nozick begins by conceding that the state may legitimately provide "protection against force, theft, fraud, enforcement of contracts, and so on." [46] The question for a democratic legal system is what set of guiding principles and what rules that flow from them will maximize both freedom to act and freedom from injurious consequences of those acts. The balance in practice will depend not only on one's philosophical predilections but also on conditions of the world. The duty of care will necessarily be greater in a world that produces and uses machinery with a propensity to cause grievous injuries.

The course the law has taken may be denoted as a movement from *contract to fiduciary*, a phrase chosen deliberately to contrast with Sir Henry Maine's famous apothegm in 1875 that "the movement of progressive societies has hitherto been a movement from status to contract."[47] Writing in the heyday of laissez-faire capitalism, Maine meant that people were no longer locked from birth into the traditional social roles—serf, yeoman farmer, nobleman. The progressive societies—that is, modern Western nations—had largely freed their peoples from legal prescription: The source of human action lay in each person to do as well for himself as he could. The central feature of this new life were the agreements that people freely negotiated. No government ordered people what to do; they ordered their own lives.

The law of contracts developed from the simple assumption of individual free will. People would be bound by the agreements they made; no superior authority would save them from their own folly, if folly it turned out to be, or else what was the meaning of freedom?

The movement from status to contract profoundly altered social relations. In particular, it helped destroy the bonds of trust that to some degree once existed between social classes, buyers and sellers, masters and servants. When the law refuses to restrain individual action, it becomes risky in a market society to trust those with whom one is dealing. The disappearance of trust is an accelerating process: In self-protection one must act more sharply toward others, further reducing trust. But a society in which trust vanishes is not only a cruel society, it is also a very inefficient one, for far too much time must be spent safeguarding one's interests. Nevertheless, such a society might work if people are relatively equal. Where there is a gross disparity in bargaining power, however, buyers are incompetent to be wary or unable to do anything about potential harms.

Political heat at the close of the nineteenth century began to turn the law around. It began to embrace notions of substantive as well as procedural fairness. In contract law, for example, as Friedrich Kessler and Grant Gilmore have described it, "the perhaps revolutionary idea [developed] that the law imposes on the parties to a contract an affirmative duty to act in good faith."[48]

In moving away from a "pure" contract regime, society constrains freedom of action by imposing a fiduciary duty° on those whose actions affect others.

° This term is used loosely. In the strict sense, a fiduciary is one who stands in a special relationship to another, as a trustee of an estate stands toward the estate's beneficiary. The trustee is obligated by law to act as prudently as possible, having uppermost in mind the interests of the beneficiary. Obviously, that the fiduciary is still recognized as something special indicates that the fiduciary principle is not legally mandated for most relationships. Yet it is possible to inter-

The objection is that doing so is paternalistic. But this characterization is misleading. A paternalistic or welfare rule is one that requires a person to act in a certain manner for his own good; a fiduciary rule is one that requires someone to act in certain ways for the good of others. Though the line between the two is fuzzy at the margin, there is a distinction that can be observed.

Many decisions are made by persons with a claim to superior knowledge on behalf of those deemed to be ignorant with respect to the decision. For example, a surgeon's unilateral decision to operate on a patient without disclosing the options and risks is paternalistic.[49] A rule of law that permits or requires this kind of paternalism may be called a "welfare rule." Though there is a fair amount of private paternalism—within the professions, for example—laws governing relationships among people are strikingly free of welfare rules in this sense. They are, rather, fiduciary. The fiduciary rule does not circumscribe the range of choices open to either party to a transaction except to say, "That which you undertake to do, do well." It may be paternal to say, "Individuals in society may only consult licensed professionals." But it is not paternal to say, "Professionals must comport themselves as fiduciaries." Thus Milton Friedman, averse to licensing, argues that "one of the protections of the individual citizen against incompetence is protection against fraud and the ability to bring suit in the court against malpractice."[50]

If the concept of fiduciary conduct can thus be squared with an individualist philosophy, its gradual diffusion through various significant social relationships nevertheless has created an important change in the legal climate. The classical individualist theory called for laws prohibiting specified conduct: Do not kill, do not steal, do not misrepresent. Such commands are generally understandable and enforceable. They can be encapsulated in formal rules that minimize a court's need to interpret and reduce its ability to stray from the purpose of the rules. But fiduciary rules are far less capable of being translated into operationally precise terms. Standards, rather than rules, become the norm, and the resulting imprecision prompts litigation.

This point is frequently misunderstood. Thus Norbert Wiener in *The Human Use of Human Beings* declared that "the first duty of the law, whatever the second and third ones are, is to know what it wants. The first duty of the legislator or the judge is to make clear, unambiguous statements, which not only experts, but the common man of the times will interpret in one way and in one way only."[51] As desirable as this sounds, it is impossible to achieve such clarity in practice.

---

pret much of the changing face of the law as an attempt to charge a variety of relationships with a fiduciary character: the trend toward a standard of strict liability from one of negligence in manufacturers' liability to purchasers and users, the increasingly broad sweep given by the courts to the ancient term *fraud*, industrial liability to the public for the effects of pollution, and so on.

One of the most significant problems in law is that of under- and overinclusiveness. A precisely worded rule tends to sweep up activity that falls within its terms but that ought not to be included, and it fails to embrace still other, often virtually identical, activity that requires protection. That is because the rule must use an ascertainable characteristic—such as age—as a predictor of the underlying behavior to be encouraged or avoided. The lawmaker achieves precison of application only by sacrificing some of his objectives.[52]

A common example is capacity to contract. A rule of law declares that a minor (someone under eighteen years of age) may not be bound legally by a contract. The usual explanation for this rule is that minors are not mature enough to understand the consequences of their agreements. The virtue of the rule is its precision and corresponding certainty. If you are over eighteen years of age, you are bound by your agreements; if you are under eighteen, you may void your contracts. The converse is also true: if you want to enforce a contract, you can do so only if the other signer is over eighteen.

This "clear, unambiguous statement" is both underinclusive and overinclusive, however. It is underinclusive because it does not protect the many who, though over eighteen, are incapable of understanding the consequences of their agreements. Chronological immaturity is not the only determinant of capacity. Likewise, the rule is overinclusive because it makes it impossible for capable minors to enter into binding commitments. So this certainty in law seemingly comes at a high price.

Rules are approximations based on prediction. By their nature they cannot accomplish precisely their intended purpose because they are proxies for our real objectives—achieving justice, fairness, safety, efficiency, salvation—which cannot be measured objectively. We do not care at all, in the abstract, whether someone drives his car at 60 miles per hour along a residential lane. We do care about traffic accidents and fuel consumption. Stated in rule form, the speed limit applies to all impartially, though it has differential consequences. In some cases the likelihood of an accident's being caused by exceeding the limit is near zero, and in others the cost of excess fuel consumption is outweighed by the need to get somewhere in a hurry. We impose the rule anyway because it is impossible to determine for every case whether other considerations moot the reasons for the speeding rule. Thus rules which in a given application may be unnecessary can nevertheless achieve considerable efficiency when consistently applied.

The United States Constitution, for example, provides for "due process" without explicit attention to its benefits and costs in each specific instance. Indeed, it can be argued that the cost of determining the costs and benefits of the due process guarantee in each instance is sufficiently great that it would be inefficient to make such a determination; the Constitutional guarantee can thus be thought of as the reflection of a judgment that, on average, through time, the resources required to carry out the requirements of the guarantee will bring benefits in excess of costs.[53]

Still, the objective, hence distorting, rule is troubling. It breeds the maddening bureaucratic response that is never supple and invariably frustrates. What can be done to make the statement of the rule and its purposes more congruent? Two alternative solutions are available.

One is to expand the number of specific rules. A capacity-to-contract rule could set forth other precisely defined characteristics that make a contract voidable—for example, prior certification, IQ level. But such refinements would impose huge costs and defeat the very purpose of rules. A rule establishing a maturation date is a legislative guess that the age selected is the most properly inclusive rule at the least administrative cost. Obviously the effort to examine each child for a contractual capacity would be self-defeating, as would the attempt to list every exception to a speed limit on the posted sign. As a rule becomes more specific it becomes less a law. Specific rules are subject to an infinite regression, each judgment calling for still another.

The other alternative is to sacrifice clarity for a *standard* that more closely embraces the subject matter of the legislation. A legal standard speaks in terms of what is reasonable, unconscionable, substantial, appropriate, or in good faith, rather than in the objective terms of age, miles per hour, or precise engineering specifications. In so doing, the standard includes every case it is intended to govern, but its boundaries are indefinite and there can be no assurance that the fact finder will properly apply the standard to a specific case. Of course, even in a case governed by a narrowly drawn rule, the problem arises. If a construction job is to be finished by March 31, what does *finished* mean, when the claim is for damages for failure to install curtain rods, apply a second coat of paint, landscape the back yard? These questions may be objectively ascertainable from the contract between the parties. But when narrowly drawn rules are dispensed with, the decision maker gains discretion, and it becomes difficult and often impossible for the observer to say whether the judge applying the standard in a particular case did so rightly or not. Did the driver act "reasonably" under the circumstances? Did the company intend to "monopolize"? Was the advertising claim "deceptive"? Was the product design "defective"?

Nevertheless, standards are inescapable even in a legal order that relies in the main on prohibitions to regulate private conduct. The age-old prohibitions against killing and stealing can without much straining be rendered in rule form, but not completely; standards inevitably intrude (for example, "justifiable" homicide). Yet these standards can be confined within manageable boundaries. A legal system that relies on case-by-case adjudication can fill in a particular standard over time, and abuses of discretion can sooner or later become known.

This complexion changes considerably, however, in an age that concerns itself with welfare and fiduciary duties. For nearly a century law has evolved from a negative or prohibitory institution ("Thou shalt not . . .") to one that declares positive or affirmative duties ("Thou shalt . . ."). These were imposed on individuals and institutions in the private sector and on government as well. Duties of reasonable care and good-faith bargaining replaced the earlier, more cut-throat notions of private action (though stated in the negative they sound like prohibitions: "Don't act unreasonably"). Administrative agencies were charged with protecting various publics from predatory conduct. The common legal denominator in this evolution has been the adoption of subjective legal standards.

The mating of standards to affirmative duties is unavoidable. If human institutions possessed a God-like ability to determine in every case what is in fact best for each person, social policy could perhaps be tailored to achieve ultimate efficiency while providing ultimate equity. The action to be taken could then be stated in rule form. ("Mr. Smith will arise at 6:19 A.M., shower for 8 minutes at a water temperature of 94 degrees, eat 248 calories for breakfast, and drive at 48 miles per hour to work.") Since it is theoretically impossible to order human society in this way, it is not surprising that the only modern societies to attempt anything like it are dictatorships that achieve neither efficiency nor equity, being inept at managing even the core of national economic planning. To avoid the bureaucratic straitjacket, while yet attempting to create a fiduciary order and redress injuries, a free society will necessarily turn to standards.

The movement from contract to fiduciary thus marks a major change in the expression of legal rules. It does more. It energizes the courts, charging them with a far greater governmental burden. This, for three separate but closely related reasons. First, fiduciary responsibilities require interpretation: Standards are inherently less knowable than objective rules. A lawsuit between private parties where a standard is at stake may affect far more people than would a lawsuit involving an objective rule. Second, public clamor over litigation will increase because government is more regularly a party to lawsuits. Common law adjudication in the nineteenth century led to the development of a body of private law, but it had little to say about the responsibilities of government, except in the negative sense of constitutional limits on its power to act. However, with the development of legislation directing the operation of a government charged with carrying out affirmative tasks (welfare and regulatory functions "in the public interest"), enormous numbers of questions are raised that cry out for answers. The roots of private law might lie in immemorial custom, but there were no roots for new governmental programs and responsibilities. Many people have an anxious interest in the shape of these governmental programs and their constitutional limits. Constitutionality could not be resolved in the legislative halls, and as a practical matter the contours of the programs could not be settled there either. Legislatures cannot with specificity define the new fiduciary order; that is the very reason, after all, that they need to resort to standards rather than objective rules. The immediate consequence of creating affirmative duties is to delegate to the courts the power to construe increasingly vague legislative mandates and thus to make law and declare social policy that, because it involves governmental powers, visibly affects large groups of people.

The third reason for the courts' growing influence is the felt necessity for patching holes in the emerging social order. The idea of redress acts like a gas in a vacuum: It rushes about filling in empty space. We are all powerfully under the influence of the idea of redress, and the courts especially consider themselves its special guardian. Where the right to redress is missing the courts will generally strive to create it, even to directing the government to act when it has failed, for whatever reason, to carry out fiduciary responsibilities. (During the 1970s, several members of Congress sued various federal administrative agencies and executive branch departments in order to have a court change rules that Congress itself could not be persuaded to enact. Though few succeeded, these suits are understandable as an expression of the belief that the courts are the ultimate authorities for creating fiduciary rules.)[54]

In short, the movement from contract to fiduciary is tending to make the judiciary the ultimate authority that defines legally redressable injury. This tendency has profound implications for our system of litigation and government.

The Changing Nature of Adjudication: Toward Total Redress

Begin with the proposition that the mission of legitimate government is to redress injury and foster well-being. The general social question is what constitutes injury and ill-being. Not every act or consequence of an act is necessarily an injury. A more efficient business that can afford to undersell its competition may steal customers away, but that is not a theft that ought to be cognizable at law (though once it was). Every society will answer the question differently, but all societies that cherish the individual will provide some mechanism not only to answer the question but to change the answer as necessary. The political question for these societies is, then, how the authority to declare redressable injuries should be vested in the branches of government.

In the United States, the textbook answer is that aside from governmental acts that the Constitution declares unlawful, the legislature serves to define the injuries that may be redressed and to create the machinery to do so, the executive operates the machinery, and the courts sit to decide whether an instance of an authoritatively determined injury has occurred. In the textbook version of this system, courts are not expected to declare acts injurious that have not been stated as such by the Constitution or some other government agency (or privately through contractual agreement). Thus a lawsuit alleging that the poor are harmed because they are not afforded health care does not seem an action that courts ought to entertain. If there is a right to health care it is one for legislative declaration.°

In this view of things, the function of a court is simple and unobjectionable: to resolve a concrete dispute brought to the court by and between two or more adversaries. This it does by first determining the existence of a specific set of circumstances that in turn should invoke a rule to whose protection a litigant can lay claim. A court is not free to make this determination arbitrarily, as by tossing a coin or—as once was done—by noting the presence or absence of a heavenly miracle. Rather, a court must proceed by adhering to three principles. First, the judge must pay attention to the parties. Second, the parties must present proofs and reasoned arguments. Third, the judge must reach and explain his decision in a manner that is responsive to these proofs and arguments.

These principles, the late Harvard jurisprudential scholar Lon L. Fuller maintained, distinguish adjudication from all other forms of social ordering. Legislators need not heed their constituents before passing legislation nor explain their reasons after, nor need explanations be responsive to arguments made at committee hearings. Voters need not listen to the arguments (or platitudes) of candidates but may cast their secret ballots for the most irrational of reasons. As Fuller put it: "Adjudication is, then, a device which gives formal and institutional expression to the influence of reasoned argument in

---

°There is a historical exception that the texts recognize for one important area of public policy: Courts have traditionally created the law of torts (civil wrongs), declaring not only the acts that will be recognized as unlawful (for example, assault, libel, fraud) but also the rules by which they may be proved. This power to declare law is not exclusive; courts share it with legislatures, which, when they act, are now understood to create superior law. The role of courts in tort law will be considered at length in chapters 2 and 3.

human affairs. As such it assumes a burden of rationality not borne by any other form of social ordering."[55]

The form of adjudication is important because it suggests that there is a conceptual limitation on the types of disputes or problems that can be assigned to courts for resolution. Questions that require judges to exercise their own preferences to arrive at answers are illegitimate. Fuller identified disputes that are not amenable to judicial resolution as "polycentric," or "many-centered," tasks in which any single decision will have ramifications for each of the remaining decisions. The polycentric task crops up most frequently when someone is called on to allocate a scarce resource.

One such problem is the allocation of broadcast frequencies. Since there are more people who wish to operate broadcast stations than the radio spectrum will allow, some allocation of frequencies is necessary. But it is not a task that courts are well equipped to handle. The general social problem of making the most efficient and socially desirable use of the airwaves is one of ultimate choice, to be made by the people's representatives, not by philosopher-kings. Fuller gives some other examples.

Suppose in a socialist regime it were decided to have all wages and prices set by courts which would proceed after the usual forms of adjudication. . . . [H]ere is a task that could not successfully be undertaken by the adjudicative method. . . . The . . . fundamental point is that the forms of adjudication cannot encompass and take into account the complex repercussions that may result from any change in prices or wages. . . .

Suppose, again, it were decided to assign players on a football team to their positions by a process of adjudication. I assume that we would agree that this is also an unwise application of adjudication. It is not merely a matter of eleven different men being possibly affected; each shift of any one player might have a different set of repercussions on the remaining players: putting Jones in as quarterback would have one set of carryover effects, putting him in as left end, another. . . .[56]

Polycentric tasks are not the only kind of problem for which courts, by the traditional criteria, are unsuited to serve as decision maker. Many disputes exhibit what Professor Melvin A. Eisenberg terms the "problem of multiple criteria." When there is no single standard for decision, authoritatively prescribed (whether by legislative fiat or contractual agreement), the adjudicator will have no guide for weighing the various relevant considerations.

In the football case, for example, [the criteria include] experience, desire, intelligence, condition, durability, discipline, team spirit, and various kinds of ability. . . . [E]ven if all relevant criteria could be listed, no criterion would be authoritative in the sense that it would trump other criteria, or even in the sense that it carried an objective weight in relation to others. One football coach may legitimately emphasize one kind of ability, a second another kind, and a third experience.[57]

This is not to say that there are not solutions to the polycentric task and the problem with multiple criteria. A football coach will assign players to their positions; a market system can fix prices of goods. But the method of decision does not demand proofs and reasoned arguments (though a coach may listen to reason). The point is simply that such preferences are for others, not for judges. If a court were to undertake a decision in these cases, its basis for decision would ultimately be preference not guided by principles demonstrable through the normal techniques of litigation (or by delegation to some nonjudicial "expert" whose decision would be made to appear scientific and hence impartial).

Of course, cases don't arrive at the court clerk's office labeled "polycentric with multiple and indeterminate (nonweighted) criteria" so that he can stamp it "refused, returned to sender." Many are docketed with disguised polycentric features. Thus (an example again from Fuller), a suit against a railroad for a negligently constructed crossing may lead to the court's determination that an underpass, rather than a roadway across the tracks, was the reasonable solution. However, "[a]s a matter of statistical probability it may be clear that constructing underpasses along the whole line would cost more lives (through accidents in blasting, for example) than would be lost if the only safety measure were the familiar 'Stop, Look & Listen' sign." If there is no reason to distinguish one crossing from another, a determination that the crossing in question unreasonably jeopardized the plaintiff's safety is implicitly a decision that the railroad should everywhere construct underpasses rather than crossings. "If so, then what seems to be a decision simply declaring the rights and duties of two parties is in fact an inept solution for a polycentric problem, some elements of which cannot be brought before the court in a simple suit by one injured party against a defendant railway."[58]

Such an analysis would show concealed polycentric elements in virtually every litigated case. If the presence of such elements were enough to foredoom the case to some other institution for resolution, there would likely be none at all, for no legislature today will consider such claims (though they once were far more prone to doing so), and rarely do legislatures enact laws specifically directing the construction of crossings, rather than underpasses, as a solution to the safety equation. As a consequence, courts will inevitably be pressed to exercise judgment, meaning a preference for one kind of activity or the other. That does not mean that every case calls for open-ended preference, for every decision is bounded by the circumstances peculiar to the case. But there will be occasions in which courts will be pressed to develop a set of rules that make it easier to determine whether a formally declared rule, based on firmly established principle, has been violated. The classic situation is in tort law, where the difficulty in an industrial society of proving what actions are negligent leads to simplifying rules that may dramatically increase the liability of certain groups, such as manufacturers.

As the foregoing example suggests, courts can get around the problems of multiple criteria and polycentricity when one of the parties seeking judicial relief claims a legal right. Whether in the form of objective rules or subjective standards, the holder of a right can demand that a court pay him heed and decide the case in response to his proofs and arguments. If, for example, a quarterback were to contract with his team for the right to play his position, the court's job would be a simple one when the quarterback charged that his coach had assigned him to play left end. In a litigious society, the principal result of law-oriented activity is the conferring on various groups formal rights that can be invoked to the exclusion of such considerations as efficiency. The oft-noted rights revolution[59] is not an aberration but an integral aspect of a society willing to entrust significant decisions to proofs and reasoned argument.

However, the principal thrust of the movement toward a fiduciary social order is the creation of affirmative duties couched in the terminology of ill-defined, and often undefined, standards. In such a regime, the only guiding beacon for such claims of right is what the courts can determine on their own. That does not mean that their decisions will invariably be unprincipled, in the sense of being based on judicial preference. There is a difference between a statute that prohibits unfair trade practices and one that requires a government agency to act in the public interest. An adjudicator can look to historical custom to ascertain whether a complained-of practice is unfair or not. There is no standard at all when the claim is that the Federal Communications Commission failed the public interest in assigning a broadcast frequency to one group rather than to the petitioners in court (and without other allegations, courts today would not accept such a case).

But a large number of rights recently created fall somewhere within these extremes (which, be it noted, are themselves rather far on one end of the continuum from narrowly to broadly drawn rules). In the guise of an antidiscrimination law, for example, Congress in the Education for All Handicapped Children Act of 1975 required the states to provide handicapped children with "free, appropriate" education. One of the law's provisions mandates special programs for children who exhibit on learning disability tests a "severe discrepancy" between actual and expected achievement. No definition of *severity* is given. New York State set the level of discrepancy at 50 percent. As a result, in New York City alone, only 10,000 out of 50,000 were placed in the special programs. The situation was ripe for judicial intervention, which oc-

curred in July 1980 when a federal court, acting on the plea of 18 handicapped children on Long Island, ruled that the state's threshold for admission
was too high.[60]

The creation of affirmative duties stated in the form of subjective standards
has activated a broad judicial discretion and thereby encouraged a new type
of litigant—or, more properly, a new class of litigants—with different objectives than the traditional suitor. Professor Abram Chayes has set forth five
characteristics of the traditional lawsuit that are being transformed under the
intense pressures generated by modern life and modern government's response to contemporary conditions. The conventional lawsuit, Chayes wrote,
is "bipolar," a contest between diametrically opposed parties in which the
winner takes all. It is "retrospective," dealing with a concrete occurrence in
the past. The remedy sought depends on the right claimed; they are "interdependent" and one follows logically from the other. The lawsuit is "self-con-
tained": Specific relief is sought and once awarded (or denied) the court's involvement is at an end. Finally, the judge is passive, the litigation being
initiated and controlled by the parties.[61]

By contrast, many suits challenging governmental operations or involving
rights statutorily guaranteed exhibit markedly different characteristics. There
may be sharply contending interests, but the parties frequently number many
more than two and are rarely precisely identifiable; they are often "sprawling
and amorphous." The victory of the eighteen handicapped children will affect thousands of others. No single occurrence need prompt the suit, which
may concern itself with ongoing activity. The right infringed may provide no
clues to an effective remedy. A quarter century after the celebrated *Brown* v.
Board of Education case the courts are still seeking effective remedies to the
seemingly simple violation of children's right not to be compelled to attend
segregated schools. The remedy for handicapped school children deprived of
special educational programs is obviously to include more children. But how
many and at what cost and to what kind of "appropriate" programs? Judges
frequently retain jurisdiction once the immediate questions are answered and
continue to monitor the workings of the decree. The parties themselves may
still initiate the litigation, but it may be shaped to a large degree by the active
intervention of the judge, who may help the parties negotiate an eventual
compromise remedy. Many of these features apply also to private suits, such
as class actions, implicating only private parties.

Though it exaggerates the extent of the change, the table on page 31 suggests the ways in which the characteristics of litigation today can differ from
the traditional model.

No assertion is intended here that every suit today possesses every characteristic of the new style lawsuit, or even any such characteristic, nor that eve-

Lawsuit Models

Components	Traditional	Emerging New Style
Actor	Identifiable individual	Abstract collection of people or nonidentifiable person, possibly predecessor of defendant
Time of act	Immediate past	Distant past, continuing, or potentially in future
Nature of act	Specific	Nonspecific or a variety of acts
Unlawful by virtue of	Specific statute or clear court precedent	No clear statutory provision or judicial precedent
Harm	Palpably injurious	Intangible
Who hurt	Identifiable individual directly harmed by actor	Many persons, not necessarily identifiable and not necessarily directly affected by actor
Relief	Narrow, directly related to injury	Broad, not necessarily deducible from the nature of the harm
Will bind	Parties only	Nonparties, potentially millions
Court's involvement	Ceases on entry of judgment	Continues indefinitely

ry suit in years past conformed to the traditional model. It is clear, however, that lawsuits are assuming more and more the characteristics of the emerging model, prompted in large part by a flood of laws that seem to dictate such terms. The growing familiarity of courts with such suits and the increasing success of the plaintiffs in winning them are contributing to an increasingly consistent judicial principle that serves as a standard for decision when no other authoritative criterion has been given: the desire to shape rulings whenever possible in order to deter injury and provide recompense for harm already done.

The judicial preference is for a social condition that can be termed "total redress." In essence, total redress stands for the proposition that no moral society can permit *any injury* to stand unredressed. The postulate of total redress has many possible operational definitions. A weak version is this: Whoever suffers harm or ill-being is entitled to recompense. A stronger version places the onus on the potential doer of harm to avert it: Thou shalt do nothing that may tend to cause anyone to suffer. A still stronger version is: Thou shalt do everything in thy power to ease the suffering of others. These hypothetical maxims express the transformation of law in a fiduciary social order: a focus on the individual harmed rather than on the putative wrongdoer, a circumscribing of his ability to act, and finally a requirement that the actor take affirmative steps on behalf of others.

It is, of course, fundamental to any humane society that a person may seek recompense from those who injure. But in a market society in which individual actors are free to calculate their own interests and in which we are all connected, any activity sends out ripples affecting all others. This means that in theory recompense may be sought for nearly anything from nearly anyone. And since courts are the primary place for seeking individual redress, a belief in the necessity of total redress will foster an incessant law making and an attendant and rampant litigiousness. Total redress is not now a reality in the United States, but it appears to be the direction in which our legal order is headed. The question is, to what degree and with what problems.

Chapter 2

Product Liability:
Transforming the Duty
to Care

DURING the middle years of the 1970s, a great cry went up from small manufacturers and insurance companies throughout the United States: They were strangling in the coils of a liability system gone berserk. The product liability crisis had hit. Insurance premiums for some small companies shot up by as much as 1,000 percent in a year. Though at least one insurance executive later conceded that the premiums were hiked up in a moment of pure "panic," most insurers justified their precipitous rate increases by pointing to the vast potential liability they and their insureds faced as a result of a legal liability system that had lost all semblance of rationality.[1]

Reduced to its essence, the complaint against the legal system was twofold: Hordes of people were seeking a "pot of gold at the end of every whiplash,"[2] and judges were going out of their way to see that plaintiffs collected enormous sums for the shakiest claims on the flimsiest proof. One commonly cited statistic, ratified in 1977 by Crum and Forster Insurance Companies in full-page advertisements, was that one million product liability suits were being filed annually.[3] An oft-told story was about the man who, despite all contrary instructions, turned his power lawn mower sideways and raised it to trim a hedge, lost a finger (or, in some tellings, a hand) in the inevitable accident, and still collected a sizable sum in a suit against the manufacturer for "defective design." As it happened, both the statistic and the story were apocryphal: After an intensive investigation, the federal Interagency Task Force on Product Liability could document no more than 84,000 product liability suits filed each year, and the so-called lawn mower case turned out to be the product of a public relations executive's overfevered imagination.[4]

Nevertheless, there was enough truth in the perception of trends to make many justifiably nervous. The general public could see for itself that liability suits, in many instances, were exceedingly profitable. An American jury first handed down a personal injury $1 million verdict in 1962, and for several years only one or two judgments of that size were awarded each year throughout the country. By the mid-1970s, such a verdict was announced somewhere in the country at least once a week, and the simple sum of $1 million was being regularly exceeded. In 1978 Remington Arms Company paid $6.8 million in an out-of-court settlement to a Houston attorney who was paralyzed for life when one of the company's rifles misfired. In that same year, a teenager, brutally burned in the crash of a Pinto in Los Angeles, won a jury verdict of $125 million (though the judge subsequently reduced it to $6.5 million). A man left quadriplegic in a diving-board accident collected $4.7 million in the District of Columbia in 1977.[5]

These sums pale next to claims sought for certain large classes of people. Recipients of swine flu vaccines asserted more than $3 billion worth of claims against the United States government (which agreed to be liable when the vaccine manufacturers refused to cooperate with President Gerald Ford's plan to inoculate the entire United States population unless they were freed from liability worries). Vietnam veterans, suing as a class on behalf of 46,000 people, are seeking what could amount to $40 billion in damages resulting from their exposure to Agent Orange, a defoliant that contained an extremely toxic poison.[6]

Worriers might well wonder whether this way lies certain ruin. The source of much of their concern is in the belief that plaintiffs collect even when defendants are blameless. To assess the scope of the problem it will be necessary to consider briefly the course of tort law during the past century.

From Duty-to-None to Duty-to-All

The story of tort law's evolution is long and tangled. If it can be summed up at all it is this: Where once the wrongdoer was responsible to practically no one, today even the relatively innocent are required to watch out for an expanding circle of people. The transformation of the duty of care has meant that a wider class of people may now sue for more extensive injuries than was possible in a distant golden age when it was every man for himself. But to see the story whole, we must go back to a time when there was no duty of care owed to anyone.

Until the mid-nineteenth century negligence, as we know it today, "was the merest dot on the law."[7] In our terms, negligence is the absence of due care, the unreasonable doing of something one has a right to do. But the term took on this meaning only in the past century. Before then, when referred to at all, negligence meant the failure of someone (usually a sheriff or other official) to do something he was supposed to do (like keeping imprisoned debtors locked up). Negligence did not carry with it connotations of reasonableness: It was as strict as any strict liability theory of today. Perhaps more so. Thus a 1795 New Jersey court imposed liability on a sheriff who demonstrated not only that he had exercised every precaution but that even had he observed extraordinary precautions the prisoner would have escaped through completely unforeseen circumstances.[8]

Likewise, the notion of fault was only fitfully a part of the more general legal action for injuries. The most ancient torts, like assault, battery, conversion (theft in a variety of degrees), and trespass, have come down to us as wrongs deliberately caused. Suits directed against intentional wrongdoers are an integral part of a civilized community. No one argues that such suits are morally wrong or impose an undue burden on society. Where the odor of fault is in the air, retribution, deterrence, and compensation are quickly sniffed.

But fault is not easy to parse. From the beginning the question was not so much whether the defendant intended the *consequences* of his act but whether he intended to *commit* his act, whether, that is, he acted *deliberately*, of his own free will. Thus, the common law imposed liability on the trespasser, though innocent of any intent to harm. A man might walk through a woods, thinking it wild land; but no matter how reasonable his belief, if mistaken, the common law made him liable for damage. Though intent to injure the owner was absent, the law concluded that by his direct actions in causing the injury—a chopped tree, a trampling of flowers, the killing of game—the defendant must pay compensation. The premodern mind disregarded blameworthiness in our sense. There was a moral sense that the victim's redress was more important than ascertaining the intent of the wrongdoer. Even where the act caused harm only indirectly (for example, by setting on one's own property a fire that escaped and did damage next door), the law did not inquire into the foreseeability of the consequences. If damage occurred, liability attached to him who did it.

During the last century, however, goaded by an industrialism that promised great riches for its proprietors and the public, tutored by a laissez-faire philosophy that embraced political and moral as well as economic concerns, and supported by a general American commitment to yeoman liberty and limited government, common law judges changed the course of their rhetoric and decisions. Individualism became the talisman that decided controversies. Where once the status quo was preserved at virtually any cost, the man of action was now freed to take risks. The community could not dictate that expectations remain settled. Freedom for entrepreneurial enterprise demanded that ensuing change not be the entrepreneur's liability. Let him be protected who looks out for himself.

As Oliver Wendell Holmes, Jr., put the matter, it was a question of freedom of choice. In discussing the old conundrum whether a person could be held liable for striking another with a stick if the other person came up unannounced from behind just as the stick was being raised to separate two fighting dogs, Holmes said: "[T]here is wanting the only element which distinguishes voluntary acts from spasmodic muscular contractions as a ground of liability. . . . [There has not been] an opportunity of choice with reference to the consequence complained of—a chance to guard against the result which has come to pass. A choice which entails a concealed consequence is as to that consequence no choice." So, concluded Holmes, in a celebrated statement, "the general principle of our law is that loss from accident must lie where it falls, and this principle is not affected by the fact that a human being is the instrument of misfortune."[9]

If Holmes had used *accident* in its most inclusive sense—that is, any untoward event that occurs although no one intended injurious consequences— tort law would have become even more constricted than in fact it was, for only deliberate acts of harm would subject the defendant to liability. By 1881, however, when Holmes penned these lines, *fault* was not limited to acts willfully calculated to injure. Negligence in the modern sense had found its way into the law of torts. Though a person could not be held liable for every consequence of every action, he could be brought to account for some consequences of careless acts.

Why the concept of negligence had not come to the law sooner is easy enough to see. In a preindustrial world, harmful contact between people resulted more from deliberate than negligent activity. A gun that can store several shells and is easy to fire is more likely to be operated carelessly than a gun that requires a good deal of attention before it can be fired—or than a bow and arrow. Moreover, compared to possibilities in the nineteenth century, the range of destructiveness of any particular action in an agrarian society was likely to be small. A railroad train will wreak more havoc than a horse. Prior to the nineteenth century, transportation was limited, mass communication slight or nonexistent, the machine's multiplication of muscle power feeble, the factory nascent. Most personal injuries in the old days were, therefore, of the kind we today consider intentional, like assault and battery. Negligence was not a necessary doctrine.

But beginning in the late eighteenth century, the increasing frequency of collisions between private ships at sea and between horse-drawn carriages on the public roads led to a new inquiry: Which party had *caused* the injury? This was never a question in assault and battery or property trespass cases because the plaintiff was clearly the victim. But the collision cases prompted consideration of causation, and that in turn raised the issue of carelessness, for if the victim had been negligent then the other party alone could not have caused the accident.

At first negligence was limited to collision cases. But in time it came to be recognized as a means of permitting risk-taking economic activity. The general trend away from strict liability toward negligence as a standard in most tort actions is usually assumed to have begun around 1840, with the development of the locomotive. As a commentator in 1895 later put it, the "quiet citizen must keep out of the way of the exuberantly active one."[10]

Of itself, negligence is a neutral concept. It need not give advantage to a corporate defendant or an individual plaintiff. It all depends on the interpretation, for negligence is a standard of almost infinite flexibility. To modern sensibilities, a railroad that has no sure way of stopping to avert collisions (which was the situation until the invention of the air brake in 1868) could easily be held negligent for all or most collisions. But that was not the course that would be followed. Judges mindful of economic progress would look for ways to contract, not expand, the scope of a defendant's duty of care.

This contraction of liability took place across a wide field. One major change concerned the obligations one stranger owed another. The pre-nineteenth century law embraced a moral notion that we must all watch out for those around us. The duty of care ran to the whole world. But the laissez-faire notion of autonomous, self-seeking man, answerable to no one save himself, led to a radical shift. Henceforth, a duty of care would run only to those to whom one directly obligated oneself. The law would not impose a duty; only individuals could do it—through contract. If a contractual relationship existed or could be implied, a duty of care (drawn as narrowly as the contract) could be enforced. But nothing more.

In the absence of contract, a social duty to others shrank, often to the vanishing point. A host of legal doctrines contained for decades the explosive pressure of the industrial age, which saw an inexorable rise in human carnage. Among the doctrines were these:

Fellow servant rule.   First announced in 1842, it said that injury to a worker was not recompensable if brought about through the negligence of a fellow employee. Recovery against a corporate enterprise was possible only if the owner or manager was personally at fault—not very likely, since owners and managers did not spend much time in factories or railroad yards.

Contributory negligence.   A plaintiff's carelessness mooted his suit against the defendant, no matter how slight the plaintiff's negligence or how great the defendant's.

Assumption of risk.   A person was assumed to have accepted the risks inherent in a situation he willingly entered, like the taking of a dangerous job.

Proximate cause.   The more indirect the connection between act and injury, the less inclined the courts were to order compensation. In one famous case, a fire in a railroad woodshed in Syracuse, New York, spread by heat and sparks and burned down the plaintiff's house and others 130 feet away. Despite clear proof that the railroad's careless operation of an engine caused the fire, the New York court in 1866 denied recovery with these words:

> To sustain such a claim . . . would subject [the railroad] to a liability against which no prudence could guard, and to meet which no private fortune would be adequate. . . . In a country . . . where men are crowded into cities and villages . . . it is impossible [to] . . . guard against the occurrence of accidental or negligent fires. A man may insure his own house . . . but he cannot insure his neighbor's. . . . To hold that the owner . . . must guarantee the security of his neighbors on both sides, and to an unlimited extent . . . would be the destruction of all civilized society. . . . In a commercial country, each man, to some extent, runs the hazard of his neighbor's conduct.[11]

Prohibition against wrongful death suits.   The common law had always considered a tort suit to be personal to the victim. Illogical in 1848 when it was first imposed in America, the ban on wrongful death actions made it "more profitable for the defendant to kill the plaintiff than to scratch him."[12]

Standard of care.   Whether a defendant acted reasonably is not mathematically determinable; it is entirely judgmental and was frequently left to juries as a factual issue (as it is today). But the courts imposed outer limits on the standard, so that a railroad, for instance, was not thought to be a "dangerous instrumentality" for which a high degree of care would be required.

These and other rules added up to a golden age, brief though it may have been, for industrial enterprises. The law permitted them to shift the burden of an enormous number of accidents onto the victims. By the beginning of the twentieth century, "industrial accidents were claiming about 35,000 lives a year and inflicting close to 2,000,000 injuries."[13] Few were recompensed at all; virtually none adequately.

So harsh were the results of laissez-faire tort law that even during its heyday courts made some attempts to blunt its most cutting edges. This the judges felt they could not do directly, however, so they piled on "exception[s] to an exception to an exception."[14] The actual law was, therefore, never quite as hard as the summaries render it, but for a long time most plaintiffs discovered that the old idea of institutions owing socially defined duties to others (as opposed to duties they contractually entered into) had all but vanished.

For us, the important point is this: Many critics of our present litigiousness look back favorably to this heyday of virtual immunity from liability for damages, even in the most serious cases, as the norm. In this they are mistaken, for it was a state of affairs that itself was a falling away from an older, sounder norm.

The no-liability rule could not last. It is impossible today to make the case for caveat emptor and its corollaries—not because the ideal of rugged individualism is any less valuable, not because people have lost their free will, not because we no longer treasure personal liberty, not because we have become enamored of socialism in the economists' sense of that pejorative and ambiguous term. We reject the rule of caveat emptor because its essential prerequisite—knowledge of risk—cannot plausibly be maintained. The ordinary consumer does not and cannot understand the engineering and safety aspects of most modern goods.[15] The world is too intricate. Few risks are obvious. It may once have been efficient to have a legal rule that puts the burden on the buyer to inspect before he buys, but the rise of organized complexity has now placed the shoe on the other foot. Efficiency lies in putting designers and builders to the test, not in forcing each individual to master several lifetimes' worth of technical specialties.

As a society we can also reject caveat emptor because the imbalance of power makes the contest between producer and consumer ruinously unequal. On so-called classical nineteenth-century legal theory[16] an automobile manufacturer could easily disclaim liability for anything that goes wrong with his car by inserting boilerplate language in the sales agreement. In a society that depends on motor transport, there is no true bargaining. We would have no choice but to accept any disclaimer offered. Twentieth-century courts came to recognize that this imbalance of power led to grievously unfair results.

With one exception—workers' compensation—the dismantling of nineteenth-century tort doctrine and the rebuilding of the older, more hospitable edifice was the work of the courts. That tort law continued to evolve judicially meant that the new structure would be jerry-built, for courts take cases only as they come. A legislature perhaps could have hired an architect to make the whole harmonious and habitable; the courts were reduced to patching corners as they came within view. Consequently, what once seemed pristine became a law of often stupefying complexities.

One change in direction was crystal clear. In 1916, Benjamin N. Cardozo, then chief judge of the New York Court of Appeals, the state's highest court, signaled the beginning of the judicial return to the older common law when he overthrew the doctrine of privity. A wooden wheel of an automobile collapsed and injured its driver, MacPherson, who sued Buick Motor Co., the manufacturer, which had negligently failed to inspect and discover the tire's defect. The company's defense was that it had no relationship with MacPherson (no privity of contract) because he had purchased the car from a dealer, not directly from Buick. Cardozo said that the manufacturer owed a duty of care to those who would ultimately use the product.[17] In a simpler world, where people bought directly from the manufacturer, the privity requirement made little difference, but an industrial age could scarcely tolerate a rule that would shield the one party that ought to have the sharpest responsibility to take pains in what it was doing.

A host of other changes, too numerous to catalog here, had the effect of redressing the imbalance that for so long weighted the system against deserving plaintiffs.[18] The burden of proving that the injury was the result of negligence was eased. Contributory negligence became less of a bar to recovery. During a nearly fifty-year period, the courts developed the fiction of "implied warranty" as an end run around the stubborn resistance of the mind to acknowledge that those whose products cause harm should forthrightly be declared to have a duty to others. In time, this doctrine would couple with a little-used rule of law, "strict liability," to become the major weapon against product injuries. In the farthest reaches of strict liability, which we are just beginning to glimpse, the courts have for the first time declared a duty to guard against harm to everyone.

Strict Liability and the Defectively Designed Product

Though it was once an important part of the common law, the idea of liability without fault has never been favored in American law. Culpability for acts of which one is blameless seems a relic of a barbaric era when members of the clan were subject to penalty for the crimes of their kinfolk with which they had nothing to do. Careless behavior, on the other hand, is a type of personal fault; therefore one justifiably could be held liable for unreasonable conduct that causes injury. Still, there was one set of circumstances in which liability might be imposed despite scrupulous attempts to be careful. That was the maintenance of something that was inherently and imminently dangerous.

One might be as careful as humanly possible about storing dynamite in one's garage, but if an earthquake set it off, or if wild and vicious animals escaped from their pen, it seems unreasonable to refer the injured to God. The harm would not have been caused but for the existence of extraordinary potential danger, and so from a comparatively early date those who harbored inherently dangerous substances in many states were held strictly liable. The test was not how carefully the keeper tried to prevent injury but whether the potential for imminent harm was present all along.

It took a while for the concept of strict liability to percolate. Courts were bothered by such questions as whether the inherent danger must also be "unreasonable" or whether if the danger was obvious the defendant was not responsible. But beginning as early as the 1920s, courts began to rule that the presence of a foreign and poisonous substance in food purchased by consumers in stores made the food inherently defective and the seller liable, no matter how much care the grocer took to package the food properly.

Some courts were bothered by the implications of this extension of liability. So they sought refuge in a fiction. They assumed that the seller warranted that the product was reasonably safe for its intended use. This sounded like a contract, which, since it was between the parties, the courts were willing to enforce. Thus was the doctrine of implied warranty born. It was a useful doctrine because it avoided a variety of metaphysical vapors that the tort law seemed to take delight in using to cloud the brains of stalwart judges. The trouble was that contract doctrine had its own wrinkles, including the nasty one called *privity of contract:* Contracts can only apply to the people who make them.

The overthrow of this privity problem had to wait until 1960 and another automobile case. Mrs. Henningsen's ten-day-old car lost its steering control and crashed into a brick wall. She sued Chrysler Corporation, the manufacturer, on a theory of implied warranty. But Mrs. Henningsen had not purchased her car from Chrysler, so the company claimed that it had impliedly warranted her nothing and that her only recourse was against the dealer. The New Jersey Supreme Court disagreed, however, and its decision cleared the way for a general rule of strict liability in all product cases. The implied warranty, the court said, "accompanies" the car from manufacturer to ultimate consumer. The court thus overcame legal niceties that troubled only lawyers. Three years later the California Supreme Court in a case involving a home power tool declared the implied warranty for the fiction that it was and forthrightly ushered in strict liability as a condition of law independent of contract.[19]

Though fault remains in the background of this new test, another explanation arose for the imposition of liability on those who did not act negligently.

The theory is called "enterprise liability," and it holds that the company that profits from the sale of a product ought to include in its cost of manufacture the harm that it may someday do. Thus, society can spread the risk so that its burden does not fall too heavily on only the few who are actually harmed. Henceforth, the product manufacturer was to be responsible to anyone who used his products (and perhaps even to those who misused them, as long as their misuse was not too gross). This shift to strict liability has had significant consequences and warrants a closer look.

In theory it is easy to state the difference between negligence and strict liability. Negligence is a standard of conduct: Did the defendant act reasonably? Strict liability looks to the product itself: Is it defective? How the product got to be defective is not at issue.

In simple cases, the distinction is not difficult to draw. Take the case of a mouse in a soda bottle. If negligence is the standard, the plaintiff must show that the mouse fell into the bottle through some carelessness on the part of the manufacturer—a loosely supervised quality control operation, for example. Strict liability does not put the plaintiff to this test. It is only necessary to show that the bottle was defective—that is, that it contained the mouse. Applied across the entire industrial spectrum, strict liability means that whenever a particular product emerges from an assembly line in a defective condition, the manufacturer will be liable for any injury that the defect causes.

This seems reasonable. Its justification is that the industrial enterprise, through both an insurance mechanism and a pricing policy, can better fund the cost of an accident than the innocent victim.

Strict liability does not do away with fault. A manufacturer is not liable for a product that is not defective and yet causes harm—a person who is allergic to aspirin cannot recover damages against the pharmaceutical company (assuming the aspirin was pure). Liability under such circumstances would be absolute and is frowned on in every state in the nation.

So it is all the more striking that the relatively rapid transformation of the tort standard from negligence to strict liability for product-related injuries appears to be moving beyond its stated purposes and toward a regime of absolute liability, consistent with the theory of total redress that those who are injured must be recompensed. The chief mechanism for this move toward absolute liability in practice is subtle: an application of strict liability to design defects and to failure to warn of potential hazards.

There are three ways in which a product can be defective. Its *construction* can be flawed, or not in conformity to specifications (for example, a weld can be weak). The product can also be poorly *designed:* The engineer may have conceived it in such a way that it will not stand up to inevitable stresses. Finally, the product can be marketed in a faulty manner: Though properly constructed and safe to use for its intended purposes, the manufacturer may fail to *warn* against using it in other circumstances, in which it will pose a danger (for example, a pill safe for women that is dangerous to fetuses).

As originally conceived, strict liability applied only to construction defects. But the initial departure from this limited application does not seem remarkable. If a piece of industrial machinery is made without safety devices and a worker's arm is severed through normal operation of the machine, it is plain enough that the machine is defective, though in design and not in construction. Likewise, if a household cleanser is toxic to the skin, a failure to warn the purchaser is to sell the product in a defective condition.

Strict liability for design defects has become a dominant part of the law governing products because it seems to be the only standard that can reach a large class of injuries left untouched by the earlier doctrines. Negligence, which requires proof that the manufacturer or seller acted unreasonably, is difficult, perhaps impossible, to prove in most cases involving a machine that is made to its engineering specifications. For that same reason, no construction defect could be shown. But thousands of people are injured by complex machines and potent pills that catch them unaware. It is the design itself, the theory of the product's operation, that is arguably at fault, and placing responsibility on the designers for a faulty decision is appropriate. A steering assembly that will impale a driver's chest and head in an automobile collision is not an intelligent approach to safety. It is difficult to quarrel with the proposition that the manufacturer of a car with sharp objects in the wrong places is a suitable target of a lawsuit.

There is also an intensely practical reason for the growth of design defect cases. Under the workers' compensation laws now in force in most states, an employee injured on the job is barred from suing his employer. Instead, he is automatically entitled to payment for his medical costs and for a certain portion of lost wages. But the wage ceilings are low. In California, for example, the general formula for recovery of wages is two-thirds of average weekly earnings to a statutory maximum of $231 per week for permanent and temporary total disability and $70 per week for permanent partial disability. Moreover, no recovery is permitted for "pain and suffering," the most significant component of large jury awards.[20] Especially when inflation makes a mockery of the statutory benefits, plaintiffs' lawyers have sought a way to bring damage suits to court. The most promising vehicle is the claim that the machine in the shop was defectively designed (it lacked a safety guard, for example) and that therefore the manufacturer should pay. In 1979, more than 40 percent of all product liability litigation dollars was spent on suits by workers against manufacturers.[21]

But given the extremely delicate balance of considerations that makes up

the design choice—performance, durability, appearance, ease of use, cost—
the question arises whether courts are capable of judging product designs defective. Professor James A. Henderson, Jr., argues that the courts cannot make
such a judgment because the task of specifying safety standards is essentially
polycentric.

Intelligent answers to the question of "How much product safety is enough?". . . can
only be provided by a process that considers such factors as market price, functional
utility, and aesthetics, as well as safety, and achieves the proper balance among them.
Ultimately the question reduces to "What portion of society's limited resources are to
be allocated to safety, thereby leaving less to be devoted to other social objectives?"[22]

In Henderson's view, the courts have strayed far from the "secure, essentially
unicentric world of early nineteenth century liability"; by his reckoning, having even to judge negligence claims plunges the courts into a polycentric
vortex.

Branding a problem polycentric may be a currently fashionable way of
condemning courts for trying to resolve it. Henderson asserts that when courts
are presented with products consciously designed without the safety features
the plaintiff alleges as legally necessary, the courts must flounder in the absence of specific legislative or administrative standards.

Confronted with the hopeless difficulties of trying to redesign products via adjudication, and presumably unable to resist the social pressures generally favoring injured
plaintiffs, courts would inevitably resort to some form of judicial coin-flipping. . . . Efforts to establish meaningful design standards would be abandoned in favor of allowing juries to determine defendants' liability upon no more substantial grounds than
their own untutored "good judgment," or whim. The shift in the basis of manufacturers' liability would be disguised, consciously or otherwise, by heavy reliance upon the
supported opinions of experts relating to the ultimate issue of the reasonableness of defendants' conscious design choices. The absence of any viable product safety standards
with which to decide these cases, however, would be obvious even to the casual observer. In effect, the adjudicative process would largely become a sham.[23]

This seems a misstatement of the problem. Courts are not called upon to
design safe products. The case that comes before a court is not, What is the
safest possible design of a punch press? but, rather, Under the circumstances,
was this particular punch press designed safely enough? Though called strict
liability, the standard it embodies, defectiveness, does not dispense with the
concept of reasonableness with which courts and juries have been working for
well over a century. "The focal point of the [product liability] case is clearly
defined," as four of Professor Henderson's sharpest critics point out. "It revolves around the question of whether the product has met a minimal level of

product safety acceptability, *i.e.*, the product is not unreasonably dangerous."[24]

In essence, the design defect case is a direct descendant of the negligence cases from the nineteenth century. We do not impose liability merely because harm was done. We inquire whether harm befell the victim because of an inept plan embodied in a physical product or a marketing scheme. The question is not whether the danger is unreasonable or extraordinary but whether the designer unreasonably created conditions for any danger.

At least, that is the theory that emerges from the torrent of words that have poured forth from the courts and the commentators over the years. But there is evidence that, perhaps not for his stated reasons, Professor Henderson may yet turn out to be right. Recent cases suggest that courts are reaching out beyond the test of reasonableness, not to judge what would be an acceptable design, but to read into the defectiveness standard their ultimate preference for total redress. Consider these cases:

• Doyle lost his leg when he fell into the gears of a screw auger machine. The manufacturer had covered the gears with a panel so solid that when repairs were necessary, Doyle's employer had to use sledgehammers and crowbars to remove it. Instead of replacing the metal panel, however, the workmen replaced it with a piece of cardboard, on which Doyle stepped as he resumed work on the machine. Doyle couldn't sue his employer so he sued the manufacturer. His theory of defect was twofold. The machine was so solidly made that it was difficult to disassemble and reassemble. It also lacked an automatic locking device that would have kept it from operating when the panels were not in place. Doyle recovered $750,000.[25]

• After drinking for eight hours, two men climbed into a new 1976 Mercury Cougar at 5 A.M. and accelerated to a cruising speed of more than 100 miles per hour on a highway in Louisiana with a posted speed limit of 55. Six minutes later, the tire tread began to unravel, the car swerved, crashed, killed the driver, and seriously injured his passenger. The Goodyear tire that Ford Motor Company had installed on the car had a maximum safe operating speed of 85 miles per hour. The question in the case was whether the tire was unreasonably dangerous for normal use. The court held that it was. Even though driving at 100 miles per hour is not normal, it is nevertheless foreseeable. Goodyear sold tires that it knew were dangerous at high speeds to an automobile manufacturer that it knew would place them on cars with speed capabilities over 85 miles per hour (Goodyear tests showed that 10 percent of the tires would break down at speeds in excess of 95 miles per hour). Ford was liable because it knew that the tire's capability and its car's capacity were mismatched. The court found the high level of intoxication of no consequence because the same accident could have occurred had the drivers been sober.[26]

• One summer evening during the course of aimless chatter, two teenage girls wondered whether a candle, sitting lit on a shelf behind the couch, was scented and concluded that it was not. On an impulse, one of the girls grabbed a bottle of Faberge's Tigress Cologne, kept in the basement as a laundry deodorant, and before her friend was even aware what she was doing, sprinkled a few drops just below the base of the flame to give the candle a scent. High flames instantly licked out and burned the friend's neck and breasts. The plaintiff's successful theory was that the failure to place "Danger—Flammable" on the label made the product defective. Evidence at trial showed that cologne consists of a substantial amount of combustible alcohol. But Faberge showed that there had been no accidents in its twenty-seven years of marketing the fragrance and argued that sprinkling perfume over a lit candle was a misuse for which it ought not be held responsible. The Maryland Supreme Court rejected Faberge's contention with the observation that "the cost of giving an adequate warning is usually so minimal, amounting only to the expense of adding some more printing to a label, that this balancing process will almost always weigh in favor of an obligation to warn of latent dangers."[27]

• A policeman was severely injured in a Chrysler-built patrol car in New Jersey. It slammed into a steel pole and crushed him against the windshield. At the trial, his expert witnesses demonstrated that the pole pushed through the automobile in a seventeen-inch gap in its noncontinuous frame. An alternative design was possible and was known to the industry; it is a continuous frame, which, according to the expert witnesses, would have prevented the accident. The experts conceded on cross-examination, however, that the continuous frame would have cost some $300 more per car and added an additional 250 pounds. The alternative design would be more expensive and less efficient—and it would subject riders to a greater risk that they would be injured in a different kind of accident (the more rigid body would transmit the shock of collisions to persons inside, whereas a noncontinuous frame would absorb and mute the force of a collision). The vehicle conformed to federal motor vehicle safety standards. But the National Traffic and Motor Vehicle Safety Act explicitly provides that such compliance does not exempt manufacturers from common law liability. Therefore, ruled the United States Court of Appeals in Philadelphia in 1980, the jury's finding that the noncontinuous frame construction was faulty and its $2 million verdict must stand, even though it would be entirely possible for a different jury to hold the alternative continuous-frame design defective in another case. Only Congress can effect the cure for this Catch-22 situation, the court said.[28]

• In 1978 the California Supreme Court moved the law a long step closer to a rule of absolute liability, under which a manufacturer would be responsible for any injury that occurs from the use of his product, no matter that his every action was acceptable or even laudable. In that case, the court reversed the traditional burden of proof. If the plaintiff can show that the product poses dangers, it is up to the defendant to prove that there was no feasible design that would have made the product safer. That is a tall order, for it will almost always be possible to suggest some modification that might have averted the accident that gave rise to the lawsuit. The effect of this decision is thus to broaden even more than strict liability does the manufacturer's duty to the world. Anyone who plausibly comes within range of the product's destructive capacity probably has suffered a legal injury.[29]

• The extent of liability may be boundless, as the DES (diethylstilbestrol) cases portend. Beginning in 1946, doctors prescribed DES to prevent miscarriages (a drug ineffective for the purpose, as it turned out). Two decades later, the daughters born to these women began to develop a highly malignant form of vaginal cancer. Because there was no way to identify the particular manufacturer of the DES taken by each mother, a number of suits (pending as this is written) seek damages against the entire industry. One resulted in a jury verdict for the plaintiffs in New York in 1979. In California the state supreme court ruled in 1980 that a similar suit could go to trial; damages, the court said, should be apportioned according to the market share of each company in the industry (some 200 at the height of DES use). Though the plaintiffs may be required to prove that the drug companies knew of the dangers, in some states (Colorado, Pennsylvania, Washington, and possibly California) the courts will presume that the drug manufacturers had knowledge of all potential dangers and ask only whether they adequately warned consumers. Since no one warns against dangers of which he is genuinely ignorant, the emerging rule, if applied broadly, spells out an absolute liability from which there can be no escape.[30]

The Consequences

Increasing, and potentially limitless, financial exposure of companies to product liability suits has a number of possible social consequences. Plaintiffs' victories encourage still more suits, insurance costs and hence product costs go up, technological innovation declines, the courts get clogged, egregious delays ensue, and plaintiffs are seriously disadvantaged and deterred altogether from the awards they deserve. That at least is the litany.

Actually, much of the conventional wisdom cannot be proved given our current state of knowledge. There can be little doubt that court calendars are overbooked; in some states cases can take up to five years to reach trial. But few of these are product liability cases. In Connecticut, which keeps good statistics, such suits increased by 58 percent from 1974 to 1976, but these were only 0.5 percent of the total cases filed in 1976. In federal courts they more than doubled, climbing 134 percent during this period, but this number represented only 2.8 percent of the total federal civil docket. Most of the cases that crowd the courts are automobile accident cases; in California in 1976, for example, two-thirds of the entire civil case load stemmed from roadway accidents.[31]

This swamping of the courts tends to hurt plaintiffs. Such statistics as exist suggest that the tort system operates "so as systematically to maldistribute benefits by overcompensating the slightly injured person and undercompensating the seriously injured." A 1971 study of auto victims showed that those whose injuries amounted to less than $2,500 received more than this sum (generally in settlement); those whose economic losses amounted to more than $25,000, however, recovered only 30 percent through the legal system. A 1976 study of product liability claims bears out the conclusion also: There was more overcompensation than undercompensation for claims involving economic loss under $10,000, whereas the reverse was true for claims in excess of $10,000. An addition of both ranges of claims shows the tort system produced an average undercompensation of $2,400 per case.[32]

Why this happens is easily explained. The threshold cost of going to trial is high enough for insurers and defendants generally to prefer to settle the smaller claims, even though inflated beyond the plaintiff's actual losses, because the payment will still be smaller than the cost of going to trial. For the large claims, on the other hand, the defendant can afford a lengthy delay before trial, unlike the plaintiff, who usually needs the money immediately.

Moreover, the uncertainty and frequent irrationality of the lawsuit itself adds correspondingly to defendants' costs in the low claims and plaintiffs' costs in the high claims. It is never possible to forecast accurately for each case how a jury will view it, so the insurer faces the prospect of a higher verdict than he thinks a case worth at the low end of the array of claims. Rather than risk this, he prefers to buy off plaintiffs with a sum that is generally more than deserved. But juries do not always make awards in deserving large cases, and therefore a plaintiff may be unwilling to gamble on a huge judgment when he can guarantee himself something early on.

It is possible that the recent doctrinal changes may in time counterbalance this tendency to undercompensate victims in the aggregate. Seemingly limitless liability for injuries, mirrored by an increasingly open-ended calculation of damages, may be an invitation to litigation whenever injury occurs. A recent study suggests that there are significant numbers of potential plaintiffs who could accept that invitation. "[A]ll available data indicate that the pool of injured persons who could file suits that are likely to win court awards under the new decision rules is still very much larger in most liability areas than is the number who now actually file." With social costs of product-related injuries conservatively estimated to be more than $10 billion annually, fewer than 1 percent of those injured are filing suit.[33]

Even before this larger class becomes aware of potential claims, the legal climate has had a significant psychological effect on defendant manufacturers and their insurers, one for which all consumers, not just those who are injured, may be paying. That is the effect on insurance rates. One study of the California Supreme Court (the pioneer of doctrinal shifts in tort law) counted forty major legal changes between 1960 and mid-1977, when the study was made.[34] Uncertain of their potential financial exposure, liability insurance companies began to raise premiums, which manufacturers pass on to consumers. For some products these costs may be significant. Product liability insurance is said to account for 18 percent of a ladder's price today, for example. Some small manufacturers were given premium increases during the mid-1970s of up to five times what they had been paying the year before; in some cases this was more than their yearly net profit.[35]

But these figures tend to be misleading and available evidence suggests that the insurance industry wildly overreacted, perhaps cynically (see Chapter 3). On an average, premiums do not exceed 3 percent of the sales price in industries that suffer from considerable litigation, such as industrial machinery.[36] Far more important, until about 1978, product liability insurance was not sold as a discrete line of coverage but was lumped in with general property and casualty policies. Not even the aggregate United States product liability premium is known with any precision.[37] Despite the sophistication of its computer programs and its actuaries, the insurance industry had no sound basis for raising its premiums as it did during the crisis years. The Interagency Task Force on Product Liability, established by the federal government in 1976 to investigate the supposed insurance crisis, concluded in its final report in 1977 that "trends in the number and severity of product liability claims cannot be determined from the available data. It is, therefore, not possible to correlate premium increases with trends in the number and severity of claims."[38] And the oft-proclaimed wild awards of juries do not agree with an analysis of the industry's own figures, which show that fewer than a quarter of all cases submitted to juries are returned with verdicts for plaintiffs. In other words, manufacturers win more than three-quarters of all cases that make it to juries, and the average product liability award, according to one study, was less than $4,000.[39]

Nevertheless, the belief that revolutionary change in tort law has led to catastrophic and unwarranted losses by defendants and insurance companies has had a significant social effect: For the first time in the history of the nation, state legislatures across the country have attempted wholesale reform of tort law. Beginning in 1977, a third of the states have reversed recent court decisions that had made it easier for plaintiffs to get to court and to prove their claims.[40] Many of these laws deal with technical doctrines, such as statutes of limitation and the state-of-the-art defense, and do not reject strict liability outright. Others impose limitations on eventual money awards. Whether these laws will have any salutary effect on insurance rates is extremely problematical, since it is not yet (and may never be) possible to correlate any legal rule with its impact on insurance. But the laws do have the effect of making it more difficult for individual plaintiffs to prosecute meritorious suits.

A decline in technological innovation is potentially the most far-reaching consequence of the expansion of manufacturers' liability for product design and packaging. But it is also the most difficult consequence to pin down. There is a paucity of data, and what little exists is anecdotal. Product liability laws have been said to be a contributing factor in the decline of companies making vaccines.[41] Since 1962 the number of vaccine makers has dwindled from nine to five and only one of six is still in the business of manufacturing measles vaccine. Certainly it is reasonable to suppose that many pharmaceutical companies will quit if they discover they are seriously in danger of becoming absolute insurers of the safety of their pills, regardless of unknowable quirks in the body chemistry of the few who will have adverse reactions. A manufacturer of diving equipment has been quoted as saying that his company, Diving Unlimited, does not pursue certain lines of applied research for fear of being held up in a lawsuit when the equipment is tested. "How can we make the unknown safe?" asks company president Dick Long.[42] But how widespread the problem is no one seems to know.

Still, if a guess may be hazarded, the decline in innovation, to the extent that it exists, is intimately linked to the effect of the liability system on the small company. Small business is stuck with two problems peculiar to size.

One is the relatively high cost of product liability insurance. Despite reports that circulated in the late 1970s that some small manufacturers were forced to liquidate because they could no longer afford insurance and were afraid to risk doing business without it, the Interagency Task Force found few that had ceased to operate. Nevertheless, the precipitous increase in insurance undoubtedly had a heavy financial effect on many small companies and may have deterred some entrepreneurs from starting up. Big business, by contrast, pays on average only a tiny fraction of its sales revenues or even profits in insurance premiums. The total product liability premium for all industry, estimated at $2.75 billion in 1978 (up from $1.13 billion in 1975), amounted to less than 4 percent of annual gross revenues of the single largest oil company. (Total premium understates the true amount paid out for product liability, since insurance policies contain large deductibles, sometimes on the order of $100,000 or more per incident, which a defendant must absorb.) This premium should be compared to the 1970 estimate of the National Commission on Product Safety that the total cost of product-related injuries in the United States was in excess of $4 billion.[43]

The second consequence of corporate size is that the ability to injure bears little or no relation to the book value of a company, its income, or its cash flow. A small manufacturer that makes tiny parts may gross under $1 million and support a tiny workforce, but if the part is used in an airplane and a defect causes a single airplane to crash, no amount of revenues or insurance within the means of the company will keep it afloat after litigation. In the large sense, this is a problem for all of modern technology: Its ability to harm is frequently out of all proportion to the revenues it can produce. That is why, for example, the nuclear power industry was desperate for a federal law (the Price-Anderson Act) to limit its liability in the event of an accident: The ceiling is set at $560 million per incident and was upheld as constitutional by the Supreme Court.[44] Still, large companies can generally finance their tort liability; economic conditions, not legal ones, determine their financial success. However, the effect on small businesses, a significant source of innovation, may be somewhat different. Independent inventors turned entrepreneur have historically been an important factor in the development and growth of new products and new industries because they have been daring and, with less to lose, more willing to bet on their products than large companies, which are usually conservative and cautious. If liability laws are preventing the entrepreneur from performing his historic function, then litigiousness and the judicial expansion of substantive law may pose a serious long-run threat to the future of American society. Such an effect is not proven, though it bears serious investigation.

Assessing Means of Curbing Suits

RETURN TO THE MARKET

The theory of regulation by market is that prices will adjust the supply of harmful products. If safe products are valued, people will pay a premium to induce companies to build safety in at the manufacturing level. Those who want to take risks can purchase cheaper, less safe products and invest their savings in private insurance. But a true market requires perfect information on the part of those bargaining, and that is no longer possible, even in theory. Companies don't regularly offer two versions of a product different only in degrees of safety, nor would the difference in price be equivalent necessarily to private insurance, even if it were regularly available. Moreover, it is likely that a true test of a market would simply force people toward a different kind of litigation. Since a product's safety is rarely apparent, merchandisers would have to advertise the safety of their products. Few would brag that their goods were cheap and flawed. That raises the specter of fraud, which would clearly require some form of policing to eliminate. Finally, it appears inescapable that historically the laissez-faire approach led to carnage, neither redressed nor deterred, whatever the theory might be.

NO-FAULT

The premise underlying the various forms of no-fault compensation is that litigation can be eliminated altogether by refusing to consider who was at fault in the event of an accident. No-fault is, of course, absolute liability. It means that payment is made even if the victim is solely responsible for the injury that has befallen him. This is a radical concept in a free society that is uneasy about collective or communitarian responsibilities toward the individual. The objection to no-fault is that it eliminates incentives to be prudent and it may increase the cost of administration because previously uncompensable events will not require cash payments and because few will resist the urge to puff the extent of the injury.

There are partial answers. When an insured is likely to be physically injured through his own carelessness, his incentive to act prudently will remain intact. This is clearly the case with automobile insurance. No sane driver deliberately risks accidents while driving because he is insured for the costs of plastic surgery and his funeral. The solution to the problem of rising costs is to impose an arbitrary limitation on the size of the payout. The victim trades the uncertainty and delay of recovery for certainty and immediacy of compensation. In return he loses the right to claim damages for the most subjective component of any tort recovery: pain and suffering.

No-fault is now operating for automobile and on-the-job accidents, with partial success. First proposed in 1917, no-fault automobile insurance was pushed seriously in the United States through the work of Robert E. Keeton, then a professor at Harvard Law School and now a federal judge, and Jeffrey O'Connell of the University of Illinois Law School. Their point was that the litigation system serves neither to compensate nor deter. It fails to compensate for the reasons discussed. It fails to deter because most accidents are unavoidable—true accidents which no amount of diligence by drivers will forestall (making the postaccident search for fault a chimera).

The no-fault plan Keeton and O'Connell proposed was simple: Every victim of an automobile accident should recover, directly from his own insurance company, medical expenses and wage losses (but no more than an established ceiling) for a period of time. In return for this immediate and fixed recovery, the victim forgoes any claim for pain. The funding mechanism was already in place because most drivers were paying for automobile insurance anyway. The expenses incident to the often-futile attempt to prove fault, including attorneys' fees, would not be incurred.[45]

There is a large literature on no-fault automobile insurance, and no purpose would be served attempting to summarize it here.[46] The most recent studies indicate that it is successful where it is allowed to work. In practice, the problem is that it can be manipulated by a lawyer's lobby that would prefer it to fail. The manipulation is possible because no-fault does not eliminate fault entirely nor banish forever the prospect of litigation.

It would be inequitable to choke off all recovery for pain and suffering for serious injury and disfigurement. So each no-fault law establishes a threshold of cost (usually medical payments) below which no claim for pain and suffering can be brought. If the threshold is too low (as it is in many states), it is not difficult for doctor and patient, collusively, individually, or on advice of counsel, to hike medical bills above the threshold, and for the victim-patient then to file suit for even higher damages. Because the trial bar is a potent lobby both in state legislatures and before Congress, national no-fault automobile insurance is a long way off.

WORKERS' COMPENSATION

If automobile no-fault is successful in reducing litigation and increasing the speed and reliability of compensation, without at the same time deterring people from driving or reducing the incentive to drive safely, the experience with workers' compensation, the first true no-fault system in America is much more equivocal. The courts remained deaf to workers' pleas for relief from the ravages of workplace accidents, so labor looked to the state legislatures. California enacted the first compulsory workers' compensation act (known until recently as Workmen's Compensation) in 1913, and within seven years Congress and most other state legislatures enacted similar laws. Again, the principle is simple: In exchange for a guaranteed but fixed schedule of benefits to be paid in any industrial accident, regardless of cause, workers gave up their right to tort recovery for pain and suffering. This enabled the financing to be placed on a fairly sound actuarial basis. Today, a high percentage of all employees in virtually every state are covered under workers' compensation plans.

In workers' compensation the percentage of the premium dollar going directly to accident victims is materially higher than is the case for product liability and medical malpractice recoveries under the tort system (65 percent versus 42 percent and 43 percent, respectively). Jeffrey O'Connell calculates that only 28 percent of the premium dollar is returned to the victim; the rest is distributed for legal and insurance administration costs.[47] In this sense workers' compensation has proved to be far more efficient than the tort system. It has also proved to be prompt: Payments normally begin to flow to victims from the time of the accident, even if there are disputes about the amount due.

But workers' compensation suffers considerably by comparison to the tort system in the actual amounts paid. Next to successful tort suits, compensation coverage is inadequate, and few workers' compensation laws provide for inflation; once an award is made, the same level of benefits is maintained, even if the disability is total and permanent.

The low recoveries and the rise of strict liability have led to a significant leakage into the tort system. The laws bar workers from suing their employers but not from taking into court the manufacturers of the industrial machinery that maims them. These suits are frequently filed by workers' compensation insurance carriers in the name of the worker to recover the amounts paid out under the policy. (A survey of 2,700 California worker suits against manufacturers from 1965 to 1975 showed that 40 percent of the dollars received in judgments came in cases in which the insurer represented the employee, who is entitled to any balance after an amount equal to his compensation benefits is deducted.[48]

Such suits against manufacturers can be burdensome. In one extreme case a rubber mill operator, seven of whose fingers were chopped off in the machine, sued the original manufacturer and six subsequent owners (not including his employer). The machine had been made in 1911, more than sixty-five years before the injury, and had been out of the manufacturer's control all that time. Indeed, it had been so altered that the only original piece of equipment left on it was the maker's nameplate. Because the manufacturer could show that the mill had been totally altered and that it had never been under contract for maintenance, repair, or service, the case against the company was dismissed—but at a cost in legal fees and expenses of $20,000.[49]

Such cases point to a significant flaw in the workers' compensation system. The employer's immunity from suit materially reduces his incentive to maintain a safe working environment. On ordinary negligence grounds, let alone strict liability, the rubber mill operator's employer was guilty, but the system of fixed payments to the workers' compensation insurance carrier is not adequate to the task of deterring harmful behavior. This is a national, not an isolated, problem. A comprehensive survey in 1976 by the Insurance Services Office, a national insurance industry rating organization, showed that employees filed 10.6 percent of the product liability claims and recovered 43.5 percent of all dollar awards; employer negligence may have accounted for 24 percent of the total payments made in all product liability cases.[50] Immunity from suit solves the employers' problem of fixing costs, but it does not achieve the important objective of deterring unsafe products from injuring a sizable body of the populace. Corporate executives who deplore the federal government's involvement in regulating safety should reflect that after fifty years' experience with workers' compensation, Congress concluded that private business had failed to curb accidents and that effective safety regulation would have to be enforced by that dreaded administrative beast, the Occupational Safety and Health Administration (OSHA). Cause and effect here run in a straight line. Those who wish to sidestep litigation have discovered something worse.

Workers' compensation systems are thus a significant source of product litigation because they are both financially stingy and economical for employers to avoid. A thoroughgoing overhaul of workers' compensation laws may considerably ease the injured worker's lot and reduce his desire to sue.

UNIVERSAL NO-FAULT

In view of this history, a no-fault plan applied generally to accidents is not likely to be part of America's destiny. Lessons from New Zealand, the one society where a communitywide no-fault plan was legislated, show the difficulties. The premise of the 1974 New Zealand legislation is that as the whole community benefits from the fruits of industry, so the community, not the unlucky individual, should bear the burden of accidental injury.

The law abolishes the tort system for all accidents and provides the injured with immediate assistance in the form of a salary supplement (up to 80 percent of prior wages) and medical and rehabilitation assistance. Pain and suffering is covered on a sliding scale up to $17,000 for paraplegia. The compensation system is highly efficient: More than 90 percent of the monies taken in to fund the compensation system are returned to accident victims. (Payments are funded with a portion of auto license fees, levies paid by employers on salaries and wages, and through general revenues.)

The Accident Compensation Act specifies a method of enforcing safety programs on industry. The theory is that rising claims for one type of accident will prompt a governmental statistical division to note that something is amiss, order an investigation, and take corrective action. In practice, however, it is working poorly, if at all, thus giving industry a relatively free ride. The statistical division is not (at least not yet) adequate for its formidable tasks, and enforcement powers are weak. Other difficulties include a narrow definition of accident so that, for example, thalidomide babies would not qualify for compensation as they surely would under the tort system; and a broad definition of *contributory conditions*, which bar recovery if an accident triggers a preexisting illness or physical impairment.[51]

Even if the act were sound in principle, its adoption here would be prohibitively expensive and would lead—as it is leading in New Zealand—to demands that the ill be covered in addition to the injured. But a national health and disability system could be still more expensive. And the adoption of any plan resembling New Zealand's would ultimately require a sound method of deterring harmful activities and the unsafe product.

Jeffrey O'Connell argues that the American legal system is equally inadequate to the task of deterring unsafe products and working conditions. As a realist, however, O'Connell proposes nothing so drastic as the New Zealand no-fault system. He advances instead a noncompulsory no-fault plan that companies could market individually. O'Connell's idea is for manufacturers to offer an insurance policy with the product. By contract with the purchaser, the company would agree to cover the medical and wage loss costs of accidents without regard to the user's or manufacturer's fault. In return, the user-buyer would waive his right to press pain and suffering claims against the manufacturer or dealer. O'Connell has put forth several ingenious variations of this concept, and surely no one can object that it would be unjust for a company to offer such a policy or for a consumer to accept it.[52] But it is not likely to make much difference. Marketing departments that are hesitant to print warnings on their labels will find it difficult to discuss the very concept of liability insurance as a service for sale. Few consumers consider the legal consequences of an accident when they are buying a new product touted, at least subliminally, as safe.

Moreover, O'Connell's plan does not address the failure of the system to deter. The reasons for the failure are many. A verdict, for one thing, will almost always be rendered years after the faulty product was marketed; by then design changes may make the decision inapplicable to a company's current product line. Liability insurance also complicates the deterrent effect. Product liability rates are not pegged to a company's actual experience with a particular product but to an entire industry's product line, and only in 1979 did most product liability insurers begin to base their rates on litigation experience. Hence most companies have rarely perceived a causal connection between the failure to market safe products and the costs of that failure. A company with a good track record may find its premiums climbing; a company with a poor safety record may be penalized only by the general increase in rates.

Despite these inefficiencies, however, there can be little doubt that liability judgments do contribute to markedly improved product design in many areas. Litigation prompts even those who are not sued to design for safety, for once a court judges that a particular way of designing or marketing is injurious, the stakes in the next suit may rise enormously (and the fear of a defendant that a product modification will imply guilt has no bearing on other manufacturers not sued). One leading case ordered a large award against the manufacturer of a vaporizer, advertised as "tip-proof," that tipped onto a three-year-old child and scalded her extensively, leaving expected lifelong deformities. Following that decision, the industry incorporated a screw-top cap and an automatic shut-off switch to prevent future scalding. Similarly, a decision by a United States Court of Appeals against Ford Motor Company for the placing of sharp objects on an automobile dashboard has led to the design of dashboards far less likely to puncture the passenger in a collision.[53] The many suits against chemical and drug manufacturers (in such areas as toxic wastes and asbestosis) are promoting widespread changes in the way workers and consumers are warned about potent dangers.

GOVERNMENT REGULATION

In dealing with the problem of physical injury in the modern world, neither the free market nor a market system supplemented by various forms of mandatory insurance is adequate. Aside from piecemeal litigation, the other general alternative is regulation. It might be supposed that government agencies could set standards in the area of product safety that would satisfy consumers and protect manufacturers from the uncertainties that beset them under the tort system. Indeed, many industrialists are pressing for such regulation. In view of business antipathy toward regulation generally, this desire for regulatory standards is remarkable—and ultimately misdirected.

The desire for regulation stems from the state-of-the-art problem. In designing a product, the engineer must satisfy a host of criteria, of which safety is only one. Others include cost, marketability, utility, and competitive acceptability. To satisfy their legal burden of producing safe products, designers may look to competing products and to industry or government standards. These standards provide a benchmark against which to measure negligent practices. A manufacturer that opted for less safety than others employed is inviting legal disaster. But how much beyond industrial standards must a manufacturer go? In the absence of any general guidelines, the industrial community may feel that it is vulnerable to claims arising out of any accident. Hence the conclusion, expressed in several current legislative lobbying efforts, that industry practices—the state of the art—ought to be the standard used to govern the manufacturers' legal obligations.

But a rule that absolves the manufacturer from liability for adhering to the ways of the past offers no incitement to search for anything new. The result would almost certainly be a lowest common denominator of safety. This is true without any inference of willful desire to injure: In the absence of incentives, few would be concerned to look beyond their accustomed ruts.

The classic case is that of the tugboat operator who lost a cargo of coal on a barge while waiting out a storm at sea in the late 1920s. The master of the tug testified at trial that he would have put to shore had he received reports of the oncoming gale, but his radio was out of order and he was not forewarned. The tugboat owner argued that the radio's malfunction was of no legal consequence, since there was no legal duty to keep radios aboard. The evidence showed that it was not an industry custom to do so. Only one tugboat line installed radios at the owners' expense, and the others were content, if they even thought about the matter, to rely on the crews to keep private radios aboard. Noting that the cost of an adequate receiver was small and that it would serve as the "ears of the tug to catch the spoken word, just as the master's binoculars are her eyes to see a storm signal ashore," Judge Learned Hand rejected the tug owner's argument. The radio's indispensability proven,

is it then a final answer that the business had not yet generally adopted receiving sets? . . . [A] whole calling may have unduly lagged in the adoption of new and available devices. It never may set its own tests, however persuasive be its usages. Courts must in the end say what is required; there are precautions so imperative that even their universal disregard will not excuse their omission. But here there was no custom at all as to receiving sets; some had them, some did not; the most that can be urged is that they had not yet become general. Certainly in such a case we need not pause; when some have thought a device necessary, at least we may say that they were right, and the others too slack.[54]

Industry standards do not develop solely through an invisible hand such as that which, unbidden by a Learned Hand, might in time have put working radios aboard all tugs. Through scores of trade associations, American business has consciously established standards for thousands of products (such as those governed by Underwriters Laboratories, the American Society for Testing and Materials, and the American National Standards Institute). But all too often private safety and product codes turn out to be the written record of a conspiracy disguised as disinterested corporate benevolence. A study of the National Commission on Product Safety in 1970 concluded of forty-eight private standard-setting organizations that their "standards are chronically inadequate both in scope and permissible levels of risk."[55] Senate Antitrust and Monopoly Subcommittee hearings in 1975 "found that the standards were used by large, established companies to bankrupt small competitors and to obstruct inventors with better ideas. For example, the committee took testimony that a company had developed a backflow valve from pipes that would cut valve costs in half but could not get the approval of the standard-setting organization, many of whose members made the more expensive valves."[56] Why we should expect manufacturers to do jointly what they would prefer not to do individually is so unclear that it remains altogether too frail a foundation on which to rest the public's expectation of safety.

A more plausible-sounding approach is government regulation. Again, the argument goes that once a governmental body, such as OSHA or the Consumer Product Safety Commission, promulgates a safety standard the manufacturer ought to be able to assert as a defense in a lawsuit that its product satisfied the code's requirements. In short, the government's judgment of appropriate safety levels should be final. But this argument, too, falls of its own weight. The DC-10 crash in Chicago in May 1979 and the debacle at Three Mile Island shortly before suggest that even if safety standards are adequate, government agencies lack the resources and the will to police the codes adequately.[57]

The adequacy of the codes themselves is a largely unfulfilled "if." Since its creation in 1972, the Consumer Product Safety Commission has managed to promulgate some three dozen safety standards, leaving several thousand as an epic task before it. Moreover, the Consumer Product Safety Act delegates the drafting of safety standards to industry and consumer groups, though the cost of research precludes consumer groups from active involvement except on rare occasions. A United States Bureau of Standards estimate puts the total cost of standards development in this country at $750 million a year. In most cases, therefore, industry alone will set the criteria, and it is not surprising that a number of government regulations may be "rubber-stamped versions of existing, voluntary standards adopted by manufacturers within an industry."[58]

To complicate matters still further, a detailed safety code, like an army prepared to fight the previous war, is at best sufficient only for old technology. The rate of technological and industrial change is always faster than the rate of legal change. The more detailed a code, the less its viability. The sustained business outcry against the numerous OSHA workplace safety and health standards was not simply an instinctive reaction against any and all regulation; the very vehemence of the denunciation—and the willingness of government to abolish or modify some of the rules—testifies to how unwieldy are minutely detailed regulatory codes. Only a general tort standard, like reasonableness, can adapt to new circumstances and embrace the whole problem it is designed to correct. The danger inherent in every detailed code is that failure to treat an important danger will be assumed to permit it.

For all these reasons, neither government regulation nor industry standards are sufficient to serve as a mechanism for deterring the myriad possibilities of injury that lurk in every workplace and product. Private regulation will be tempted to cheat, either unconsciously because the standard-setters will not look closely or broadly enough at the whole field that should be regulated or consciously because it is cheaper to stint. Government regulation, often delegated to private, self-interested parties, is painfully slow in coming and unlikely to cover every nuance. To the degree that it is comprehensive, through the use of standards rather than detailed rules, regulation will invite litigation to test meaning and coverage. There is thus no escape from litigation if we desire to redress injuries and deter injurious conduct.°

OVERHAULING THE LAW

That litigation is inescapable does not mean that all of it currently experienced is necessary. Changing the legal rules can reduce it; but of the more than thirty separate aspects of tort law that industrial lobbyists would like to see altered, most would bar deserving plaintiffs from filing or prosecuting damage suits. Shortening a statute of limitations, for example, will prevent old claims from being presented but will also preclude plaintiffs whose injuries did not manifest themselves until years after their cause from pursuing redress.

Similarly, eliminating the contingent fee would substantially reduce litiga-

---

°This conclusion does not invalidate private or public standards as thresholds of safety. That legislatively mandated codes are not sufficient does not mean that they are unnecessary. Codes can obviate injuries that would frequently occur in their absence and save the judicial system from an enormous strain.

tion and is politically unfeasible for that very reason. The contingent fee is a financial arrangement whereby a lawyer agrees to charge nothing if he loses the suit and to take a substantial percentage, usually between 30 and 40 percent, if he wins a money judgment for his client. The justification for this arrangement is that justice does not come cheap. The cost of proving a case is almost always beyond the means of those injured. To win one case, a leading negligence trial lawyer, Philip H. Corboy of Chicago, once commissioned a 40-foot model of a railroad crossing, including special lighting to simulate moonlight reflected from the night snow, at a cost of $23,000.[59] Paul D. Rheingold, a New York negligence specialist, says that expert witnesses are paid at least $1,000 a day for court time; travel, duplicating, and transcript costs can consume extra thousands of dollars. Rheingold estimates that the average automobile accident case costs between $10,000 and $20,000 to prepare for trial.[60] These costs are exclusive of the lawyer's fee, which if billed by the hour would amount to many more tens of thousands of dollars. Unless those who prevail can be permitted to help subsidize those who fail through the contingent fee, few suits would ever come to trial or result in settlements.

Surely much of the lawyers' rhetoric about the nobility of the contingent fee is self-serving, for no one compels them to take on all comers and few are not highly selective. The case that is not worth, these days, at least $50,000 is not one likely to excite much interest in the bosom of the true specialist if there is the least bit of complexity, because the cost and time of preparation will outweigh a fee of even half a recovery. Similarly, a lawyer will try to avoid a deserving client with a case that is difficult to prove unless its potential outcome will be quite large. It is not surprising, therefore, that through rigorous selectivity some of the most successful negligence lawyers earn in excess of $1 million a year and many earn several hundred thousands of dollars. This is more money than is necessary to induce most people to take on an onerous job, much less one of championing the underdog, as most plaintiffs' lawyers profess they are doing. Such large incomes represent instead a skewed legal system that puts large chunks of the victim's recoveries in lawyers' pockets for relatively few risks. Proposals to scale down the size of contingent fees would be just but would not eliminate the personal injury suit. Abolition of the contingent fee would but would not be just. Changing the law in this manner is to throw the baby out with the bathwater.

A more sensible approach is to square liability law with the purposes implicit in a fiduciary social order. The fiduciary is not, and ought not to be, an insurer of every consequence of his actions, no matter how remote. Such a standard would force the actor to scrutinize too carefully those toward whom he would extend his products or services, shrinking the productive base of the community. In failing to rely on the capacity of clients and consumers to use

any degree of common sense, a standard of absolute liability would be inefficient. The fiduciary standard does require, however, a high degree of watch-
fulness and care by the actor: A complex society is one in which it is generally
more efficient to impose on the producer the duty to mind the consequences
of his action.

In the area of product liability, these considerations suggest that uniform
federal legislation setting forth a standard of care would be helpful in cutting
through the muddle of the thousands of state court decisions that now purport
to define the law. Both in clarifying the standard and making it uniform
among the states, congressional enactment could go a long way toward ameliorating the fears of those who now see nothing but open-ended liability. The
intent is not to abrogate the concept of strict liability but to rationalize it by
making clear that it is based on the twin concepts of fault and reasonableness.

In 1979, the United States Department of Commerce drafted a Model Uniform Product Liability Act that attempts to accomplish just such clarity and
uniformity. The section dealing with liability for defective design follows.

1.　In order to determine that the product was unreasonably safe in design, the
trier of fact must find that, at the time of manufacture, the likelihood that the product
would cause the claimant's harm or similar harms, and the seriousness of those harms
outweighed the burden on the manufacturer to design a product that would have prevented those harms, and the adverse effect that alternative design would have on the
usefulness of the product.
2.　Examples of evidence that is especially probative in making the evaluation
include:
　　(a)　Any warnings and instructions provided with the product;
　　(b)　The technological and practical feasibility of a product designed and
manufactured so as to have prevented claimant's harm while substantially serving the likely user's expected needs;
　　(c)　The effect of any proposed alternative design on the usefulness of the
product;
　　(d)　The comparative costs of producing, distributing, selling, using, and
maintaining the product as designed and as alternatively designed; and
　　(e)　The new or additional harms that might have resulted if the product
had been so alternatively designed.[61]

To the uninitiated eye, this section might seem vague and open ended. But
it accomplishes two important objectives.

First, it makes clear that the standard of liability is one based on fault. It is
a negligence standard, viewed from the perspective of the defendant as an expert held to a high degree of knowledge and care. The proposed standard
does not require every precaution to be taken. Only the unreasonably dangerous product, not every product that could conceivably be made less dangerous, will subject the manufacturer to liability.

This weighing of risk, benefit, and burden makes explicit what has been implicit in most product design cases. If, for example, adding to a vaporizer an inexpensive screw-on top would not interfere in its operation but would substantially reduce the risk that scalding water would burn someone who accidentally tips it, then it is reasonable to hold that the vaporizer was defectively designed in the absence of such a top.

The second achievement of this proposed standard is that it explicitly sets forth the various factors that bear on the decision, both as a guide to the designer and the trier of facts. To be sure, it does not weigh them, but that is because no such legislation could. At what point the cost of installing a vaporizer top is no longer inexpensive cannot be determined abstractly.

As a society we are too much imbued with the image of courts as institutions for chastising those who concededly have violated law. But the notion of courts searching out a preexisting truth, as though legislatures were capable of laying down a series of dots that courts can connect according to a predetermined order, is adequate only for a narrow range of cases. Legislatures cannot decide cases. The impossibility of defining a legal principle with any greater specificity than through a standard such as that quoted above does not mean that a case claiming to be governed under it is unfit for adjudication. A zone of uncertainty necessarily will surround any dispute submitted to a tribunal for resolution. Otherwise we could resolve it routinely without courts.

As with defective designs, so with defective warnings. It is illegitimate to impose liability simply because the manufacturer has failed to warn against the danger that actually materialized. As Professors A. D. Twerski, A. S. Weinstein, W. A. Donaher, and H. R. Piehler have explained:

The warning process, in order to have impact, will have to select carefully the items which are to become part of the consumer's mental apparatus while using the product. Making the consumer account mentally for trivia or guard against risks that are not likely to occur imposes a very real societal cost. Even when the risks are significant, one must consider whether the consumer will perceive them as significant. If the only way to ensure that the consumer will consider them significant is to oversell the warning by increasing its intensity, one may again face the problem that all warnings will come into disrepute as overly alarming.[62]

In short, reasonableness of design and warning should be the critical considerations. And part of that calculus inevitably must be the conduct of the victim. A return, no matter how partial, to the old concept of contributory negligence will make many uncomfortable. Professor Twerski of Hofstra Law School notes that barring or reducing a victim's recovery by the amount of his own fault undercuts the premise of strict liability. "We shouldn't cut a plaintiff's recovery by X-percent because he's a *schlemiel*, when the reason for saying there's a design defect in the first place is that it didn't protect the

schlemiel."[63] Nevertheless, some *schlemiels* ought to lie beyond the protection of the law because the costs of guarding against their folly are too great.

Given the variety of factors that can comprise a product liability case, reform legislation thus will not immediately or inevitably reduce litigation. Any
change will breed uncertainty in the short run, so even legislation intended to
narrow the classes of cases that are winable may produce more lawsuits at
first. But comprehensive and sensible legislation that sets usable standards can
shape the kinds of suits that are filed. Over time, as courts gain experience
with the standards, understanding what constitutes reasonable safety diffuses
throughout the manufacturing and legal communities. Short of a bald legislative declaration that a product design can never be defective, more cannot be
asked of standards.

REFORMING INDUSTRY

In the final analysis, supposing that liberal tort laws are the cause of litigation is like arguing that liberal constitutional rights for criminal defendants
prompt crime. Personal injury suits are more properly attributable to personal
injuries. For every frivolous case—the drunkard who argues that it should not
be his misfortune that the highway department built the center divider into
which he crashed out of stone rather than pliable plastic—the data suggest
hundreds of bona fide cases. The ultimate reduction in litigation can come
only from a substantial change in the methods of industry and a public perception that business is devoting major attention to safety. The growth of formal safety committees and "risk managers" in many companies during the
late 1970s indicates that the biggest lesson of product liability suits is being
learned: that safety engineering is cheaper than subsequent litigation. For example, Montreal-based Bombardier-MLW Limited, a snowmobile maker
with half its market in the United States, puts steady pressure on its employees to be safety conscious, and the policy seems to be working: By 1980 the
number of suits against the company had dropped 80 percent and insurance
premiums, which soared in 1970 from $10,000 to $600,000 in 1973, settled
back to $150,000.[64]

But American industry has a long way to go. Systematic investigation of accidents and their causes is still in "the Neanderthal stage," asserts Professor
Twerski. The only people regularly in the business of investigating all types of
accidents are insurance claims adjusters and their level of professionalism is
frequently wanting. Texas-based Johnson Ladder Company gave up on regular insurance coverage and began to self-insure jointly with other ladder manufacturers when it discovered "a case in which our insurance company settled

for $200,000 a $3 million claim against us for a defective ladder we never manufactured."[65]

How industry can most effectively cope with the demand for safety is far beyond the scope of this book. But until ways are found, litigation will continue unabated, one may confidently predict, and in the great run of cases with quite good reason.

Chapter 3

Medical Malpractice:
The Uneasy Balance

Blaming the Doctor

On June 29, 1980, a Sunday, more than 150 doctors, all incoming house staff, gathered somewhat grumpily at 9 A.M. in an auditorium of Mt. Sinai Hospital in New York City. They had been summoned to their first official meeting at the prestigious hospital where most would begin working a few days later as residents during the coming year. An assemblage for filling out forms and getting assignments? No, it was too odd a time for the usual welcome, and it developed that Mt. Sinai had other things in mind. That Sunday morning was devoted to a lecture on the perils of medical malpractice.

For three hours, four attorneys and a hospital physician described New York as a hostile environment for the doctor. The lecturers explained that some doctors were litigation-prone and repeatedly stated that a good rapport with the patient was crucial in avoiding suits. Most of the lesson was general, but there were some specific rules to remember. One had to do with the nature of informed consent, how to tell the patient beforehand what you intend to do to him. Another rule governed resuscitation of a dying patient. In most hospitals a patient who has died will automatically be revived if possible. Since this rule makes no sense for old, terminal patients, most hospitals permit an instruction canceling automatic resuscitation to be written in the patient's chart. Not at Sinai. No such instruction is to be recorded anywhere, the lawyers said. Just imagine what the family of the deceased would do if they saw that. Doctors can still cancel resuscitation efforts, however; they just must do it orally. Otherwise, the lawyers said, write down everything. It is the best defense, next to a calm bedside personality, against malpractice suits.

That the new doctors' introduction to the world of medical practice should concern itself with lawsuits is symptomatic of the times. No other area in which litigation is vigorously pursued is so rife with charges of perversion of justice than that of medical malpractice. To be sure, malpractice suits are not confined to doctors; other professionals, including accountants, architects, and increasingly lawyers are targets of unhappy clients. In recent days, even clergymen have begun to buy liability insurance.[1] But in the medical arena, malpractice litigation erupted earlier and cut deeper.

On the face of it, malpractice litigation ought to be easy to justify. A doctor bungles, the patient suffers, a lawyer brings suit on behalf of the injured patient to compensate for economic losses and trauma. As a president of the Association of Trial Lawyers of America, Robert A. Cartwright, has repeatedly asserted, "The sole cause of medical malpractice cases *is* medical malpractice."[2] And beyond immediate redress, a larger good is ostensibly served: Risk can be spread through widely held insurance, and bad medical practices can be deterred. Thus, says Cartwright, "successful medical cases have caused hospitals and doctors to utilize such safety techniques and procedures as sponge counts, instrument counts, electrical grounding of anesthesia machines, padding of shoulder bars on operating tables, the avoidance of colorless sterilization solutions in spinal anesthesia counts, and colored bandages."[3]

Whence, then, the belief, widely shared within the medical profession, that malpractice litigation is a system gone berserk? An American Medical Association spokesman summed up the prevailing, though considerably exaggerated view. "You end up with a situation where every time medical care doesn't effect a cure, there's a law suit filed."[4]

The issue emerged publicly during the middle 1970s when doctors felt the sting of liability insurance premium hikes and cancellation of policies. In 1975, a New York City hospital saw its insurance go to $558,000 from a mere $40,000 the year before. From 1965 to 1975, rates for nonsurgeons jumped 540 percent and surgeons' premiums increased by 950 percent. In most states and for most specialists, these increases came almost entirely in the years 1974 to 1976.[5]

The profession's first instinct was to blame the insurance companies, but the doctors' wrath was soon visited on a more visible enemy: the lawyers, who were depicted as voracious ambulance-chasing suing machines, abusing the contingent-fee system to the destruction of the medical community. As par-

tial proof of their charges, doctors offered various statistics showing that between 66 percent and 80 percent of malpractice cases that ultimately went to
trial ended in verdicts for doctors.[6] The implication was that lawyers were
ploughing ahead with spurious lawsuits, hoping for a big strike. Given that in
1977 one out of every nine doctors was hit with a malpractice claim, it was no
wonder that the profession was up in arms.[7]

But the ultimate victory figures are deceptive, and the evidence is rather
more equivocal. Not every malpractice claim goes to trial; 40 percent are
never followed up. Nor does every payment result from a claim. Federal and
state figures indicate that 28 percent of all payments are made without the injured party even asserting a claim (in many cases, no doubt, these represent
settlements by insurance companies anxious to pay patients who might press
large claims if they have time to reflect on their injury and its causes).[8] When
a claim is asserted, frequently more than one doctor is named. Some of these
doctors won lawsuits in the sense that they were not found culpable, even
though the plaintiff may have won the case against the remaining doctors in
the suit.

Charting the total number of cases in which a plaintiff who asserted a
claim was actually paid (these include claims paid without a suit being filed,
prior to trial, during trial, and after a trial verdict) shows the medical malpractice plaintiff winning 78.5 percent of the time.[9] To be sure, not every
payment is necessarily a valid one; some represent the nuisance value of filing
a lawsuit. But this turns out to be a minor factor. An insurance industry study
indicates that claims of $5,000 or less (the study's definition of a nuisance suit)
account for 50 percent of all claims but only 1 percent of all monies paid
out.[10]

Seen in perspective, these figures are understandable. Hospital studies show
that 7 out of every 100 persons[11] are injured as the result of hospitalization,
where 80 percent of all malpractice incidents occur.[12] Conservative estimates
are that 29 percent of all medical accidents are caused by negligence.[13] These
estimates are based on data from hospital medical charts and omit all incidents of misdiagnosis, injuries coming to light after a patient has left the hospital, and injuries occurring in doctors' offices. These statistics translate into
some 400,000 negligent injuries committed against patients each year. Knowl-
edgeable physicians also estimate that some 5 percent of the nation's physicians are incompetent; although they are not necessarily the same doctors
who perform carelessly, these amount to 20,000 doctors with 10 million patients each year.[14]

Moreover, that many doctors are needlessly sued scarcely diminishes the
gravity of the malpractice problem from the patient's perspective. Many
causes contribute to the litigiousness of patients, but the least of the forces im-

pelling the litigation is the legal system itself. For despite the tendency elsewhere toward total redress, the law has not changed the ground rules by which doctors are required to conduct themselves.

The Standards of Practice

The doctor has three potential liability concerns, akin to those of the manufacturer. In the product field, liability can be imposed for harm arising from defects in construction, design, and warnings. The analogous areas in medicine are the actual performance of the medical skill (diagnosis, surgery), the particular course of treatment chosen (whether or not to operate or prescribe a particular drug), and the advice given to the patient beforehand about potential risks (informed consent).

For the first of these—how the doctor actually performed—the standard governing liability is negligence. The law dispenses with an examination of the reasonableness of the manufacturer's conduct (for example, was his quality control program reasonably proficient) and holds him liable for every defective product that slips through. No such strict liability is imposed on the doctor. That his ministrations caused a new injury or worsened an old condition is not sufficient. The doctor is not a guarantor of cure and has never been so held. The plaintiff must show that those ministrations were carelessly carried out. In the largest class of these cases—those involving surgery—that means there must be proof that the doctor did not operate up to par.

Par is defined by what other doctors do. The major criterion of reasonableness is whether other doctors, similarly situated under like circumstances, would have done the same thing. Because it is usually impossible after an operation to reconstruct the doctor's precise maneuvers, a rule borrowed from the general negligence law is applied. This is the rule of res ipsa loquitur (the thing speaks for itself).[15] In its simplest form, allowed in most states, it would be used in a case in which, for example, sponges were left in the body. The assumption is that a careful doctor would not do so; their existence thus proves carelessness. Doctors do not like this rule, judging by their attempts to have it legislatively abolished, because it substitutes for an expert witness. Nevertheless, the reasonableness of some medical acts can be judged from certain consequences by the average jury without assistance.

The courts are rather cautious in the use of this doctrine. Only the most obvious defaults are left to common, rather than expert, knowledge. This is not strict liability. The doctor is held liable not solely because something went wrong but because it could not have gone wrong without negligence.

Occasionally the doctrine of res ipsa loquitur has been given a somewhat broader role. In Washington State, for instance, proof of negligence in the specific case may be dispensed with, even though the facts are beyond the common understanding, if expert testimony establishes that the injury could never happen without imprudent conduct by the treating doctor.[16] A few states allow the doctrine some leeway in cases against hospitals, where untoward events happen while patients are unconscious. Only one state, New Jersey, has broadened the rule still more, in a case in which it was impossible to show whether the doctor or the manufacturer was at fault when the tip of a forceps broke and fell into the patient's spinal canal.[17] The New Jersey court gave the decision to the plaintiff and left it to the codefendants to sort out the liability between them. None of these modest extensions of a common sense rule makes any inroads on the standard of negligence. Nor does res ipsa loquitur figure heavily in malpractice cases. In a 1974 study of all malpractice claims resolved that year, this rule was involved in only 8 percent, and played a prominent role in much less than that.[18]

The second area of a physician's liability is faulty choice of a course of treatment. (Though choice of treatment is analytically distinct from actual performance and so is considered here separately, in practice the two often overlap.) A common instance is unnecessary surgery that leads to complications. During the 1970s there was a major legal development, but it did not alter the basic legal standard of liability that the doctor is to be governed by the accepted practices of the medical community. What the courts did do was to change the community.[19]

Until the past decade, the conventional measure of prudence adhered to in most states was whatever doctors generally did in their *local community*. As a practical matter, that meant that only local doctors could testify as expert witnesses, and this in turn had a severely retarding effect on the production of experts at trial. It was a hallowed convention, amounting almost to an ethical prescription, that one doctor would not tattle on another, and this feeling was enforced by the geographic proximity and brotherhood of potential witness and defendant. Thus, nearly three-quarters of the Boston doctors participating in one study said they would not testify against a fellow surgeon for negligently removing the wrong kidney.[20]

But in the 1970s, the courts began to recognize that specialty areas of medical practice were not defined discretely by city or state. That pediatricians in Chicago and Los Angeles would test for phenylketonuria (PKU), a condition that leads to retardation, was relevant in Detroit, where pediatricians apparently did not test for it. How anesthesiologists in Boston conducted their work ought not be foreign to the practice of similar specialists in New Bedford, an urban center 50 miles away. The locality rule had needlessly prevented experts from other cities from testifying to national standards. (They could not testify of their own knowledge of local standards, since they did not come from the community.) But doctors are not trained at schools teaching local medicine, certification is according to national standards, the most significant medical discoveries are circulated nationally. In 1968 and 1970 the supreme courts of Michigan and Massachusetts recognized the national scope of the medical community and permitted experts from out of town to testify. Other states followed.[21]

This change pierced the doctors' shield of silence. Less constrained by bonds of fraternity, these doctors began to supply expert testimony and soon local doctors took to the witness chair. The consequence of this change in perception was to permit many more plaintiffs to present a full case and thus to prevail on the merits. But it did not change the basic rule that it was the medical profession which defined the acceptable standard of practice.

When the accepted medical standard is well known, there can be no quarrel with holding doctors to it. But medicine is an evolving discipline, and standards are frequently in flux. Doctors could thus be exposed to liability by an uncomprehending jury. The Kalmowitz case is frequently cited as bearing out this possibility.[22]

Gail Kalmowitz was born prematurely in 1952 and soon became blind from a rare disease called RLF (retrolental fibroplasia), which scars the eyes several weeks after birth. From the early 1940s into the mid-1950s, RLF was the primary affliction of premature babies. The cause was not established until 1956. Some thought the disease was a natural outgrowth of prematurity and that it had become predominant only because medical advances were finally saving so many infants who formerly had died. In 1953, following "a frenzy of research,"[23] the medical journals began to cite a variety of factors that could be the cause: light, vitamin lack, cow's milk, excess electrolytes, low body temperature, effects of oxygen. By 1956, the cause was finally isolated: too much oxygen, routinely administered to nurture the premature baby to health. The study that led to this conclusion began three months after Gail Kalmowitz's birth. In 1975 she sued the hospital and the doctors who administered oxygen to her in excessive quantities. What made the case famous was her decision, minutes before the jury would have returned with a verdict of $900,000, to accept a settlement of $165,000 because she was afraid she might lose altogether.

That her lawyers persuaded a jury at all is troublesome. "Note the dilemma of the doctor accused of negligence," says Jeffrey O'Connell.

Each month dozens of medical journals publish numerous articles reporting on research of a technical nature, often conflicting in their conclusions. Hypotheses are advanced; inconclusive tests are reported; advocates urge their solutions. How much evidence of danger is needed before a doctor will withhold a treatment like oxygen and perhaps risk killing an infant? . . . [A] skillful lawyer, using hindsight, could sway a jury into condemning doctors who failed to heed early warnings. What is a doctor to say when confronted on cross-examination with those earliest studies in reputable medical journals implicating oxygen? That he hadn't read them? That he had read them but ignored them? That they seemed inconclusive? Maybe a group of his peers at a pediatrics convention would sympathize with such understandable confusion, but think of the reception such testimony would meet in a courtroom where a blind girl sits as living testimony to the consequences of ignoring those studies.[24]

In retrospect, Gail Kalmowitz's blindness was an iatrogenic injury—one caused by medical practice itself. But it does not follow that the practice was unreasonable or that the doctors should pay for what turned out to be a mistake. To do so, to impose strict liability on the doctors, is to make them vicariously liable for the failures of the body. The complexity of the body makes it impossible to predict with accuracy the side effects of measures undertaken to treat in an emergency (here the life or death of the infant). Nature might have killed the infant altogether; modern medicine—in conformity with the wishes of most of society—substitutes itself in part for nature. This human intervention represents a shift from nature to man and permits a legal system to shift the risk from nature (which cannot be sued) to the human agents (who can). But to ask doctors to serve as risk-bearers for nature could have catastrophic effects on the practice of medicine and the course of medical research, for no society can afford the costs of untoward effects properly attributable to nature. The attempt to force some segment of society to do so (doctors, taxpayers, or whomever) could lead to doctors refusing to attempt to save premature infants.

However, the Kalmowitz case was not one in which a strict liability theory was argued or won (since it was settled before the verdict, there was no court ruling at all). The case was presented as one of negligence—hence the necessity of convincing the jury that the attending physicians should have heeded the hints about oxygen. This puts doctors at the mercy of a jury, to be sure, but does not fix liability on them at the outset, as a rule of strict liability would. If juries were to hand out verdicts against doctors in such circumstances frequently enough—if, that is, the techniques of law are not appropriate to resolving questions that are at bottom medical—then malpractice litigation can be said to be socially disruptive and might hamper research and innovation.

The available evidence shows that doctors lose only 29 percent of cases that eventually reach a judge or jury. There is no way of telling how many of these suits are illegitimate like the Kalmowitz case, but there is no reason to suppose that a significant number are. Indeed, anecdotal evidence points the other way. O'Connell recounts another RLF case in which the evidence was more damaging to the doctors than in the Kalmowitz case, yet the doctors won. In this case, the premature infant was born in 1969, thirteen years after research demonstrated the danger of using excessive oxygen. Unlike Gail Kalmowitz's doctors, these could be expected to know well the medical risks. But later research also showed that lowering the oxygen concentration could increase both the death rate and the chances of mental retardation. Finding the balance is a delicate business. The jury in the latter case was unwilling to conclude it had been struck negligently (though, as in the Kalmowitz case, the nervous parties agreed to a settlement of $500,000 upon hearing a knock on the jury door from the inside, signaling that a verdict was forthcoming).[25] Since these cases were settled, neither the trial judge nor appellate courts had the opportunity to consider the legal soundness of the jury's conclusions.

In the foregoing cases, the doctors' course of treatment was measured against a medical standard. The question was whether or not the standard was observed. If it was, then there could be no liability. Suppose, however, that a doctor was adjudged at fault though he faithfully adhered to the prevailing standard. Under this circumstance, it might be fair to conclude that the malpractice system could force fundamental changes on the medical system. Such a decision was reached in Washington State in 1974.[26] Characterized by a leading torts scholar as "one of the most important [malpractice] decisions to come down in recent times," it has been read as placing the burden of strict liability on doctors and for that reason is worth exploring at some length.[27]

The case arose from the failure of a Washington State ophthalmologist to detect a case of glaucoma. In 1959, Barbara Helling, then twenty-three years old, sought treatment for myopia in the office of Dr. Thomas F. Carey, who fitted her for contact lenses. Four years later, complaining of irritation caused by the lenses, she twice returned to Dr. Carey for consultation. Beginning in February 1967, still bothered by the lenses and complaining of visual field problems, she paid him eight more visits. On the eighth trip, in October 1968, Dr. Carey for the first time tested her eye pressure and field of vision. These tests showed that she had primary open angle glaucoma; her peripheral vision had virtually vanished and her central vision "was reduced to approximately 5 degrees vertical by 10 degrees horizontal"—a severe and permanent loss of sight.

The following year Helling filed suit, charging that the damage to her eyes was directly caused by her ophthalmologist's negligence. (If detected early enough, glaucoma can be kept under control through drops, medication, or, if necessary in a severe case, surgery.) At the trial, medical experts for both

Helling and the doctors established that it was standard practice not to give routine pressure tests for glaucoma when the patient is younger than forty years of age because its occurrence in young people is rare (estimated to be 1 in 25,000 persons). Above forty, however, the incidence climbs to "two to three percent" and so the test becomes routine. Dr. Carey testified that in his opinion Barbara Helling had had glaucoma for at least ten years.

The jury gave its verdict to the doctors, and an appellate court affirmed, judging that the evidence amply supported the finding that Dr. Carey was blameless because he had followed the applicable medical norm. In 1974 the Washington Supreme Court unanimously reversed.

The courts ruled that as a matter of law failure to give the test at an early enough stage of the disease's onset was negligence. Recalling Learned Hand's declaration in the tugboat case that "there are precautions so imperative that even their universal disregard will not excuse their omission," the court concluded (in a sentence of doubtful syntax) that "the precaution of giving this test to detect the incidence of glaucoma to patients under 40 years of age is so imperative that irrespective of its disregard by the standards of the ophthalmology profession, it is the duty of the courts to say what is required to protect patients under 40 from the damaging results of glaucoma."

Clearly influencing the court's decision that the failure to test is negligence per se was the special nature of the test itself. The accepted pressure test is done by a tonometer, a device that is standard equipment in every ophthalmologist's office. The tonometer tests the intraocular pressure of the eye by lightly flattening the cornea and measuring the resistance, a procedure that takes only seconds. The test is considered foolproof; no case of glaucoma can escape it and no ophthalmologist can misread the test results. The test itself is harmless (assuming the physical condition of the eye permits). These circumstances suggest that at minor inconvenience the impending glaucoma would have been caught and that the only benefit of the standard practice not to test is the trivial amount of time saved. The consequence of adopting that rationale, however, is that 1 person in 25,000 under forty years of age is condemned to suffering glaucoma-induced blindness. In overruling the medical standard, the court was in effect declaring the cost it imposed too high—and also reiterating that finally judging whether a particular medical test should be withheld, given its consequences, is for the courts, not for the medical profession.

The immediate concern for a doctor in a case such as this is his being branded as having been negligent. Dr. Carey did not cause the glaucoma; at worst he failed to arrest it. The court's ruling sounds rather more like strict liability than negligence. The defect in the service provided was not a quirk of the defendant doctor; no personal flaw or act of carelessness, as we usually conceive negligence, accounted for the failure to perform the pressure test. The defect was, rather, in the theoretical principles of medicine, principles in which ophthalmologists are instructed as interns and residents and from which Dr. Carey did not deviate. The defect, in fact, is strikingly similar to a product's design flaw. It is the conception that is wrong, not the manufacturer's execution of the models to which the design gave birth. By shunning the negligence label, three concurring justices said, the court could avoid "imposing a stigma of moral blame upon the doctors who, in this case, used all the precautions commonly prescribed by their profession in diagnosis and treatment."

In the usual product case, the company found liable for a design defect is also the company who employed the designer. The defect, in other words, was developed "in house." Not so, however, in the case of the ophthalmologist: He did not collect the statistics that suggested the need for glaucoma testing over forty years of age only, nor did he initiate the practices that became the professional norm. Doctors do not work for the medical profession the way engineers work for companies. In a product liability case, the company as a whole bears the burden of the damage award; in the malpractice case, only one of potentially scores of ophthalmologists bears the brunt of the attack on the inadequacy of the medical practice. This consequence of the court's ruling is not necessarily wrong or bad, but it understandably worries physicians, who may now be faced with the unenviable difficulty of evaluating all the norms of their art as they affect each individual patient.

It may be that the court's ruling is simply wrong, and that the concerns of doctors could be alleviated by supplying the courts with a rationale that would permit them to avoid heaping the burden of risks on the doctor. Richard A. Epstein, a University of Chicago law professor, has suggested that the entire direction of malpractice liability law has been misconceived, as this case shows. Tort law has not held the putative Good Samaritan liable for failing to rescue the drowning man, even when it would have been easy and safe for him to do so. The law imposes liability only when the defendant in some way *causes* harm by performing some affirmative act—for example, by pushing the victim into the water or by placing for sale a dangerously defective life jacket to be used in the normal way. Similarly, if a doctor at a party chanced to see a person with symptoms obvious only to the doctor, no court would hold the doctor liable for deterioration in the man's condition because he went undiagnosed.

Liability requires a relationship between doctor and patient and that relationship, Epstein says, is contractual. Only a contract imposes a duty on the doctor to act. The appropriate liability principles, therefore, "should be drawn from contract, as they concern the level of care that the physician must demonstrate in order to discharge the duty he has assumed."[28]

What would a contractual approach do for the doctor? For one thing, an economist could argue, it would permit doctors to perform their responsibilities in an efficient manner by providing care less expensively to those who do not wish to pay for a warranty of care. The theory is that a warranty, as opposed to the treatment itself, is a separate economic good that should not automatically be included in the fee for service; otherwise, everyone will be forced to pay for it, even those who do not wish to or who cannot afford it.

The difficulty with the argument is the meaning attached to the word *warranty*. If the warranty offered were a guarantee of full recovery then we could not object to its being offered separately at an additional charge. No professional relationship is undertaken with the understanding that a definite result can be delivered. The warranty is, rather, that the professional will undertake his duties carefully. This is not a separate good; it is part and parcel of the service that the patient entreats the doctor to render.

Besides, what in practice would it mean for a doctor to be able to offer two types of treatment: fully warranted and discount? At the least it would presage a disparity in treatment between rich and poor, which would no doubt exacerbate tensions over the issue of medical coverage and prompt public appropriations for a broader segment of the public than presently receives money.[29] It would not, however, obviate the need for some legal process. It would instead shift the focus of inquiry. Courts could not deny patients who waived liability a hearing to determine whether the doctor fully explained the risks. The complexity of the medical service and of the doctor-patient relationship that so bedevils analysis in terms of what is reasonable will not become simple when shifted to a contract. The same difficulties would have to be overcome and would transform the already tangled issue of informed consent into a nightmare of forms, lectures, and legal consultation. Under such a regime, one would start out with a lawyer before ever entering the doctor's office.

Moreover, it is hard to see how the contract, even one that waived all liability, would prevent a court from pondering a tortlike standard of due care. A doctor offering different classes of service to his patients would quickly appreciate the economic need to devote most or indeed all of his attention (subject to the dictates of conscience—which, we can assume, would be slight given the doctor's willingness to negotiate standardless care to begin with) to those whom he will have to pay if he makes a mistake. Those who purchased the discount service would soon resent the bargain they struck. A court presented with the case in which injury befell the discount shopper could say the contract was unconscionable (if the contract explicitly recited that the doctor promised no professional standards of care) or it could infer a standard of care (if the contract left the root matter open). How could a court do else? Medical service in the absence of fidelity to some standard is neither professional nor medical care; it is butchery. In the end, therefore, treating the standard of care as a contractual matter between doctor and patient would not keep the doctor away from the courts nor markedly decrease legal uncertainties. To the contrary, a contractual regime might increase them.

These difficulties arise because the notion of a doctor-patient contract is a simplistic one that straitjackets the relationship. A professional relationship is not identical to a formal business dealing underwritten by contract. In the business setting, a contract is hammered out following negotiations over a variety of contingencies that may arise. As understood in classic contract doctrine, the parties bargain as equals. That is not the situation between professional and patient or client, where necessarily the former possesses information unknown to the latter. This is why professionals have codes of ethics and purport to be different from merchants. The patient seeks out the doctor and places himself in the doctor's hands. The patient cannot dictate to the doctor (I'll pay you a sum of money, you give me a bag of drugs). Nor can the patient know what is the best course of treatment or what precautions ought to be taken. The professional is a fiduciary, one who is committed to a higher degree of care than that countenanced as the morals of the marketplace. This is so whether an individual doctor agrees or not. The law, in other words, underwrites a portion of the doctor-patient contract.

The proponent of the contract view could retort that the foregoing is mere caricature. Obviously no one would suggest that the law should permit professionals to escape all liability nor do the professionals themselves suggest it. Even if, therefore, the contract theory would not permit economic fine tuning of costs and risks, it can still be beneficial in the formulation of the proper standard of care to be applied. Thus Epstein argues that the Washington State Supreme Court's analysis in *Helling* v. *Carey* was flawed because it failed to recognize that the relationship between Barbara Helling and Dr. Carey was consensual; the harm caused was not that done to a stranger, as, for example, a defective product may harm a consumer who did not purchase it from the manufacturer.

Given that the doctor-patient relationship is consensual, says Epstein, a standard other than one created by courts is available: the custom of the profession—the very standard that courts have traditionally used. "The law of negligence is simply trying to establish the implicit terms of the bargain between physician and patient."[30] In other words, as a matter of law courts ought not look beyond what doctors themselves do. Why? Because this is what patients, at least impliedly, agree to.

This is a curious argument. There is no reason to believe that when Barbara

Helling first entered her ophthalmologist's office, he explained that his service would accord with the common custom in Seattle and no more. She may have assumed so; she may have never thought about the matter. Epstein argues that it does not matter that the doctor and patient have not agreed that liability will rest on how faithfully the doctor adheres to medical mores; what counts is only whether or not they have agreed to *reject* the custom of the local practitioners. "Custom is relevant to the extent that it helps determine the class of risks that the plaintiff assumed in his dealings with the defendant."[31] Epstein's argument, therefore, reduces to the old "assumption of risk" doctrine. In the absence of evidence to the contrary, he asserts, the patient's willingness to consult the physician should signal the court to enforce against her the professional norms of practice.

The argument is not persuasive. Why should patients have to assume risks of which they were unaware because of a custom of which they were ignorant? Unless the doctor discussed the meaning of normal care in the state of Washington, it is unreasonable to reject an argument that the custom was defective. Epstein's argument would be plausible only if it were a true contract: if the doctor had obtained the patient's informed consent. As before, this new ingredient would not eliminate the legal inquiry, only change its focus.

Does this mean that doctors will remain at significant legal risk? That courts will constantly search, at the behest of importuning litigants, for ever more stringent standards to impose on hapless physicians, counter not merely to the instincts but the informed judgment of the medical profession? That strict liability is now to spread to other areas of medical practice? As will become immediately clear, the *Helling* case, though rightly decided, stands for none of these propositions.

First, as a historical matter, not a single court in the United States has adopted the *Helling* rule in the same or even different circumstances (as of this writing). During a six-year period, in other words, when countless medical commentators voiced fears that the courts were extending liability willy-nilly, no court has availed itself of a published opinion squarely doing so. The *Helling* case, in fact, has been cited in only six other cases, three of them in Washington State, and each of these expressly disavowed the applicability of *Helling* because its unique facts were absent. In 1975, one year after the state supreme court decided the case, the state legislature enacted a law requiring a plaintiff in a malpractice case "to prove by preponderance of evidence that the defendant or defendants failed to exercise that degree of skill, care, and learning possessed by other persons in the same profession and that as a proximate result of such failure the plaintiff suffered damages"—a rule that a Washington appellate court declared in 1978 "decently inter[s]" the *Helling* case.[32]

The reason that it has had no discernible judicial effect is that it is unique. Few situations are imaginable in which a particular test is regularly given to one segment of the patient population and not another, though both come to the same doctor's office, in which the machine for administering the test has been purchased of necessity for the one segment of patients, in which the cost of administering to the other segment is nil, in which the risk of harm to the patient undergoing the test is virtually zero, in which the test is not underinclusive (that is, fails to detect instances of the disease), and in which the benefits to be realized in the untested patient population will be huge though only infrequently realized. This uniqueness suggests that the case stands squarely for the proposition that the majority announced: Under these circumstances, ophthalmologists who fail to administer the pressure test are negligent. In the final analysis, this is not a holding of strict liability and such a holding is therefore not likely to spread to other areas. Fears that it will are imaginary.

Second, as a practical matter, the actual effect of the holding is likely to be slight because the facts as reported in the opinion are open to serious question. For one thing, doctors do not uniformly bypass the opportunity to test for glaucoma on patients under forty years of age. I had such a test in 1966 at the hands of an optometrist when I was exactly Barbara Helling's age on her first visit to Dr. Carey. The optometrist, whom I had not consulted before, wanted as complete a medical picture as he could get. More generally, though ophthalmologists do not routinely test for glaucoma on people in their twenties, it is not unheard of and is certainly undertaken, according to ophthalmologists in New York City, whenever there is any sign of difficulty. Moreover, a visual examination of the optic nerve through the retina will reveal enough signs of glaucoma to tell any ophthalmologist to perform a test immediately. The visual inspection is part of a routine eye examination and would certainly be performed at the hint of the kind of trouble Barbara Helling was experiencing. Helling, after all, was not a patient whom Dr. Carey saw only once and then routinely; she had been in his office on seven occasions before the first glaucoma test. Why only then did he administer the pressure test? The court's opinion is silent on this obvious question. Why? Perhaps because the judges wished to spare her a retrial. To avoid ordering a new trial they could not dwell on the time at which the symptoms first became noticeable because the question of negligence then would be one for the jury. Only by reaching back to the initial visit could they hold that as a matter of law the failure to test was negligence. It was an adroit move (if such was the motivation), suited to the unique facts.

What, then, does the Helling case tell us about the impact of litigation on medical practice generally? The answer is in what the decision did not do. It did not instruct physicians how to treat patients, it did not issue a rule such as might emerge from a regulatory agency, it did not direct the American Board of Ophthalmology to change its standards or even to reassess them. The ophthalmologist remains free to disregard it without penalty unless a patient who has not had the test develops glaucoma (and sues)—and the odds are at least 25,000 to 1 (or a lifetime of patients for many) that the individual practitioner will never be presented with such a suit. If the doctor does become a defendant, his insurance (the cost of which he will ultimately have passed on to patients or taxpayers) will cover any ultimate damages. This is about as minimal an interference in the private doctor-patient relationship as is possible to imagine. Those interested in preventing early glaucoma might see rather more virtue in a law compelling the test.

Some may object, however, to the unfairness of a court's declaration of even such a minimal rule in the context of a particular case. Legislation to accomplish the same end would at least act prospectively and would not punish the doctor ex post facto.

But legislative action is improbable. Legislatures may ultimately succumb to reason, but reason rarely initiates. The Young Person's Glaucoma Lobby, which on the face of it is an unlikely group to coalesce, would ordinarily be impotent to persuade the legislature to direct doctors to administer glaucoma tests. That is too specific a rule for legislation, even if it were to pass constitutional inspection.

The legislative inclination is almost always to draft a rule in the form of a standard such as reasonableness, thus delegating the matter to the courts. The legislature could, to be sure, create a regulatory agency with the power to promulgate authoritative rules for the practice of medicine. But such a step is likely to be less welcome to both the public and the profession than the present arrangement. Doctors would detest it because it would directly threaten freedom of action; the public would discover that its slowness in publishing medical guides was providing little or no protection.

Our general social preference for freedom of professional action ultimately requires that the question of limits on harmful action be referred to courts for answer. This process may be less than ideal, because it is a system of incremental change by constant testing of norms under the unique circumstances of each case. Case-by-case adjudication does not always generate appropriate rules or appropriate behavior. But patently unworkable rules and clearly burdensome standards established through litigation are not likely to be perpetuated. It is important not to confuse an outlandish rule (for example, "a doctor must in every circumstance administer every conceivable test") with the standards we actually have, standards designed to test behavior at the margin.

The third type of liability to figure in the malpractice equation is summed up in the term *informed consent* [33]—the duty to warn the patient of the risks inherent in the proposed course of treatment. In its original form, this duty was a purely legal requirement, contractual in nature, and independent of medical practice. It meant that a physician could not treat without consent. The first word in the phrase became relevant when the circumstances showed that the consent was derived through fraud.

A change in the meaning of *informed consent* arose during the 1960s, when the courts began to treat the word *informed* as a standard of fair dealing that imposed an affirmative duty on the physician to disclose the relevant risks. This altered view took the matter out of the realm of contract and called into focus professional medical standards. What risks should be disclosed to the patient depended on the disease to be treated and on the doctor's assessment of the patient's capacity to deal with the information. Again, the standard of liability was negligence: whether or not the doctor conformed to professional standards of the community.

Two problems developed. One was that there turned out not to be any professional consensus. How much should be divulged was within the personal discretion of each doctor. The second problem was that in leaving the question to doctors, the courts were in effect ratifying their personal biases, and these have profoundly personal, as well as medical consequences, for the patient. Deference to medical judgment resulted in loss of autonomy for many patients, who were not informed that they were dying or that certain pains and risks were associated with preferred treatments.

Therefore, during the 1970s, some courts changed the legal perspective. The standard—reasonableness—remained intact, but the reference point was different. Henceforth, the point of view was that of the patient, not the doctor. What a reasonable patient would wish to know about what his doctor proposed to do became the test.

This change, which so far has spread to about one-fifth of the states, has distressed doctors because it limits their autonomy and subjects each practitioner to second-guessing by a court. But the burden is not onerous, and the profession wildly overreacted. In the first place, the standard is not based on the subjective state of mind of the individual patient. That is to say, the question is not whether this particular patient desperately wanted irrelevant information but whether an objective, reasonable person would consider what was withheld relevant in reaching a judgment whether to proceed with treatment. The plaintiff must also show that the undisclosed risk was sufficiently serious that a reasonable person might have refused treatment. In the second place, the doctor should have little difficulty complying with the new informed consent rule. He simply needs to view his patient as a human being who is entitled to be treated as an equal when it comes to making decisions critical to his life and well-being. Furthermore, observing the spirit of the informed consent rule should spare many physicians considerable litigation that now arises out of disputes over the proper course of treatment. When the state of medical art is uncertain, speaking candidly with the patient will force the doctor to think through his options and allow the patient to assess the uncertainties for himself. In any event, the rule of informed consent is not one of strict liability and does not provide the sick with a means of suing the doctor for every worsened condition.

By the same token, it should be noted that the tendency of judges in ruling on such a policy issue is to substitute a legal for a medical model of man. Judges trained in the common law are not apt to think of an individual as a biological organism whose care is best entrusted to a medical professional. Rather, the judge will consider the individual as an autonomous being with rights, among them the right to make up his own mind. On occasion, the physician's medical duty to care for the individual who truly cannot tolerate information about risk or about his condition will conflict with the political judgment that each person *must* be free to determine his own course. Some exceptions may therefore have to be made, and it will take a courageous physician to assert them.

Some Social Consequences of Malpractice Litigation

THE MALPRACTICE INSURANCE "CRISIS"

The most widespread perception about the consequences of rising medical malpractice litigation is that it has led to an insurance cost crisis for doctors. In fact, the swelling tide of lawsuits seems to have served as an excuse rather than a cause. One cannot be certain of this conclusion because good statistics (that is, those that are comprehensive, nondeceptive, and comparable to each other) are notoriously difficult to locate in the insurance industry. Nevertheless, the available evidence tends to suggest that "the malpractice crisis was a crisis of insurance, not of medical practice" and was not caused by the legal system.[34]

Insurance companies earn money in two ways: through premium income from policyholders and from market investments (stocks, bonds, public securities, ownership of other income-producing assets). The insurance contract requires the insurers to defend policyholders in malpractice suits and to pay for any damages awarded or agreed on in settlement of claims. With a large enough pool of claims, such as exists in the automobile insurance field, an actuary can determine with remarkable accuracy the premium dollars the company must charge to cover judgments against policyholders, plus administrative costs.

Since claims against the insurer are not made immediately—only 52 percent of the medical malpractice claims are reported within a year of injury, and as late as four years after the injury some 4 percent of eventual claims are unknown[35]—a considerable amount of money from the premium receipts must be placed on the insurer's books in an account known as a loss reserve. Three types of potential losses comprise the reserve: claims actually asserted against an insured, estimates of claims that may arise from reports of injuries forwarded to the insurer, and an amount known as "incurred but not reported" (IBNR). This last is an insurer's guess that it will be hit with some claims about which it has, as yet, heard nothing.

The loss reserve account is open to considerable manipulation. Claims can be placed in the reserve at face value, even though few will ultimately be settled for as much as the claimant seeks. Reported injuries do not all materialize as actual claims; a Department of Health, Education, and Welfare (HEW) study found that 40 percent of all reports never led to claims of any sort.[36]

As open to question as this part of the loss reserve is, that for IBNR may verge on pure fiction. In 1971 Employers of Wausau applied to the New York State Insurance Commissioner for a hefty rate increase. Part of its justification was the growth in its loss reserve, of which $36 million was for IBNR expenses for 1970. It won the rate increase. The following year Employers restated its IBNR account for 1970, cutting it in half. Of the $18 million that suddenly disappeared, $6 million represented claims paid and transfers of claims actually asserted. That left $12 million, or one-third of the previously reported IBNR, as essentially a fake figure, which could now be restated as profit.[37]

Exaggerated loss reserves reduce the book showing of a company's profits (or increase its losses), providing an excuse to seek higher premium rates. But that is not the only effect. The cash itself, tax free as long as it is kept in the loss reserve account, is available for investments. In a bull market, earnings from such invested cash can be far higher than profits available from the underwriting business. In fact, the profits from investments can be enormous. In 1972 the property/liability insurance industry as a whole (of which medical malpractice is estimated to comprise between 1 and 7 percent) reaped $2.5 billion in investment profits.

From the late 1960s there had been clear signs of the rise in malpractice claims, as the table shows.[38]

Year	Percentage of Increase/Decrease (−)
1966–67	11
1967–68	−5
1968–69	15
1969–70	1
1970–71	16
1971–72	31
1972–73	29

But there was no outcry from the industry until 1973 when the stock market finally soured. The industry lost $1 billion on its investments that year.[39] By 1974, there was a real financial crisis: Rising claims, coupled with inflation, led to underwriting losses of $1.8 billion; stock market losses totaled $3.3 billion for the industry as a whole.[40]

Losses on the underwriting business are tolerable if the cash generated by competitive premium rates can earn large sums in the financial markets. This seemed to be the motive of the most notorious malpractice insurer, Argonaut Insurance Company, a subsidiary of Teledyne, Incorporated, a large and aggressive conglomerate. From 1971, when it first wrote medical malpractice policies, to 1974, when most of its officers were fired, Argonaut went from insuring 1,300 doctors to nearly 30,000; during the same time it took over the insurance of one-quarter of the country's hospitals. It did this by keeping its rates low and in at least one state even by cutting its rates—this during a period in which claims were clearly rising. Its demands in 1974 for huge rate increases and its subsequent decision to pull out of the malpractice market altogether, threatening to leave a significant number of physicians uninsured, were instrumental in giving birth to the crisis. Significantly, its decision to quit came not when it lost money on its underwriting business but when stock market reverses finally forced it into the red.[41]

Many industry spokesmen deny that there is any connection between investment losses and the request for premium rate increases. The rate-making process and the decision to invest, the insurers uniformly assert, are rigidly separated within the corporate walls.[42] One company testified before a United States Senate subcommittee investigating the malpractice insurance crisis that state insurance commissions would never permit companies to recover marked losses through rate increases. This assertion is false. Few state insurance departments before 1975 even collected information about the companies' experience with malpractice claims. Threats to withdraw from malpractice insurance were usually sufficient to scare insurance commissioners to ratify proposed rate increases. "The capitulations that occurred provided the casualty insurers who wrote malpractice with a billion dollar booster shot at exactly the time their stock market losses made that infusion necessary."[43] A careful analysis of the malpractice insurance expenses and income between 1970 and 1976 shows an underwriting profit of $1 billion, representing a 30 percent return on the industry's premium income.[44] Moreover, even if the underwriting side is not profitable, investment opportunities when the market is rising make the business worthwhile.

Peter H. Foley, executive vice-president of INA Underwriters, is forthright about the economics of malpractice insurance. In 1980, with no significant changes in the legal climate, INA (Insurance Company of North America) expanded its malpractice business. "We will not make a profit on our underwriting," he said, "but the premium investment will make us money."[45]

That doctors, the legal system, and ultimately the public were forced to bear the industry's investment reverses seems clear not only from the data but from the example of the "one malpractice insurer that didn't ask for big rate increases between 1974 and 1976." As John Guinther points out:

Its non-action stands as testimony to the relationship between the market losses and the rate increases received by the other companies. The holdout was Medical Protective, the only company that writes only malpractice and the only company to admit it makes a profit doing so. Medical Protective, unlike its giant cousins in the malpractice field, had conservative investment policies and threfore took no bath in the stock market and had no losses to recoup. As a result, between 1974 and 1976, its rate requests were both few and in keeping with actual perceived increases in claims liability.[46]

In the end, the malpractice crisis was a function of insurer malpractice.

DEFENSIVE MEDICINE

A second asserted consequence of malpractice litigation is the rise of defensive medicine. This usually is taken to connote more, and usually unnecessary, laboratory tests, second consultations, hospitalization. It has also been taken to mean a greater willingness by nonspecialists to defer to ever more rarefied classes of specialists for the treatment of disease.

It seems intuitively correct that defensive medicine is on the rise and is an outgrowth of the perceived trend of malpractice litigation. Few who have been to a doctor since at least the middle 1970s can fail to be impressed with a sense that doctors are increasingly covering their tracks. But it is a rather more difficult matter to quantify the defensive medicine phenomenon. Dollar figures vary wildly. In 1975, HEW variously estimated the cost at $1 billion, $3 billion, $5 billion, and $7 billion. Polls of various physicians' groups reflect the rise in one form of defensive medicine or another.[47] According to a 1976 poll of Virginia doctors, 73 percent (of a sample consisting of half the state's doctors) say they are X-raying and testing their patients defensively, and a 1975 poll of California physicians arrived at a figure of 59 percent who do likewise. These same polls reflected a practice of shifting patients to those specialists deemed more qualified.[48] Forty-two percent of the Virginia doctors reported that "they can no longer afford to treat patients considered to be 'high risk' because of the nature of their illnesses."[49] Though no one has attempted a sound estimate of the increased cost of such referrals, it is clear that when patients who once would have been treated in a doctor's office are hospitalized or sent along to specialists who command higher fees, the total bill to the public for medical care must rise, perhaps steeply.

That more doctors are ordering more tests does not prove, however, that the tests are unnecessary. If the fear of being sued prompts a doctor to perform tests he should perform, then litigation is serving a needed deterrent function. Many of the doctors surveyed in polls disclaim the necessity for more extensive testing. But there are reasons to doubt the disclaimers.

Defensive medicine can only be explained by litigation if there is a large class of diagnostic situations in which the medical norms are poorly understood or articulated. Where the standard is unclear so that a jury would have difficulty determining whether a doctor had complied, it would behoove physicians to do more than is technically required by the professional norm as they perceive it. This circumstance may be present in most malpractice cases not involving a factual dispute over what the doctor did. But the clarity of medical standards is more properly a medical problem than a legal one.

Moreover, as generally defined, defensive medicine is only partially rational—that is, responsive to the perceived threat. It should stress not only more tests, consultations, and hospitalizations but also fewer operations, prescriptions, and tests (for example, X rays) that pose the risk of iatrogenic injury. Yet much that could be eliminated continues. A 1976 study of unnecessary surgery revealed a startling pattern: 70 percent of the 724,000 tonsillectomies, 14 percent of the 472,000 gall bladder removals, 22 percent of the 787,000 hysterectomies, 22 percent of the 223,000 prostatectomies, and 17 percent of the 200,000 hemorrhoidectomies were found to be contraindicated. Together they resulted in 12,500 deaths (or a sixth of the 70,000 deaths following elective surgery annually).[50]

Equally startling are statistics on the incidence of iatrogenic injury resulting from faulty medication. One study put the number of people hospitalized from adverse drug reactions at 300,000 annually; another study showed that at least 25,000 died annually from adverse reactions to antibiotics.[51] Applying the HEW estimate that 29 percent of all medical accidents are caused by physician or hospital-related negligence, then 90,000 hospitalizations and 7,500 deaths may be due to an overhasty prescription of drugs.[52] Studies investigating the problem of overprescription tend to bear out this conclusion. Between 1967 and 1971, for example, doctors doubled the number of prescriptions they wrote for antibiotics, despite lack of evidence that bacterial infection had increased in frequency.[53] In 1980, the Food and Drug Administration called for a halt in the routine prescribing of Valium and Librium for daily stress, calling them the most abused drugs in the nation.

Much of what is called defensive medicine thus springs from factors other than fear of lawsuits. The most obvious explanation is that doctors are paid for every extra test, consultation, and hospitalization. Comparisons of surgery rates between England (where doctors are primarily salaried) and the United States have shown that the British tend to operate only half as much as American doctors.[54] They perform only 40 percent as many hysterectomies as are done in the United States where the leading cause of malpractice claims is operations on the female genital system.[55] Comparisons of salaried versus fee-for-service surgeons in the United States also tend to suggest that payment is a strong inducement to operations: Again, the salaried doctors tended to operate only half as often as the doctors who are paid separately for each operation.[56]

LEGISLATIVE BACKLASH

A third consequence of the malpractice crisis has been the successful demand that legislators statutorily modify the ground rules that govern the malpractice suit. In just two years, 1975 and 1976, forty-nine state legislatures enacted 250 bills responding to the threat that doctors felt; this was "a flood of legislation, a torrent unparalleled . . . in the history of medical law in this country."[57]

Many of the 250 bills created alternative insurance mechanisms to guarantee continued coverage. Equally important, from the doctors' and the insurers' perspective, were laws intended to limit the ability of plaintiffs to seek and recover damages.

The many laws took a few common forms. But none was in fact responsive to the underlying causes nor was likely to have any deterrent effect.

One was the limit on large damage awards. Eleven states decreed that no successful plaintiff could recover more than $500,000; Idaho restricted the patient to a maximum $150,000. Limits were also placed on the size of the lawyer's contingent fee. As unfair as these ceilings may be in a deserving case, they would at least be defensible as a policy judgment if large awards contributed to the rising costs. But the facts seem conclusively contrary. A National Association of Insurance Commissioners (NAIC) study in 1976 of 24,000 closed claims showed that less than 1 percent of the claims and 6 percent of the damages paid were attributable to verdicts or settlements in excess of $500,000.[58] Statistically, therefore, the large claim is insignificant as a factor in insurance rates. But it is highly significant for patients who suffer from grave injuries. Of ten cases in which settlements of $1 million or more were reached, NAIC reported that the insurers themselves defined the injuries as "grave," including quadriplegia, severe brain damage, lifelong care, or fatal prognosis. Awards above $100,000 involved what the insurers termed "major" injury: paraplegia, blindness, loss of two limbs, brain damage. As with injuries stemming from defective products, "incidents associated with small amounts of economic loss are generally overcompensated, while incidents with very large amounts of economic loss are often 'undercompensated.' "[59]

Other legislative changes in the substantive law of tort included elimination of the *ad damnum* clause (a trivial change that simply means a lawyer may not state in his legal complaint how much the plaintiff is seeking in damages), abolition of the collateral source rule (which allows a plaintiff who recovers part of his economic losses from some other source, such as private medical insurance, to recover it again from the defendant), restoration of medical standards as the definition of informed consent, shortening of the applicable statutes of limitation, abolition of the res ipsa loquitur doctrine, and creation of arbitration and mediation schemes designed to circumvent the trip to the courthouse.[60] To varying degrees, however, these changes do not address the underlying problems but deal, instead, only with symptoms.

Abolishing the *ad damnum* clause will curtail headlines when a suit is filed (no longer, the doctors assumed, will people be able to draw ideas from news articles headlined, "Woman Seeks $10 Million for Sore Thumb") but will make stories about eventual recoveries ("$700,000 for Permanent Paralysis") all the more pointed. The informed consent rule has never been a significant factor in malpractice litigation. In New York State in only one case was money ever paid solely on an informed consent claim, yet the legislature was pressured to abolish it, so that now only local medical standards apply.[61] The NAIC study discovered that informed consent figured in only 3 percent of the cases, in which only 2 percent of total payments to plaintiffs were involved. The study also showed that 94 percent of all claims were reported to the insurers within three years (well within the shortened statutes of limitation) and that these claims represented 89 percent of all dollars paid out.[62] Even under the modifications to the statutes of limitation some further percentage of the remaining claims could still be filed. Finally, the arbitration and mediation schemes, touted as a creative way of avoiding the stumbling blocks and delays of court suits, do not seem to have produced the desired effect. Enormous backlogs have arisen in many courts, and though perhaps enough time has not yet elapsed to provide a true test, some screening panels are already being abolished. In September 1980, the Pennsylvania Supreme Court voided a state law requiring that all malpractice claims first be submitted to arbitration panels. The court ruled that the law infringes the right to a jury trial. In four years the panels had resolved only 27 percent of claims submitted.[63]

Much of the legislative hullabaloo stems from medical ignorance about law and the legal system. As of 1978, "not a single medical school in the nation requires a course in which physicians in training are introduced to the basic law affecting their practice, and 40 percent of the medical schools do not even offer such a course."[64] And as usual, ignorance only begins in school. The level of misinformation passed around in professional medical circles about legal currents is high, making for shrill and uninformed debate and leading to misplaced and useless public action.

The clearest example is the Good Samaritan Act, which in more than forty states immunizes from liability any doctor who provides emergency roadside medical service. State legislatures responded to physicians' fears that the potential for suit was too high given the need to act quickly under harrowing circumstances. The legislators responded also to threats that, without protection, doctors would cease to offer emergency care altogether. But the basis for this legislation is chimerical. "There is not one single reported case, in any state, in the entire history of the country, in which a doctor has been held liable because the treatment he provided at a roadside accident or on the street was below professional standards."[65] The legislative response is thus not only unnecessary but dangerously overbroad, because it immunizes grossly careless conduct that even in an emergency ought not be tolerated as well as the kind of reasonable mistake that someone might make under pressure. Nor have even these laws penetrated the medical community: An American Medical Association survey reported that "even after enactment of these laws, only half of the doctors studied said they would stop to help at a roadside accident."[66]

In short, most of the new laws passed during the 1970s were neither responsive to the perceived problems nor directed at those lawsuits that can reasonably be termed spurious. They will thus result in unfairness to some plaintiffs who deserve to win but whose costs and burdens will increase. The tort changes will not slow the filing rate, thought to be the heart of the problem.

THE SPIRAL OF DISTRUST

For all its supposed effects for good and ill, malpractice litigation scarcely addresses the larger problems of medical care in the United States, nor can tinkering with the legal system aid professional medicine or the public in the long run. Litigation is only a narrow approach to the structural problems of medical care; indeed, in some ways it serves to aggravate them. Perhaps the most serious consequence of the rise of malpractice suits is the spiral of distrust that blinds all parties to the real problems and effective solutions.

The cause of malpractice lies below the surface of a litigant's complaint that someone erred. Doctors know more, have more powerful tools, operate more efficient services, and receive more esoteric training than ever before. Surely doctors are not as a class more negligent now than decades ago. Equally clearly, there has been no change in the legal system that can account for the appearance of rampant medical incompetence: Contingent fees have been the rule in such cases for the better part of this century, and no startling reformulations of tort law have beckoned lawyers where they once refused to tread (though a specialist trial bar has become far more sophisticated). Why, then, are doctors being sued more? The answer lies in the one major factor that has changed considerably: the delivery of medical services to the American public.

The growth in medicine has been dramatic. In 1940 less than $4 billion was spent on health and medical care; this figure rose to $70 billion in 1970 and is estimated at $175 billion in 1980. Hospital revenues increased from $650 million in 1930 to $40 billion in 1970; 1980 estimates put it at $50 billion. From 1930 to the mid-1970s physician income rose from $1 billion to $18 billion. Financing much of this growth was a spreading insurance system that encouraged hospitalization, treatment, and surgery.[67]

Rapidly expanding patient-physician contact in an increasingly bureaucratized setting would inevitably result in more accidents. Once general practitioners who saw patients in homes or offices, doctors more and more have become specialists with subspecialties. In the urbanized society into which the nation has been transformed, doctors have shifted their professional lives to large, impersonal clinics and hospitals; the house call and other signs of personal service have virtually disappeared. In their place a forbidding panoply of technology—machine and chemical—is available to the specialist, who sees before him a particular symptom or disease. The whole person vanishes. The office that once contained perhaps a single nurse has given way to a hospital of bewildering bureaucratic complexity. Separate lines of authority, faulty communication between doctors and nurse, and minute subdivision of work all conspire to dehumanize the patient, prevent important information from being assessed, maximize the possibilities of error, and multiply the chances of iatrogenic injury.

The very sophistication of medicine is an important contributing factor to the litigation boom. Error is easier to commit, and its consequences can be far graver than in days not so long gone. A simple slip of the knife in operations not attempted until recently can cause permanent damage where previously death or suffering would have been of natural causes and not attributable to a doctor's intervention.

The mushrooming outlay of public funds and private insurance plans has served during the past quarter century or more to place an ever-expanding part of the population (especially the growing ranks of the elderly) in the hands of physicians so that the number and complexity of physician-patient contacts has multiplied to an astonishing degree. These financial incentives have made doctors as a class rich and have gone a long way toward insuring that medicine as practiced is treatment-oriented rather than preventive. Add to these conditions the perceived, and often real, arrogance of the doctor, who has little time for the patient in his office, whose staff demands that insurance forms be signed first, whose magazines deal with how to invest in tax shelters, and who frequently refuses to take a patient's described symptoms seriously, and there is created a social situation ripe for the spreading distrust of doctors, hospitals, and their associated paraphernalia. Let that distrust smolder long enough and it will ignite into a flame of anger at the doctor when the patient fails to recover from his injuries or is further injured by what seems to him to be inept care.[68]

Like the patient confined in a hospital, so the doctor in a lawsuit finds himself in an alien and threatening world. He becomes anxious and frightened: He stands to lose money and he runs the risk of losing face and autonomy. He may be shorn of dignity on the witness stand as the disrobed patient is shorn of dignity in the hospital bed. He will be forced into an adversary posture from which it will be nearly impossible to view the proceedings neutrally.

Moreover, the very principles of malpractice may force the proceeding into one that is more irrational than need be. The lawyer, increasingly plagued by malpractice suits himself, will not hesitate to practice defensive law and will (often erroneously) join all possible defendants in the suit, even doctors and support staff only remotely connected to the alleged injury. Escaping the snares of a malpractice complaint is not easy, though being made party to one is as simple as typing a name on a piece of plain white paper. Though they are ultimately acquitted of any wrongdoing, often without a great deal of involvement in the suit, many doctors may be left permanently embittered and convinced of the essential evil of the legal system.

The result is medical distrust of the legal system. Though doctors would not for an instant wish to be deprived of their right to sue their investment advisers for fraud or perhaps incompetence (financial malpractice), they will view the legal system from the medical perspective as a swimmer views a shark. "I look at every patient as a potential malpractice suit when she first enters my office," said an obstetrician, responding to a *Medical Economics* poll.[69] "Thus," writes Louise Lander, "patient hostility, of which doctors constantly complain, can become a self-fulfilling prophecy—the patient coming to the doctor with a desire to trust, being met with a screen of suspicion and wariness, and inevitably feeling resentment that in his search for an ally he has been branded an enemy."[70]

The matter, of course, can be overstated. Most doctors are not sued. Most patients, we may suppose, are satisfied. But the knowledge that angry patients sue doctors is close to universally circulated within the medical profession. Doctor and patient may become adversaries, if not immediately, then long before any legal cause arises for suit. Collectively, medicine and law become adversaries, each distrustful of the other, unwilling to confront the other on the other's terms, and unable to see that the solution is neither more suing (as the trial bar confidently advocates), nor less suing (as medicine belligerently suggests), but something different altogether.

Sketching a Solution

The problem of medical care in the United States is a cluster of related but separable issues. They are linked, but not indissolubly so. Thus one component is the cost of health care. The malpractice suit "solves" this problem for a relatively small class of people: those who are wrongfully injured, have large enough damages, find skillful lawyers, and persuade insurers to settle or juries to award damages. Lawyers find this solution appealing because the solution of the cost problem also serves as a self-executing mechanism to deter future wrongful behavior. It is the lawyers' invisible hand, their analogue of the market system: no heavy-handed bureaucracy, no labyrinthine set of rules need interfere in the system's natural efficiency.

Unfortunately, the litigation system very expensively serves few. Those who may have been wrongfully injured but cannot prove their cases—or who remain ignorant that they have cases to present—recover nothing. The vastly greater number who suffer from natural causes cannot look to litigation as a means of paying the bill. The problem of cost is beyond the capacity of litigation to remedy, and whatever direction public policy takes, the problems of incompetence and the nature of health care remain. To absorb the cost of faulty medical treatment by paying for all medical care or to ignore it by throwing a patient onto his own resources will not put an end to maltreatment.

That will not begin to happen until the profession itself recognizes its long-standing obligation to clean up its own house. Medical discipline, like that of other professions, has been moribund. In more than half the states, incompetence historically has not been a ground for losing the license to practice medicine. The usual grounds are drug addiction, criminal offenses, acts or conditions like sexual abuse of patients, alcoholism, and mental illness. As sluggishly as have medical boards performed in branding these doctors unfit for practice, their record against incompetent physicians has been far worse. From 1970 through 1975, medical boards revoked or suspended licenses of only eight doctors in the entire United States on grounds of incompetence (against an average of seventy a year for drug addiction and the like). Doctors and hospital administrations, furthermore, are notoriously protective of their errant colleagues, and if a doctor's conduct is so flagrant that it can no longer be tolerated, the usual remedy is to induce him quietly to resign and move elsewhere by assuring him a good reference. Even while under official investigation doctors can generally establish new practices elsewhere because state agencies so rarely exchange information and are so slow to act.[71]

Effective medical discipline is a far more direct route toward elimination of incompetence than a subsequent lawsuit. But it will require a will on the part of a profession notably lacking the stomach or the interest in effective self-policing. In a few states during the late 1970s, professional public agencies with adequate funding have been created. Any lessening of autonomy is the fault of a profession (in common with others) which refuses to recognize that self-regulation for the specialist is justifiable only as long as it benefits those using his service. Furthermore, for the profession as a whole to remain out of the reach of a remote bureaucratic governing body has never meant complete autonomy, heedless of responsibility, for the individual practitioner.

Whether real change will occur from agencies explicitly designated disciplinary is problematic. But there is another route that may be more promising simply because it appears to be less legalistic, governmental, and punitive: the management of risk within the most important medical institution, the hospital. This will become legally imperative, if not socially imperative, as courts begin to hold hospitals liable for failure to monitor the competence of their medical staffs.

Still more is involved. The immediate cause of the alarums in the 1970s was an insurance system that reacted to an inbred set of incentives not rationally tied to the service it promised to deliver. The medical profession should not be held hostage to the fate of insurers' stock market investments. What has just been said about medicine—the need for discipline and for restructuring—has its analogue for insurance. There, too, the question is whether structural reforms can be devised and implemented. Most legislation aimed at the insurance industry has been cosmetic. One authority has described state insurance laws as "a rubbish heap without parallel in the law-making of modern man."[72] There has been no serious undertaking to provide greater resources or power to state insurance commissions or otherwise prod the regulators out of their somnolence. It is no coincidence that the malpractice crisis hit one of the least-regulated major industries in the nation.

In an age that decries regulation, is more regulation an even passable answer? In the absence of an effective private deterrent it must be. There is no private legal mechanism by which insurers can be made answerable to their customers and the customers for which doctors stand proxy, the public. Insurance is a necessary service; its provisioning is akin to that of a public utility. Too much of the business remains hidden from effective check by the consuming public; too much is at stake to let it remain so. No less than other major instrumentalities of modern life, insurance must be made subject to a fiduciary ethic.

It would, indeed, be simpler to live in a society in which patients, and consumers generally, bore more of the burden of accidents. Doctors, and producers generally, would be able to plan their lives more intelligently. The argument is beguiling and on its face innocent. William J. McGill, past president of Columbia University and chairman of the New York State Special Advisory Panel on Medical Malpractice, writes, "We are now in an era of high technology in which medical injury is a risk that must be accepted either in the practice of medicine or in the conduct of hospitalization."[73] If they are true risks, unpredictable contingencies that no one yet knows how to avert, we should not hold doctors responsible. But there is another breed of risk, the chance that injury will befall a person unlucky enough to be subjected to the hazards of an ill-designed institution or plan of action. We need not immunize medicine on the ground that the patient, knowing a hospital's routine is akin to a game of Russian roulette, assumes the risk. We can, instead, punish those who proffer the game. Determining which type of risk is involved in a given case may not be easy. It remains a job for the courts.

Chapter 4

Redressing Social Harms: The Rise of an Environmental Ethic

Boundless Opportunities for Delay

THE Natural Resources Defense Council (NRDC) is a public interest law firm, a handful of lawyers supported by foundation grants whose primary function has been to litigate against the government in environmental cases. It has had some spectacular successes. "Some of the NRDC's victories or near victories include delaying offshore drilling in the Baltimore Canyon and off Georges Bank, opposition to the leasing of public lands in the West for coal and timber production, forestalling nuclear power plant construction and demanding stricter enforcement of air quality standards." But these successes may be viewed as strategies for delay. The bottom line, according to a petulant *Wall Street Journal* editorialist is that "in the name of the public interest, the NRDC has gone a long way to impede the development of an effective energy program in the United States."[1]

Corporate executives do not wholeheartedly appreciate the virtues of environmental litigation. And no wonder. A lawsuit under the Mineral Leasing Act held up construction of the Alaska pipeline nearly four years and re-

quired an act of Congress to reverse the court that stood in the way. A series
of legal actions against Consolidated Edison Company, the electric utility in
New York City, to prevent it from building a nuclear power plant along the
shores of the Hudson River began in January 1963 and was not settled until
December 1980. The hearings before the Nuclear Regulatory Commission, its
predecessor agency the Atomic Energy Commission (AEC), and the courts
have consumed hundreds of thousands of pages of testimony and millions of
dollars in legal fees.[2]

NRDC is not alone in its fight against private and government action that
environmentalists consider socially harmful. In Midland, Michigan, Myron
Cherry, a Chicago attorney, has been battling the Consumers Power Company for nearly a decade to prevent it from going forward with its nuclear
generator. By 1978, owing in no small measure to his tenacity in staying in
court, the company reckoned it had lost eight years and its construction costs
had skyrocketed from an original estimate of $350 million to $1.75 billion.
The key to his various suits against nuclear plant construction, Cherry ex-
plains, is "to hold up funding, for once a utility starts pouring millions of dollars into a project, it is almost impossible to stop."[3]

Holding up major industrial plans has proven tedious but relatively easy
under the web of environmental laws that came into being during the 1970s.
So complex are the issues, so vague are the standards, that the attempt to
build an environmental ethic has given its proponents boundless opportunities
for delay. Whether that is a bad thing is, however, another issue. So, too, is the
question whether there was any practical alternative to the path that environmental protection took in its first decade.

National Environmental Policy Act: Broad and Opaque

A society that blesses private ordering as the basic mode of human interaction
justifies this arrangement by hoping that on balance whatever harms occur
will be fewer and less intense than in a society in which a central government
regulates human conduct. In the usual preconditions for market society—
many actors, full information, equal bargaining power—the assumption is
that whatever harms occur will be felt as palpable injuries by identifiable individuals and will have been caused by a discrete act of another individual—
murder or fraud, for example. Where these conditions prevail, after-the-fact
redress can be sought easily enough through adjudication, and the fact find-

er's decision will have little or no effect on those unconnected with the act that caused the harm.

But this is not the only possible picture of redressable injury. Some harms are cumulative, only partially caused by any single act. The impact may be distributed widely, so that no single individual can claim to bear it all. These can be called social harms, and they require some form of public intervention if the ills they create are to be treated and cured. Such intervention is not antithetical to a private market system. The economists recognize that various externalities are beyond the reach of self-correcting market mechanisms.

One of the clearest examples of such externalities is damage to the natural environment. By now it is a commonplace that air is a free good. We do not pay to breathe it, and no one charges the polluter for the waste gases that he pours into it. Polluted air may be responsible for the death of certain persons each year, and it may cause or aggravate diseases. But no cancer victim can point to a particular factory and show that its discharge of effluents was responsible. Suits for injunctions or damages are not entertained unless the harm can be particularized (dense smoke poured continuously into someone's back yard). Neither the market system nor the conventional legal system is adequate to the task of cleaning up the environment because the social harm is the cumulative result of trillions of actions by individuals in their homes, cars, and places of work.

Redress for environmental depredations can only be structured, in the first instance, by a legislature, registering a public preference for cleaner air, water, and land, despite increased costs and decreased economic growth. But on closer inspection, it turns out to be devilishly difficult to write a law that will accomplish these objectives. The drafter cannot say simply, "Do not pollute," because every human action has some effect on the environment, and any enforcement scheme would quickly run afoul of constitutional prohibitions against vagueness. As the Committee on Pollution of the National Academy of Sciences has noted:

To insist on clean air is meaningless. How clean? At what cost? And for what purpose? Even before man there were occasional excesses of natural pollutants, such as too much volcanic ash or too much water. A little solid material in the air—salt nuclei and dust—is essential for natural rain. Too much—a great dust storm—is a pollutant. . . . So it is with manmade pollution. There is a necessary and acceptable amount of each pollutant that society will tolerate; but because of the varied uses of land, air, and water, the right amount is not the same everywhere. . . . The right amount of pollution must be planned with criteria set somewhere between the ideal of complete cleanliness and the havoc of uncontrolled filth.[4]

But Congress cannot set forth the proper balance in a comprehensive code: In an interdependent industrial society, any legislative interference at one point

will have ramifications throughout. Attempting to dictate specific action for
everyone—or even for the seemingly most obvious culprits—would lead to a
host of unanticipated and unwanted consequences.

Congress's response, therefore, to the mounting political demands that
something comprehensive be done about the deteriorating environment was
to pass the problem on to other governmental agencies. This was scarcely novel. Congress almost always solves major problems by delegating rule-making
authority to the executive branch or to the so-called independent agencies.
This legislative solution is inherent in the nature of modern democracies.
Members of Congress have neither the time nor the expertise to oversee programs that will invariably require continual monitoring. Moreover, because
the problems pressed on Congress always implicate values over which there is
widespread discord, the only feasible approach is to draft legislation in the
most nebulous possible language to satisfy each interest group that has won or
at least can remain hopeful that it has not lost. Congress can then breathe a
sigh of relief that someone else will be called on to answer the tough questions. Once a legislative consensus is reached on the language of generic statutes—like antitrust, civil rights—there will be the greatest reluctance to review the handiwork of a previous legislative session.

By 1980, Congress had enacted scores of laws delegating authority to dozens of federal agencies to direct the actions of private corporations in the interests of environmental protection. But the broadest statute of all, enacted in
1969 as the first great success of the environmental movement, was the National Environmental Policy Act (NEPA). It undertook to regulate the activities of the entire federal government, declaring that every bureau and agency
must "create and maintain conditions under which man and nature can exist
in productive harmony." This means, the act says, that insofar as is practica-
ble, the government must assure "safe, healthful, productive and esthetically
and culturally pleasing surroundings," and "attain the widest range of beneficial uses of the environment without degradation."

Because it would be easy for any agency to ignore these grand sentiments,
the act set forth a process of compliance. It detailed techniques agencies must
use in integrating environmental considerations with their central tasks. It
also prescribed a specific affirmative duty: Before any "major federal action"
affecting the environment is undertaken, the agency concerned must present
a prediction of its proposal's effects. This prediction has become known as an
environmental impact statement (EIS). The impact statement must note unavoidable adverse effects, set forth alternatives to the proposed action, discuss
the "relationship between local short term uses of man's environment and the
maintenance and enhancement of long-term productivity," and indicate any
"irreversible and irretrievable commitments of resources which would be in-

volved in the proposed action should it be implemented." In other provisions, the act created the Council on Environmental Quality and empowered it to put flesh on the skeleton of the EIS that Congress had stitched together.

Nowhere in NEPA, however, is any particular conception of environmental health set out. It does not tell the government how much environmental protection is requisite. The act's only instructions are that the government is to put environmental concerns at the forefront of its deliberations and to consider what it does in the light of environmental impact. It would be within the letter of the law for environmental considerations to be submerged in or missing altogether from the ultimate conclusion of an agency to issue a regulation, a license, or a monetary grant. In the words of Judge Henry J. Friendly, NEPA is "broad and opaque";[5] potentially it covers both waterfronts and all the land and air in between, yet it sets down no substantive standards whatsoever. That NEPA has produced such squawks from business executives and editorialists is a tribute to a special breed of litigants who have seen how to prod the courts into fashioning an environmental ethic.

The Courts Discern a Standard

Courts derive their power to decree substantive legal principles from three sources. The first is the common law. Within this body of precedents, customs, and traditions, courts have considerable flexibility in articulating legal standards that govern private conduct. But the domain of the common law is not coextensive with the realm of human conduct; it is confined, rather, to the kinds of transactions between individuals that can give rise to direct physical injuries and pocketbook losses. The common law in this sense is a creature of state courts and is normally beyond the power of federal courts to interpret and change.

The second source of judicial power is the Constitution; all courts may apply the policies and standards it declares when proper cases are brought before them. But neither of these sources confers authority on the courts to act in environmental disputes. Only the third source, legislation, does so.

Some statutes give the courts a power to act akin to that of the common law. The Sherman Antitrust Act, for example, declares that all contracts "in restraint of trade" are unlawful. With these few words, federal courts for nearly a century have been able to build an impressive body of commentary on commercial dealings. But not every statute gives the courts such freedom.

One type of statute in particular, the laws delegating power to administrative agencies, limits the courts severely. Since the 1930s the courts have deferred to the agencies' "primary jurisdiction." When Congress entrusts policy to an agency—communications, land development, trade relations, commercial practices, securities dealings—then the power to give shape to the policy by promulgating rules, granting licenses, and enforcing substantive provisions of the law must rest with the agency. A court that substitutes its own judgments usurps the agency's role and counters congressional intent.

In giving the federal government responsibility and authority to weigh the environmental impact of its decisions, Congress thus seemed to be excluding the courts. Environmental policy, unlike antitrust law, would be shaped in the numerous agencies, boards, bureaus, and departments of the federal government. This makes intuitive sense. The only environmental policy actually laid down was the order to be mindful of the environment as the government goes about its other business.° The job of balancing ought to be left in the hands of those who are empowered to oversee specific enclaves of the private sector.

The principle that agencies are masters of their own house does not, however, prevent the courts from all involvement. The question remains whether the agencies have stayed within the confines of the statutes committed to them and have abided by its procedural requirements. These common sense principles were to give the courts a larger role than most thought possible in defining a national environmental ethic, and interested litigants took full advantage of the opportunity.

By the late 1960s, the spread of nuclear power generation had become an issue for both environmentalists and those more single-mindedly concerned about nuclear hazards. One of the earliest targets of citizen activists, therefore, was the AEC (now the Nuclear Regulatory Agency), which licenses the construction of nuclear reactors for public utilities. When President Richard Nixon signed NEPA on January 1, 1970, the AEC was engaged in eighty licensing proceedings. The first question that arose was the applicability of NEPA to these projects.

Though it had once denied it had the power to consider environmental factors, the AEC now agreed that they would have to be given some weight. Near the end of 1970, the agency amended its operating regulations to comply with NEPA. The published rules took the position that the AEC need not look anew at ongoing construction nor consider environmental issues in licensing hearings already scheduled. "By excluding the existing plants from NEPA, the regulations made the statute a dead letter in just those cases where

---

°In other legislation, the Environmental Protection Agency was given specific enforcement powers under a number of other statutes, like the Clean Air Act. These laws regulate private activity, unlike NEPA, which applies only to the federal government.

the controversies were most acute, and in which the environmentalists had hoped to employ it to mount a major challenge to nuclear plants."[6] Other issues lurked in the AEC's regulations—for example, whether the AEC could ignore any environmental problems not raised by a party, such as the utility, to an agency proceeding.

The AEC's regulations and, by implication, those of every other agency (some of which had not yet formally complied with NEPA) were quickly hauled into court in a case involving the construction of a nuclear plant at Calvert Cliffs on the Chesapeake Bay in Maryland. The AEC had given a construction permit to the Baltimore Gas and Electric Company before Congress passed NEPA, and the agency now refused to reopen its decision to consider the environmental impact. A group called the Calvert Cliffs' Coordinating Committee, charging that NEPA required all ongoing projects to be reassessed, took the AEC to the United States Court of Appeals in Washington, D.C., which has jurisdiction to hear challenges to federal agencies' rules.

Writing for a unanimous panel, Judge J. Skelly Wright (now chief judge) declared the AEC's rules to fall far short of the law. The court's duty, Judge Wright said, "is to see that important legislative purposes, heralded in the halls of Congress, are not lost or misdirected in the vast hallways of the federal bureaucracy." Since the statute committed the substance of environmental policy to the agency, the court, as all subsequent courts, had to speak in the language of procedure. The court could not dictate the substance of an agency's decision, but it could review critically how the decision was reached.[7]

The line between substance and procedure is a thin one. Though frequently useful, it is a semantic construction that when squeezed allows substantive standards to flow through into procedural containers. Judge Wright showed how to squeeze. NEPA requires agencies to come up with data on the environmental impact of federal actions and to consider the data before acting. On the face of it, there is no reason to accuse the court of overreaching in reminding the agency of its affirmative duties. The problem is that the duty of considering is far more subjective than the duty to issue an EIS. If Congress directs the government to issue a report and it fails to do so, a court is the proper place to call it to account. But the failure to consider a matter is more difficult to detect or to mandate.

Suppose the licensing bureau or the agency chief says, "I looked at the information, I considered it, and I rejected it." The question is how thoroughly the agency considered the data. Judge Wright said that an agency must show that it gave weight to the predicted environmental damage its action will cause and balanced the damage against the benefits sought. Without more, however, the subterfuge is still relatively easy: The responsible officer need simply list an exhaustive collection of figures, which, since they represent apples and elephants, are not directly comparable, and opt for apples—nuclear plants rather than preservation of a river's natural temperature and its quantity of fish. To this the court had an answer: If "the actual balance of costs and benefits that was struck was arbitrary or clearly gave insufficient weight to environmental values," then a court was required to reverse the decision. From this and other similar points in his opinion, "[w]e can see the nose of a substantive rabbit peering over the rim of Wright's procedural hat."[8]

The AEC chose to accept the court's decision and not to appeal. Within two months the commission issued "far-reaching" new procedures, "including what are generally recognized [in 1974] to be the most comprehensive cost-benefit analysis guides which have been formulated for projects regulated by the Federal government," in order to adhere scrupulously to the court's interpretation of NEPA.[9]

The effect of the decision was not solely on the rules. The AEC itself was reorganized, the regulatory staff and licensing boards were enlarged, and environmental specialists were recruited. Within three years the commission's staff doubled to 1,200. Its regulatory budget climbed from $15.7 to $46.5 million. The new procedures affected 110 nuclear plants (operating, in construction, and in design), and for seventeen months no new licenses were issued.

The *Calvert Cliffs'* case was the seminal decision. Hundreds soon followed, as the courts poked into every byway of government operations that affected the environment. A significant number of the cases dealt with the adequacy of the EIS. As before, a statement that said merely "no impact" or "big impact" would scarcely meet the affirmative burden on the government to assess the environmental impact on the proposed course of action. By nudging government agencies to draft a comprehensive EIS, on the grounds of complying with NEPA's procedural requirements, the courts came closer to forcing the government's hand on making environmentally favorable decisions. A process that, for example, calls forcefully to an agency's attention an expert's opinion that a million fish or 20 percent of the striped bass population would be killed annually from the operations of a nuclear power plant,[10] will impress on the agency the prudence of taking the findings into account.

In another key decision, the United States Court of Appeals held that an agency may not disregard an alternative solely because it will prove less effective than the preferred course. This decision also forces the government to the hard task of comparing disparate goals. One alternative to a nuclear power plant that will kill fish through thermal pollution is a plant with cooling towers. However, the towers make the plant less efficient. If the agency could always defer environmental considerations to those of effectiveness, there would rarely be a choice for environmental protection.[11]

Strict judicial scrutiny of the contents of the EIS and the methods of prep-aration also forced agencies to undertake their own environmental review and not to rely on studies by applicants.[12] It also opened the door to public partici-pation in agency decision-making by giving citizen groups the right to com-ment on drafts of the EIS. This right in effect gives outsiders the power to ne-gotiate and to alert influential people, like members of Congress, to forthcoming actions before they were announced as a fait accompli. Judicial interpretation of NEPA thus opened up the federal government to an inter-play of interests that were formerly barred and gave voice to the public in agency deliberations.

The burgeoning legal requirements also imposed serious burdens. These can be glimpsed in the second major NEPA decision, also by the District of Columbia Circuit Court of Appeals. NEPA requires the agency to consider al-ternatives in light of environmental factors. The issue was whether the De-partment of the Interior could confine its consideration of alternatives to those under its control or had to search out alternatives even though it had no power to implement them. The court held that all alternatives were required to be analyzed in the EIS.[13]

In the case, the district court had enjoined a proposed Interior Department lease sale of offshore tracts in the Gulf of Mexico for oil and gas exploration. The flaw was the omission of numerous alternatives to such exploration. These included elimination of the oil import quota, which held down the number of barrels imported annually (an alternative, in 1971 when the court spoke, that would have an odd ring only two years later). Other possible alter-natives were "freeing current domestic oil production from state restrictions, an acceleration and increase in nuclear power development, and the abolition of natural gas producer price regulation."[14] In calling for an assessment of changes that only Congress could bring about, the court was assigning govern-ment branches a potentially endless task.

Attacking the adequacy of the EIS became a favorite tool of environmental litigators during the early 1970s. Because the requirement was new and large-ly untested, they were successful in halting several major projects—at least temporarily. During the first four years, the courts enjoined the construction of eleven dams and water resources projects. For a time there was hope among public interest lawyers that the courts would retain the ultimate au-thority to veto government action, if not to dictate what that action should be. In 1972, the Eighth Circuit Court of Appeals, following *Calvert Cliffs'*, opined in a water case that courts could scrutinize agency action to see whether "good faith consideration" was given to the environmental problems; the wrong conclusion ("insufficient weight to environmental factors") might suggest that good faith was lacking.[15] But the principle of substantive review remained a principle; pressed to enjoin projects permanently because an agency like the Army Corps of Engineers had badly weighed the alternatives, the courts demurred, and the focus remained on the adequacy of the EIS.

"Berserk Proceduralism"

Adequacy of an EIS is not a simple concept. Assessments must be made of factors that cannot be quantified, of risks that are difficult to gauge, of effects that remain unknown. In view of the many doubts associated with an EIS, a court presented with the claim that the impact statement is inadequate may desperately desire to know whether the methods the agency employed to uncover the data it has assembled are sensible. This is a difficult point. The question is not whether the data are correct. It is, instead, whether the agency used appropriate procedures to verify the information on which its final decision is based.

When Congress wants to enact a law, it is not required to hold hearings or to conform the statute to the arguments or evidence brought before it. True, if the law bears no rational relationship to the matter it is intended to control and significantly impinges on constitutionally protected values, courts will upset it. But its method of decision-making is fundamentally different from that of a court. None of the three attributes of adjudication—attention, proofs, responsive explanation—is a requisite of legislation.

This distinction is troublesome when the question is how administrative agencies may properly proceed. When they promulgate rules, they seem to be acting like legislatures. But when they hear cases, they act as courts. Because these hybrid bodies are only uneasily fitted into the constitutional structure of American government, courts have tended to view them suspiciously unless they have conformed to procedures that the judicial mind supposes to be proper. Though all federal administrative bodies have been governed since 1946 by the Administrative Procedures Act, which spells out different approaches for rule-making and quasi-judicial hearings, the courts have tended to impose a judicial model on every agency action with external effects.

Part of this tendency has already been mentioned: the review of an EIS to ensure that it is adequate and the full disclosure of alternatives to the proposed course of agency action. These requirements are, of course, founded in NEPA. But the next step is not. As Judge J. Skelly Wright put it:

I suggest that the time is not far off when in some cases agency action will be vacated without judicial review because the record as kept by the agency is inadequate, confused, or incomplete. . . . There is simply no reason why this record, since it may be subjected to court review, cannot be kept as court records are kept. . . . Presenting the public with a mass of uncatalogued documents, at best, barely meets the minimum requirement of making a public record available. At the very least, with [a] simple docket system the agency, the court, the parties, and the public would know what documents are missing from the record. We would also know that unless a document has been entered on the case docket, it is not part of the record. . . . What the agencies must now understand is that courts reviewing informal rule-making proceedings operate on the basis of a record. We are not mind readers; nor are we unduly impressed by pretensions of expertise unsupported by the record.[16]

This drive to ensure that the record of agency actions is procedurally sound and the increasing tendency of courts to disregard the once fashionable claims to expertise that administrative bodies make means that there is a considerable potential for reversible error in virtually any agency action. Even though the substantive outcome may be correct (or at least beyond the competence of the judge to assail), the matter at issue can always be returned to the agency for further consideration because of procedural defects. Oversight will nearly always yield nits to pick. Agencies unaccustomed to supporting their decisions by reasoning responsively to the parties' proofs and arguments—unaccustomed, that is, to acting like courts—have fared poorly before judges bent on scrutinizing the record.

An example may make the point clearer. After a prolonged hearing on licensing of the Seabrook Nuclear Power Station in New Hampshire, the Environmental Protection Agency, which is empowered to review the safety of the proposed seawater cooling system, gave its approval. Thereupon the Nuclear Regulatory Commission (NRC) issued a construction permit. Thereafter the EPA official who passed on the cooling system changed his mind. Construction stopped. The EPA administrator appointed a panel of six experts, EPA scientists, to provide more information on one aspect of the cooling system. They submitted a written report, which the administrator accepted as a finding that the cooling system would not adversely affect the ocean. An ad hoc interest group, the Seacoast Anti-Pollution League, sued the EPA for violating the Administrative Procedures Act, which governs the methods by which all federal agencies may reach decisions. The United States Court of Appeals agreed with the plaintiff.[17] Its principal reason was that information presented by the administrator's expert panel had not previously appeared in the hearing record. Thus the administrator, in reaching his ultimate conclusion that the cooling system was acceptable, relied on information that, while perhaps entirely accurate, was not made available to the parties before the agency. Commenting on the court's decision, the *Wall Street Journal* acerbically denounced the legal point as farcical or worse.

Approval of the plant has been overturned, in short, not because of any real remaining question about the merits of the Seabrook design, not because of any question about the soundness of Mr. Costle's decision, not because of any question about the merits of the scientific advice he received. Approval is being voided, and future supplies of energy in New Hampshire are being jeopardized, over the question of who delivered the advice, and in what kind of ribbon was it wrapped? . . . When we wonder why we have an energy problem, or why economic growth fails to meet our hopes, we ought to notice that we are being bled to death by berserk proceduralism.[18]

In reversing the administrator's decision in this case, the court may have been sticking to the letter of the Administrative Procedures Act. But in a number of other cases, the courts have begun to impose affirmative duties on agencies to follow certain procedures not found in the law. In 1978, the Supreme Court finally called a halt—perhaps.

Two license applications to build nuclear power plants were at issue in the case, one in Vermont (the Vermont Yankee plant) and one in Michigan (the Midland plant, which lawyer Myron Cherry had for so long been battling). The critical question in each was the increased hazard to the environment that would occur from the waste nuclear fuel that would have to be stored. This is probably the most vexing problem in the use of nuclear power. The NRC chose to confront it once and for all through a "rule-making proceeding" rather than tackle it every time a prospective licensee knocked on the door.

Under the Administrative Procedures Act, the NRC gave notice of the proceeding and accepted comments from its staff and outside parties. These comments were in the form of written reports, replies to these reports, and some oral statements. But the formalities of the courtroom were omitted. The NRC allowed no cross-examination of those making statements, for example. On the issue of waste management, the NRC apparently relied primarily on a twenty-page written statement by one of its staff scientists, who concluded that the problems of waste disposal would in due course be resolved. In turn, the NRC concluded that the risks posed by nuclear waste were minimal. On the strength of this general finding, it issued construction permits to Vermont Yankee and Midland, without assessing the risks associated with each plant individually.

Environmental plaintiffs took NRC to the United States Court of Appeals in each case and won what appeared to be significant victories. The court of appeals held that the NRC's rule-making procedures were inadequate because they did not sufficiently "ventilate" the waste disposal issue. The lack of proper ventilation fatally doomed the license grant, the court said, because it tainted the factual record. In short, improper procedures in compiling the record meant that it was too weak to support the agency's conclusions based on it. What would appropriate procedures have been? The court suggested quite a few, among them limited cross-examination of witnesses, informal conferences with the parties and staff, and the use of technical advisory committees consisting of "outside experts with differing perspectives."[19]

Reviewing the court of appeal's decisions, the United States Supreme Court unanimously reversed, condemning as "Kafkaesque" the judicial philosophy that permits judges to "nullify" the results of exhaustive administrative proceedings on the ground that the agency failed to follow procedures called for by no explicit statutory provision.[20] The NRC followed the rule-making provisions of the Administrative Procedures Act to the letter, Justice William H. Rehnquist said for the Court. That act requires only that the agency give notice to the public and that it permit interested persons to submit information and opinion. The agency is free to accept or reject their advice, and it may consult any other material it chooses. In rule-making, in other words, agencies may act like legislatures and need not act like courts. Extra procedural steps cannot be compelled, Justice Rehnquist said, because it is "the discretion of the *agencies* and not that of the courts [which is] to be exercised in determining when extra procedural devices should be employed."

The Supreme Court's decision in the Vermont Yankee case has been taken as a stern rebuke to lower federal courts which have too frequently, so it is said, heaped extraneous requirements on administrative agencies in order to control their decisions. Will the Supreme Court's order to the federal judiciary to give agencies breathing room end "berserk proceduralism"? Not likely. For the Supreme Court specifically recognized the need for courts to review the record on which an agency's decision is based. When the record is inadequate, the courts may order the agencies to improve it. Though they may not detail the means by which the evidence is to be placed in the record, it will not take much ingenuity for the courts to achieve practically the same thing by dictating what in their view comprises an adequate record. The prospects for delay are not much less. Indeed, they may be even greater. If a court can direct the procedures that must be followed on remand to build an adequate record, then the agency has a guide and the court cannot complain later if the procedures are followed. Absent a guide, "[s]ensible administrators will wish to avoid the risk of a remand and thus conservatively may engage in extensive extra proceedings to be sure the proceedings are adequate. . . . The result will be to slow down the administrative process."[21] In short, as long as some questions may be raised, litigants will continue to have an incentive to bring the government before the bench.

The Incoherence of Policy

Assessing the impact of environmental litigation depends very much on where one looks. On the one hand, it is decried as the principal impediment to the development of a national energy policy because the litigators can tangle up in so many knots the oil and gas explorers and the power plant builders. On the other hand, environmental lawsuits are credited with saving lives and property and even the delays are said to be beneficial.

Delays caused by environmentalists' taking their case to the courts have in almost every major instance resulted at least in improvement in the methods of resource development. For example, the Alaska pipeline is admitted by both Government and industry spokesmen to be far safer and more efficient than it would have been without environmentalists' objections. If their advice on siting had been heeded, the pipeline would not have been put in what former Energy Secretary James Schlesinger now concedes is "probably . . . the wrong place."[22]

These contradictory assessments may both be true. If there is fault in that, it lies rather more with the legislation than with those who have attempted to enforce it. We have no national energy policy because Congress has failed to prescribe one, not because litigators succeed in slowing down energy projects (which are not, be it noted, parts of any comprehensive plan). Likewise, we have ad hoc environmental decisions because Congress has prescribed no substantive environmental policy either. In the main, the litigation conforms to the policy that Congress did lay down: to stop and think about the consequences of action before it is undertaken. Judges who have absorbed an environmental ethic look for ways to advance the cause of environmental health, but just because they do not know precisely what that is, they have stopped short of making substantive decisions or imposing affirmative duties on government to take the environmentalists' line.

Indeed, the very lack of standards makes it difficult to discern a direction in which courts are moving. American industry has discovered that it can bend the environmental laws to its purposes by making the simple observation that actions the government intends to take adverse to industrial interests will also likely have an environmental impact. As early as 1971, National Helium Corporation succeeded in delaying cancellation of a contract it had to supply the federal government with helium, a byproduct of natural gas processing. Its argument was that helium is a resource that would be irreversibly and irretrievably lost if the government stopped purchasing it and that before it did it was obliged to prepare an EIS. The court agreed, the statement was prepared, and the contract was eventually canceled, but not before the government paid $30 million for helium during the two years it took to prepare an acceptable EIS.

Other such suits demanding the preparation of an EIS have led the Environmental Protection Agency to reverse a decision denying a permit for the use of DDT and resulted in a federal court injunction against the Interior Department for attempting to enforce a law regulating the size of land holdings on which federal irrigation water is used. The department wanted to break up large ranches, as the law seemed clearly to require. But the court agreed with angry farmers that the department's law enforcement activity could adversely affect the environment by leading to increased use of water and pesticides and stayed the department from enforcing the law until an EIS was drawn up.[23]

If there is no pattern to the suits, and if the results in individual cases seem to contradict each other, that is the consequence of a law that directs institutions to think through the ramifications of individual actions. NEPA is an important experiment. It is an attempt to see whether a fundamental national policy can be carried out in the absence of a master plan. In this sense, it is closely analogous to the system of private ordering that it is intended to monitor.

Postscript

One may regard the cries against environmental litigation with a certain degree of cynicism, since the business community that now complains pioneered the art of delay. It was, after all, business that subsidized the practical education of lawyers who have best defended their corporate clients by stretching out proceedings in order to force those to yield who are financially or emotionally unable to stay the course. Indeed, one of the reasons that litigiousness has become the focus of public debate is that large corporations have been running a full court press against each other and have begun to feel the pinch. What elephants trample beneath their feet we can easily miss; but when they fight each other, we all notice their wounds.

Nevertheless, the lure of the courtroom is bewitching and despite the rhetoric, the business community, it seems, would rather preserve and even enhance the powers of judges than hew to a foolish consistency. The clearest example is the so-called Bumpers amendment to a bill pending in Congress during 1979–1980 that would make several changes in the structure and powers of the federal courts. This amendment, sponsored by Senator Dale Bumpers of Arkansas, was aimed at reversing half a century of legal precedents that give a presumption of regularity to rules promulgated by administrative agencies. The theory is that when Congress delegates authority to executive agencies to issue rules, the author of the rules should be the agencies, not the courts. A litigant unhappy with a particular rule will assume a heavy burden in trying to persuade a court to upset it. The Bumpers amendment would put the burden on the agency to justify its rule-making: Unless the agency can show by the "preponderance of evidence" that its rule is valid, the court must void it.[24]

The Senate's passage of the Bumpers amendment took most observers by surprise. It should not have. It was introduced at a time when the fever against meddlesome government regulation was high and was viewed as a means of attacking excessive rules that seem to, and often do, interfere with business operations. Though some lawyers opposed the amendment, it appealed to many others. The American Bar Association overrode its own section on administrative law to endorse the proposal.

Should it ultimately be signed into law, the Bumpers amendment would foster litigation not thought worthwhile today. Virtually every administrative regulation would be ripe for searching review, judges would have a markedly greater power to play the role of policy maker, and the prospects for delay would increase by several orders of magnitude.[*]

Congress could, of course, legislate against most administrative rules if it chose to. What the Bumpers amendment expresses is the belief, so prevalent in our political scheme, that litigation and the courts can be trusted to remedy our ills, that it is far easier to hand the job over to the courts.

In the cases examined up to now, the courts have not seen fit to tell private

---

[*] Speaking of the relationship between courts and administrative agencies, shortly after the Bumpers amendment was approved in the Senate, Chief Judge J. Skelly Wright noted that

[w]hile opposition to economic legislation at the administrative level is like trench warfare compared to attacking its constitutionality in court, in the long run it can be very effective, particularly because of the potential for delay. Indeed, most lawyers opposing implementation of legislation at the administrative level, if put on their Boy Scout honor, will agree that delay [through invocation of a federal court's jurisdiction] . . . is the most effective weapon against implementation. . . . [I]f the industry leaders and their lawyers succeed in heavily involving federal judges in the administrative process, both during and after it eventually comes to an end with a final order, time will always be on their side and the opportunities for frustrating implementation of the legislative mandate will be virtually endless. (*Legal Times of Washington*, November 12, 1979, p. 9.)

individuals or public institutions what they must do. The fiduciary ethic that the law embodies generally speaks only to what people or institutions may not do. This is clearly the case where standards of conduct are known. The law says that a company is liable for building a defective product that causes injury. But the law does not direct the manufacturer to build a safe product nor does it tell the company how to organize itself to avoid making unsafe products. Likewise, even where standards are unknown and the harm for which redress is sought continues, as in environmental law, the courts have imposed at most a duty to follow certain procedures or to gather certain information. The courts do not dictate the outcome—for the good reason that they are forbidden to do so.

But eschewing affirmative decrees, decisions that tell people to carry out specific assignments or to act in specified ways, is not an inherent limitation. In other ways the courts do move closer to total redress by actively determining social policy—not its procedural ghost but its worldly substance.

Chapter 5

Courts on Their Own: Restructuring Public Institutions

Right and Remedy: A Discontinuity

IN recent years a broadly voiced complaint is the failure of our public institutions. The detractors' concerns are not novel. Few governmental bodies have ever escaped criticism, informed or otherwise. What is new in our time, however, is the hope that judges can repair the failures.

There can be no principled objection to challenging some kinds of governmental conduct in court. If the sheriff puts a citizen in jail without a trial or other hearing, some form of judicial review is necessary to preserve due process. If the President orders a steel mill seized because he fears for the public safety if it should shut down, the owners ought to have some chance to argue that the government may not take their property. In a constitutional regime, the government, like any citizen, is subject to law and should be held accountable when officials violate it. That is why legislation has always been subject to constitutional attacks in the courts.

But it is one thing for judges to release a prisoner unlawfully incarcerated or even refuse to permit public schools to offer prayers and quite another for courts to order congressional and state legislative districts reapportioned, school children bused, police precinct procedures reorganized. It is even more remarkable for courts to take over management of prisons and mental institutions.

Each of the decisions leading to these orders originated, traditionally enough, in a claim that government had infringed upon a constitutional right. But unlike traditional litigation, the conduct complained of did not have a discrete impact on a single victim, could not be characterized as a single act, nor had it ceased. The complaint was, rather, that an ongoing course of governmental conduct was injuring a class of people in violation of a constitutional provision.

The novelty of the courts' response to these claims lay less in the declaration of a constitutional right (though there was frequently novelty there, too) and more in the remedies devised. Instead of narrow prohibitory injunctions ("you may not incarcerate the defendant without a trial"), the courts issued sweeping affirmative decrees that in some cases put to public institutions a detailed set of tasks and in others restructured basic governmental units.

Traditionalists decry the emerging affirmative decree as a primary example of judicial overreaching. "All too many federal judges," the late Alexander Bickel declared in a memorable line, "have been induced to view themselves as holding roving commissions as problem solvers, and as charged with a duty to act when majoritarian institutions do not."[1] Nathan Glazer accuses the courts of becoming an "imperial judiciary," of going "beyond the wrong presented to them to sweepingly reorganize a complex service of government so that the wrong can be dealt with—in the Court's mind, at least— at its root." Glazer finds the stated reasons for such remedial orders inadequate:

The justification in these and many other cases is that the legislature and executive won't act. This justification will not hold water. The legislature and executive have far more resources than the courts to determine how best to act. If they don't, it is because no one knows how to, or there is not enough money to cover everything, or because the people simply don't want it. These strike me as valid considerations in a democracy, but they are not considered valid considerations when issues of social policy come up as court cases for judgment.[2]

Beyond academic criticism, these decisions have led to heated public protest. In many cases, judicial intervention into the realm of public policy has prompted street demonstrations, aggravated the tendency toward single-interest politics with all its distortions of the political process, and created several serious attempts, so far none successful, to amend the Constitution (for example, to deal with busing, reapportionment, and abortion). The reason for

public hostility is not far to seek: In almost every case in which they have declared a constitutional right, the courts have acted contrary to the discernible
wishes of a majority of the people.

But majority disapproval is scarcely conclusive. The lowly and despised
have rights that the public may not legitimately deny. The problem is that
the rights are not self-evident because they are applications of Delphic constitutional standards. Sooner or later, any attempt to pour meaning into the
standards will embroil the courts in public controversy and lead them to take
a position that is arguably opposed to some definable majority. More importantly for our present purposes, any line of constitutional interpretation will
lead to a remedy or set of remedies that will appear to be legislative in nature
and that will lack continuity with the right infringed.

For example, the Fourteenth Amendment requires states to guarantee each
person the "equal protection of the laws." When the Supreme Court confronted the issue of racial segregation in 1896, it declined to overturn what
had become established practice in a number of states but opted instead for a
formula of "separate but equal." Black may be segregated from white, the
Court declared, as long as the separate facilities (railroad cars, schools) are
equal facilities.[3] Fifty-eight years later, the Court reversed itself in *Brown* v.
Board of Education. A unanimous Court said separate but equal was no longer a valid criterion, sparking the most significant social revolution of our
time.[4]

Suppose, however, that the Supreme Court had not decided *Brown* as it
did. Just as surely as *Brown* that decision would have been but the beginning°
of a series of lawsuits that would have tested the meaning of equality in every
appropriation, school program, building construction, curriculum, and teach-
er-hiring process wherever segregated schools were maintained. If a new high
school were built for whites, would one need to be built for blacks? If 75 percent of a white high school's teachers took their college training at, say, the
University of Mississippi (which would have remained closed to blacks),
would students at a black high school enjoy equal educational opportunity if
their teachers came from an inferior black college? The issues would have
been endless, and the courts would have been plunged into a morass of policy
dilemmas no less difficult than the questions they are compelled to tackle
now. In desperation, the judiciary would likely have laid down a code to
avoid taking on so complex a problem in piecemeal fashion, as the Supreme
Court laid down guidelines for the police in interrogating criminal suspects.

° Actually the middle. *Brown* was not the first but the continuation of a series of lawsuits
brought by the NAACP's (National Association for the Advancement of Colored People) litigation arm to test the limits of—and ultimately to overturn—the separate but equal doctrine. (See
Richard Kluger, *Simple Justice* [New York: Knopf, 1976].)

Limits of patience and judicial resources lead the courts to attempt to define what the government must do if it is to stay out of constitutional hot water. This result will accompany any process that permits courts to interpret the Constitution at all.

The remedial problem remains a serious one nevertheless. That some remedy is necessary cannot be denied, but the shape of the remedy is not forgone. In institutional cases, right does not often contain the contours of the remedy, as the right to redress for physical injury dictates the tort damage award. In fashioning affirmative remedies, the constitutional court is frequently adrift, and its understanding of the wrong may shed no light on the efficacy of the remedy proposed to it. The conduct of an institution is not the same as the conduct of a person; to pretend that law can grapple with institutional behavior according to a psychology that applies to individuals is like plotting a rocket's course to the outer planets according to the Ptolemaic theory. That is at once the necessity for affirmative decrees and their drawback.

Right to Treatment and the Minimum Standard

In April 1972, a judge of the United States District Court for the Middle District of Alabama, Frank M. Johnson, issued a sweeping decree containing more than fifty specific mandatory changes in policy, plans, and operation of three state-run mental hospitals. Some sense of the decree's magnitude and detail can be glimpsed from the following: Patients, Judge Johnson declared, are entitled to a minimum of 80 square feet of floor space in multiperson rooms, and 100 square feet in single rooms. Every 8 patients are entitled to at least 1 toilet, installed in a separate stall. The hospital temperature may not fluctuate beyond 68 degrees F. and 83 degrees F. Minimum numbers of employees per 250 patients were prescribed in 35 categories: unit director (1), psychiatrist with 3 years residency (2), M.D.'s (4), orderlies (10), social workers with the M.S.W. degree (2), social workers with a B.A. (5), clerk typist (3), two categories of cooks (5), food service worker (15), messenger (1), and so on. At one hospital, this meant a minimum of 45 M.D.'s, where there had been only 17. The professional staff was told how to keep and what to include in patient records and how to construct and maintain an individualized treatment plan.[5]

These orders, and there were many more, are undeniably intrusive. At the time, they were probably the most extensive federal judicial intervention in a state-run institution. A hurried and sentimental reading of the lengthy decree might convince those who believe state sovereignty ranks with Mom's apple pie that something fundamental had gone awry in Judge Johnson's court.

But it is necessary to understand the conditions in the mental hospitals of Alabama. A parsimonious legislature condemned them to near penury. Three hospitals comprised the mental health facilities of the state: Bryce Hospital in Tuscaloosa, Searcy Hospital in Mount Vernon, and Partlow State School and Hospital, an institution for the mentally retarded, also in Tuscaloosa. The newest of the three, Partlow, was built in 1919. Bryce goes back to the 1850s, and Searcy had been an abandoned military reservation to which 302 patients were transferred in 1902 from a then woefully overcrowded Bryce.

By the late 1960s, the overcrowding had intensified by several orders of magnitude. Bryce housed 5,000 patients, of whom fewer than half were mentally ill under the terms of the commitment statute. Some 1,500 to 1,600 were geriatric patients, with no incidence of mental illness; another 1,000 were mentally retarded. Of the 1,600 staff members, there were only 17 physicians, 21 registered nurses, and 12 psychologists, in addition to 850 psychiatric aides (required to have but a tenth grade education), and 13 social workers. Of the professional staff "whose duties involved direct patient care in the hospital therapeutic programs" only 6 had sufficient training (3 M.D.'s with some psychiatric training, though none were board-certified psychiatrists; 1 Ph.D. clinical psychologist, and 2 M.S.W. social workers). Expenditures per patient were so meager that Alabama ranked lowest in the nation ($6.55 per day in 1970, up from $3.86 in 1965). Only fifty cents a day was spent on food for each patient. So thin was staff spread that the state's own consultants testified at trial that Bryce created "extreme stresses for individual aides, who at times must cover one or two or three wards, housing as many as 100 or 200 patients."

Out of these conditions grew many serious problems. There was virtually no privacy; indeed, "for most patients there is not even a space provided which he can think of as his own." Health problems were severe: "Patients with open wounds and inadequately treated skin diseases were in imminent danger of infection because of the unsanitary conditions existing in the wards, such as permitting urine and feces to remain on the floor; there was evidence of insect infestation in the kitchen and dining areas."[6] Patients were perpetually malnourished. Safety hazards were legion. Patient treatment was virtually nonexistent.

At Partlow, the institution for the mentally retarded, conditions were even graver. According to testimony of Dr. Donald L. Clopper, Associate Commissioner for Mental Retardation for the Alabama Department of Mental Health, the institution was 60 percent overcrowded, and 70 percent of the inmates should never have been committed. Three hundred inmates could have been discharged immediately. Most performed unpaid labor, a system that amounted to peonage, outlawed by the Thirteenth Amendment and Congress a century before. Brutality and inadequate supervision and staffing led to at least four deaths: "One resident was scalded to death when a fellow resident hosed water from one of the bath facilities on him; another died as a result of the insertion of a running water hose into his rectum by a working resident who was cleaning him; one died when soapy water was forced into his mouth; another died of a self-administered overdose of inadequately stored drugs."[7] To prevent one resident from sucking his hands and fingers, the Partlow staff placed him in a straitjacket for nine years. Still another was kept for several years in a seclusion room; these were so small that there was space enough only for a bed and a coffee can, which served in lieu of a toilet.

These facts came to light when five of the ninety-nine employees of Bryce who were discharged when the budget was slashed following a legislative cut in the state cigarette tax filed a class suit in 1970 to regain their jobs. They alleged that without their continued employment the patients at Bryce would not receive adequate treatment (forty-one of the ninety-nine employees were typists, mechanics, and the like; twenty-six were involved in social and recreational activities; only the remaining third, including two doctors, one dentist, and three nurses, had been directly concerned with patients' health). A second class of plaintiffs, represented by Ricky Wyatt and two others, were patients at Bryce.

The original pleadings did not complain of inadequate treatment at Bryce before the firings. The immediate concern was the effect of the budget cuts on continued care. But the focus quickly shifted "to questions of the overall adequacy of the treatment afforded at the Alabama state mental hospitals." The appellate court, reviewing Judge Johnson's eventual order, said that the reason for the shift in focus was "not entirely clear from the record before us." That was because the reason—Judge Johnson's concern—was not placed in the record. At a pretrial conference in chambers, Judge Johnson said the employee grievances could be resolved in state courts; the larger issue of patient care was the one that troubled him.[8] His concern prodded the lawyers into rethinking the premise of the suit. The employees dropped out, patients at Searcy and Partlow were added to the class, and the complaint was broadened to allege an unconstitutional denial of a right to treatment.

From our perspective, there are two general considerations. The first is constitutional. The second relates to the wisdom and efficacy of a judicial order defining the scope of the right.

The constitutional question need not detain us. Although the Supreme Court has explicitly reserved judgment on the question,[9] the federal appellate courts have begun to endorse the principle. The concept is simple. Patients confined to mental institutions are locked up. The process through which they lose their liberty contains few procedural safeguards: In Alabama there was no right to notice of charges, to a lawyer, to confront witnesses, to present evidence, or to a trial by jury.[10] The justification for this relaxation of the normal safeguards is that the state's benevolent purpose is to provide needed treatment. A failure to provide adequate treatment is, under the circumstances, therefore, a violation of a patient's right to due process of law.

There are, of course, other purposes to be served by civil commitment of the mentally ill. The most important is to prevent danger to others and to the patient himself. But treatment aside, society's right to lock a person up for his own or the general protection cannot be exercised in the absence of procedural safeguards. The states may not indulge in a "pea and shell game" whereby a patient loses procedural rights on the claim that he will be provided with treatment and then is denied that treatment on the ground that the real purpose of incarceration is to prevent danger to himself or others.[11] As the United States Court of Appeals put it in upholding the principle: Where the justification for commitment is treatment it offends the fundamentals of due process not to provide it. Where the justification is danger to self or to others, then treatment is the price of the extra safety society derives from the denial of the individual's liberty. This principle goes to the core of a society that pays more than lip service to freedom.°

Of course, a constitutional conclusion is not a practical solution. That the courts espy constitutional grounding for a right to treatment does not mean that they are saying something meaningful. Can they define the right they are talking about? Can they force it on an unwilling public? Can they implement it? Are the courts the most expeditious institution for overseeing the right? This last question answers itself: Courts are the only institution that will tax the public itself and its unwilling legislative and executive representatives with the failure to observe that right. The other questions are more worrisome.

Was there, first of all, a less intrusive method of judicial intervention? Alabama argued that the plaintiff patients had what lawyers call "adequate rem-

°Governor George C. Wallace argued that the real reason for commitment in Alabama was to provide care, as distinguished from treatment, for the mentally ill and retarded, who are unable to care for themselves. Wallace's argument proceeded from a mischaracterization of Erving Goffman's *Asylums*, in which "relatives, police, and judges" were said to be the "true clients" of mental hospitals. According to Wallace, the primary purpose of commitment was to relieve the burden that mental illness places on the families and friends of the afflicted; the governor (one supposes, that is, his lawyers) failed to appreciate that Goffman was scarcely approving the function to which mental hospitals were put. The court held not only that the Wallace position would not wash constitutionally but that in the case at hand, the patients were not even being provided with custodial care.

edies at law." By this they meant that any patient could have sued individually for medical malpractice or for the commission of some other tort (like
assault and battery, false imprisonment, and the like). Indeed, charged the
defendants, the failure of the plaintiffs to proceed individually belies their
claim that what they really want is individual treatment.

The argument is something of a non sequitur. The usual tort suit, as the
court of appeals pointed out, is for after-the-fact damages; in this case, the patients needed injunctive relief to "assure in advance that mental patients will
at least have the *chance* to receive adequate treatment by proscribing the
maintenance of conditions that foredoom *all* mental patients *inevitably* to inadequate mental treatment."[12] Moreover, the likelihood is small that those
trapped at Bryce, Searcy, or Partlow, placed there by families who could not
afford or did not want to keep them at home, would be able to sue their way
to freedom or to treatment. In fact, none ever had. This suit only came into
being when action was initiated by employees. In legal *theory*, a wave of tort
suits might have scared the staff into some kind of reforms if damages were
high enough. But it is unlikely that the staff would have personally paid or
that the reforms would have been refined or comprehensive.

At the time, damage suits against the state-run hospitals for failure to provide treatment probably would have been dismissed because of the state's traditional immunity from tort actions. The picture is rapidly changing and
damage suits are likely to burgeon against state-run facilities. Decrees em-
bodying appropriate standards of care in other types of hospitals may emerge
from malpractice suits charging negligence in the internal organization of the
facility.

In any event, the theory was untestable because as a practical matter the
suits could not be brought. Moreover, a single tort suit might have done more
harm than good because the relationship between plaintiff and defendant was
ongoing: "Individual suits may produce distortive therapeutic effects within
an institution, since a staff may tend to give especially good—or especially
harsh—treatment to patients the staff expects or knows to be litigious."[13]

But if individual patients were not suing, who was? In essence, the lawyers
were. A plaintiffless case is widely at variance from the historical norm,
which requires parties with a personal stake joined in issue. Without a personal interest, it is feared, the concrete issues stand a good chance of being overlooked or of not being forcefully or intelligently presented. Interested citizens—philosophers or lawyers not affected personally by the outcome—
would engage in abstract argumentation and might be willing to settle for answers that a real plaintiff would not accept.

This question of representation was not present in *Wyatt* v. *Stickney*, however, for there were real plaintiffs. Whether any lawyer may reasonably rep-

resent a patient who does not and cannot know his own mind is not an issue unique to litigation. It is the root of the mental patient's problems, medical and legal. Civilly committed mentally disabled persons must conduct their affairs through state-appointed guardians.

No one has suggested that the lawyers betrayed a trust or sought what was inappropriate in terms of treatment. They did not seek a standard treatment plan for all, a concept inconsistent with the premise of the suit. They could not get and did not want individualized treatment plans spelled out for each. The lawyers did secure a set of minimum conditions without which no treatment could be effective. This was an operating structure that the professional staff could use to develop appropriate treatment tailored to the needs of each patient.

Uneasiness about judicial intervention on so massive a scale stems from doubts about judicial competence to achieve the desired end, not from doubts about constitutionality or lawyers' responsibilities. Governor Wallace argued that the court's holding that patients were constitutionally entitled to adequate treatment presented questions that were not "judicially manageable" and that "ascertainable standards" were beyond the competence of the court. The argument has surface plausibility. What does Frank M. Johnson, LL.B., learned as he is, know about the proper administration of a mental hospital? How can any court, busy as it is, take the time to reflect on the nuances of psychiatry (or penology, or educational theory, or whatever)?

This line of attack, however, misconstrues the way the judicial process has worked in cases such as these. Judge Johnson did not go home with several fat volumes on psychiatric administration tucked under his arm, read late into the night, and pen out a grand plan of reorganization, like Jeremy Bentham remaking the world, to assure perfect congruence between the most advanced and respected medical theory and a patient's particular needs. Judge Johnson did not dictate individual treatment plans at all. Instead he decreed an administrative structure, a setting for treatment, and the details were not original with him. The most revealing aspect of the case is that the judge for the most part accepted standards previously negotiated and agreed to by the parties.

The suit was originally filed on October 23, 1970. On January 4, 1971, the lawyers formally asked that Bryce be enjoined from operating unless it conformed to acceptable minimum standards of treatment, those to be set by the court. Plaintiffs' lawyer was a private practitioner, George W. Dean, Jr., of Destin, Florida. Dean sought to have a "master" appointed to oversee implementation of whatever plan was ultimately decreed. On March 12, Judge Johnson issued his first and landmark order in which he agreed that a constitutional right to treatment plainly had been violated.

But he did not order immediate relief. Observing that Dr. Stonewall B. Stickney, Alabama's commissioner of mental health, was implementing a new approach to mental health care at Bryce, Johnson refused to refer the case to a master to set standards. Instead, he gave the hospital ninety days to submit a report evaluating the Stickney program and to tender a plan for upgrading patient treatment. The court set six months as an outside date "to implement fully a treatment program." If this were not done, Judge Johnson warned, he would appoint a "panel of experts in the area of mental health" to devise a plan. The court also brought other lawyers, requesting the Justice Department to participate as a friend of the court, with the aid of officials from the Department of Health, Education, and Welfare and the United States Public Health Service. Their explicit mission was to aid the state defendants in meeting federal health standards as well as to advise the court.

The final order was still thirteen months away.

The March 12 order was not the first notice Alabama's health officials had had that something was amiss. Four years earlier, in 1967, a study team from the American Association on Mental Deficiency had visited Bryce and discovered that it was far below accreditation standards. No significant change had been made in the interval.[14]

In August 1971 Judge Johnson added Searcy and Partlow residents to the suit as plaintiffs. He also permitted several organizations to join the suit as amici curiae (these included the American Psychological Association, the American Orthopsychiatric Association, and the American Civil Liberties Union [ACLU]).

On December 10, having received the defendants' reports, Judge Johnson decided that the hospitals had failed the constitutional test by not providing three fundamental conditions: "(1) a humane and psychological and physical environment; (2) qualified staff in numbers sufficient to administer adequate treatment; and (3) individualized treatment plans."[15] Johnson agreed that the failure stemmed from the legislature's refusal to finance staffing at an adequate level, but he chastized the defendants for not at least formulating the appropriate standards. More hearings were set. The court continued to resist referring to a master the formulation of minimum standards (largely because both Stickney and the new superintendent of Bryce had demonstrated good faith in attempting to meet the court's demands).

Between December 10, 1971, and April 13, 1972, when the lengthy decree came down, Stickney realized that the proceedings presented a rare opportunity for the state mental health establishment: Court-mandated standards could be just the thing to wake the legislature from its lethargy.[16] One commentator has characterized the state's default as the Alabama Punting Syndrome (more formally, the Alabama Federal Intervention Syndrome). Calling on federal courts is an elaborate ritual that shields state officials mired in a social-political system that prevents leaders from effectively prodding the electorate to reform.

The tendency of many state officials is to punt their problems with constituencies to the federal courts. Many federal judges have grown accustomed to allowing state officials to make political speeches as a prelude to receiving the order of the district court. This role requires the federal courts to serve as a buffer between the state officials and their constituencies, raising the familiar criticism that state officials rely upon the federal courts to impose needed reforms rather than accomplishing them themselves.[17]

The phenomenon is scarcely peculiar to Alabama nor to judicial intervention into the affairs of state-operated institutions. Especially in the era of single-issue politics, with conflicting demands crushing legislators, the safest course is to avoid writing laws altogether or to enact legislation that is murky, ambiguous, and that holds out hope that the protagonists may yet win in court—as, of course, someone eventually will, to the anguish of the losers and the accompaniment of their cries that the courts have continued to tread where they are incompetent or unwanted.

Where broad social policy is at stake, the courts must act, but they too punt, though rightfully and in their own special way. They do so by ratifying the negotiated agreement of the parties. That is what happened in the *Wyatt* case. The decree was the work of the parties: "Virtually all the specifics of the court's order were taken verbatim from the Memorandum of Agreement signed by the parties, and none of these standards [was] challenged on appeal."[18] Where there were changes they appeared to be in the state's favor. Thus the expert witnesses had recommended that Bryce employ 168 psychiatrists; Judge Johnson cut the number to 45.[19] For the most part, the staffing ratios adopted were those of one of the defendant's consultants, a former superintendent of Bryce.

The constitutional question answered, the minimum standards decreed, the question remains whether anyone is going to do anything about them. Massive resistance to the Supreme Court's desegregation decision kept a generation of black youngsters out of white schools and moved the integration controversy onto a much different and more difficult plane—busing. Suppose the state had ignored the decree? Or told Judge Johnson to come down any time he liked and write out a personal check for $60 million to cover the costs the decree imposed? Would contempt have been the only or even a reasonable solution? Wouldn't Governor Wallace have enjoyed being marched off to federal prison as a palpable political martyr? Would President Nixon have committed federal troops to the Alabama legislature as President Dwight Eisenhower sent them to keep peace in Little Rock, Arkansas? In short, would defiance have worked and is the implementation of a court order any concern of the court, which might be presumed to have done its duty simply in stating the requisite constitutional standards?

There can be no definitive answers to these questions. To what degree a court should be concerned that its orders are upheld depends on the issues, the cases, and the nature of the slight. A court whose orders are never obeyed is an impotent institution, and so at a personal level, if not from an institutional perspective, a judge must constantly worry whether he is spending his life in something other than futility.

In the normal case, in which the judge oversees a jury's decision or renders a judgment not calling for affirmative relief (for example, injunction against continued use of dynamite next to a neighbor's fence), the judge may consider that he has done his duty regardless of the eventual outcome of the case. That is because the political process normally enforces his judgments. Most defeated litigants will pay the damages they have been ordered to pay. Most will stop doing what they have been ordered to stop doing. When they prove recalcitrant the sheriff can usually be persuaded to seize property to enforce the victorious litigant's claim to reparations. But an affirmative decree is something else again. How the decree is written, what it contains, how it is structured are fundamental to the relief. If the decree is unworkable, the judge has failed in his duty.

As courts become more enmeshed in litigation calling for affirmative decrees that substantively change institutions in ways that are not preordained—that is, as courts move from adjudicating facts under rules toward the less certain task of assessing performance under still-evolving standards— the likelihood that their decisions will be met with substantial resistance increases. For this reason, if for no other, courts ordering broad-scale affirmative relief will be concerned about its impact and will necessarily consider framing the decree in such a way as to maximize the chance that it will produce the desired result.

To be successful at this game, a judge must have something more than an instinct for precedent and a mind attuned to the subtle nuances of "legalism." [20] To endow a decree with sufficient strength to withstand defiance of entrenched resisting powers, a judge must have political sense and a shrewdness about the nature of bureaucracies. The judge cannot simply direct; he must structure the remedy. He cannot set the decree adrift; he must oversee it.

Judges occasionally are willing to invest a great deal of time in oversight. Judge Joseph Tauro, active in several right-to-treatment cases in Massachusetts, has been quoted as saying that having invested "literally hundreds of hours in conference time" he would promise "the parties that if they wouldn't lose patience with each other and with the project, that I would continue to buy the coffee."[21]

But few judges engage in direct oversight. Judging is no less a full-time job than administering. The judge, however, can attempt to keep informed, and the fear that he will learn how much progress is or is not being made may insure that on the whole it will be. Whether it does depends on the quality of his delegated eyes and ears.

To help implement the standards he promulgated, Judge Johnson appointed overseers for each of the hospitals involved in the litigation. These were seven-member Human Rights Committees (HRCs), with a writ to review all research and rehabilitation programs, to assist patients complaining about violations of the order, and to contract with outside specialists for consultation concerning the commissions' duties. Judge Johnson named each member of all the commissions, appointed the United States Attorney in Alabama to serve as their counsel, and retained jurisdiction of the case.

The difficulty with this approach to implementation is that an adversary relationship tends to develop between the monitor and the administration, calling for frequent trips to the courthouse. In part this development is the natural outcome of any system in which different groups have competing loyalties. It is abetted by the inevitable shocks that occur when a particular problem bumps against a generally worded order. The HRCs had no staff and had to rely almost entirely on hospital staff for information about reforms and results. Understandably this shortcoming can lead to conflict. Relations between the HRC and staff at Partlow became so strained during the first year that the commission called in the United States Attorney, who in turn summoned the Federal Bureau of Investigation to study various patient complaints.[22] Many battles were fought between the commissions and the staffs over dozens of issues, but Judge Johnson refused to settle most of them, though he did strike down an order of Partlow's superintendent that all contracts between patients and HRC must be screened by his office, and involuntary sterilization procedures at Partlow were eventually referred to a three-judge federal court (which ruled against the Alabama law).[23]

Much of this tension is unresolvable as long as the administration remains unsympathetic to the judicially imposed regime. It is instructive that Judge Johnson foreswore further effective intervention (including appointment of a master, expansion of the HRC's powers, contempt proceedings, or a financing order) until the court of appeals ruled on the validity of his constitutional decision and the specific details of the decree. This gave the state mental health board and the hospital administrators a two-year reprieve from judicial enforcement. The state officials could have used this opportunity to press forward relatively quickly on their own in order to demonstrate good faith and to make the court thereafter more receptive to their continued direction of the facilities. In fact, however, "implementation . . . proceeded slowly during this period . . . [and] was widely regarded by members of the Human Rights Committees and attorneys for the plaintiffs as frustrating the purposes of the decree."[24]

A more extreme, and efficient, solution is to designate a master, responsible directly to the court, to supplant the state administration altogether. In effect, the master becomes the hospital superintendent, often with subpoena and other powers to exact compliance. Courts have resorted to masters only sparingly, however. (Despite his threats, Judge Johnson never appointed a master to oversee any of Alabama's mental hospitals.) This failure to work through masters, it has been argued, is "unfortunate: They are most appropriate in lengthy and complex litigation in which there is need for personal action, specialized knowledge, and continuous supervision because they combine monitoring, dispute resolution, and enforcement functions in a figure closely tied to the court."[25] But whether through masters or less powerful delegates, the major lesson of these cases is that the courts inevitably take on an administrative burden. Affirmative decrees move courts well beyond the traditional judicial model.

Nor is this due solely to the adversary nature of the underlying dispute. The order itself may present unanticipated consequences. For example, the Wyatt decree forbade hospital officials from running a peonage system that required patients to labor without pay at activities that essentially supported the hospital. The response of the Partlow administration was to prohibit patients from working altogether because there was no money to pay them. As a result, the HRC determined, "these residents are now bored and anxious to be doing something." The court had to amend the order to permit uncompensated labor for therapeutic purposes.[26]

The existence of a judicial blueprint does not guarantee that anyone will consult it to build the new institutional structure it describes. The principal obstruction is the lack of money. The problems that cause patients and inmates to sue invariably stem from the state's decision, conscious or not, to starve its institutions financially. In the mental health field, a vastly greater budget was needed to support staffing increases and building reconstruction. This need raises an acute constitutional and political difficulty: whether courts may direct the expenditure of funds.

Of course courts do so routinely, but in an indirect manner. Awards of damages against governmental units require the state to pay. But legislatures anticipate these cases and have provided various officials with authority to settle and with funds to pay. Legislatures do not provide courts with the authority to reorder the basic state budget. The power to tax and to spend public revenues is as exclusively within the legislative province as any power one can point to.

Yet the logic of the affirmative decree brings the court to the abyss. On a few occasions, courts have jumped across it. A federal district court in Boston in 1973 directed state authorities to construct a new prison facility to be financed by sale of public lands—owned by the prison system.[27] In most other cases, the courts teeter on the edge.

Thus in a proceeding against the Alabama state prison system, in which he declared a constitutional right of rehabilitation under the Eighth Amendment's prohibition against cruel and unusual punishment, Judge Johnson came close, in effect, to seizing state assets to finance the massive rebuilding and retraining programs necessary to comply with his order. The ultimate judicial decree would be an order to a state to tax its citizens. (Governor Wallace refused to accept this as a political option, and a direct order to tax is not likely to withstand a constitutional test should it ever be pressed.) But there are lesser degrees of control. Judge Johnson had in mind directing the state to eliminate nonessential expenditures, such as the Junior Miss Pageant held annually in Mobile. He also believed that it would be sensible for the prison system to sell off thousands of acres of timberland that it owned to finance the necessary improvements. In the event, none of this came to pass, partly because on appeal the Fifth Circuit Court held that there is no "right to rehabilitation" and struck down several of the particulars in the decree and partly because the state legislature itself began to act.[28] *

In the mental health litigation, Judge Johnson's orders did not need to be so intrusive; he had other equally effective means. Orders barring further admissions, closing down facilities, and releasing a number of patients put pressure on the legislature to act. The Department of Mental Health's budget climbed from $26 million in 1970–71, when the suit was filed, to $72.2 million in 1974–75 after the court of appeals affirmed the decree.[29] The legislature's response was not solely a function of judicial threats, however. A good deal of publicity, the sort that always attends such suits, about conditions in the hospitals put independent pressure on the legislators to increase the budget. Nevertheless, the primary ingredient in the budget rise was the litigation.

Whether it is ever justifiable for a court to come so close to usurping the sovereign power of the people to decide what and how they are going to

---

* Prodded by the litigation and by newspaper coverage of the shocking conditions in the prisons, the state legislature itself began to investigate. A committee found that prison officials grossly misused prison funds. They purchased caviar in goodly quantities to entertain visiting legislators, and they bartered fifty-two head of cattle (owned by the state board of corrections) for three "Tennessee walking horses" that were said to have been acquired for breeding but turned out to be geldings. Public support of funding for rebuilding the institutions began to grow. (See Frank M. Johnson, "The Constitution and the Federal Judge," 54 *Tex. L. Rev* 913 [1976].)

spend public revenues is not easily answerable. It might be said that it was the state's own witnesses, after all, who agreed on the programs that made imperative increased spending. But the impartiality of such witnesses is open to question. In the final analysis they testify as experts within a discipline, and as experts their interests in advancing the cause as they professionally understand it may not be congruent with the state's interests, as fiscally conceived. However, in the absence of congressional legislation removing from the federal courts the power to issue such decrees, the courts will find reasons and ways to enforce the affirmative decree in those cases where official depravity is the only possible explanation for the conduct under challenge.

The adequacy of budgets is not the only difficulty in implementing a decree aimed at restructuring. A major problem is whether doctors, nurses, and other professionals can be attracted to serve in state mental hospitals, even if salaries are competitive. Still another problem, rarely thought out in advance, is whether aggressive recruiting of professionals for the institutions will have a deleterious effect outside. It has been pointed out, for example, that "the doctor-to-patient ratio in Alabama has been one of the lowest in the nation." Bringing some Alabama doctors into the hospitals may serve to deplete the supply of physicians available to the rest of the people in the state. "Even if we assumed that the mental hospitals could recruit the professional personnel required (a highly dubious assumption), it does not follow that meeting these standards would be the most reasonable allocation of such resources."[30]

Has judicial intervention in the administration of mental hospitals worked? Has it changed conditions for the better? Are patients being more humanely and professionally treated? The tentative answer to these questions is yes.

A substantial part of the hospital population was discharged in the years after the litigation was instituted. Although this trend began in 1968, when overcrowding had reached its physical limit, it accelerated once the litigation was underway. In September 1970, just before the suit was filed, 9,116 persons were confined at Bryce, Searcy, and Partlow. Five years later, the total population had been reduced to 4,345. Most of the former patients were released into the community and given varying degrees of support. Community mental health centers jumped from 22 in 1970 to 85 around the state by 1974. New admissions to the hospitals declined also, 30 percent fewer in 1974 than in 1969, and this compares to a national decline of only 5.5 percent (and to an actual increase in the admission rate in neighboring states). The patient-to-staff ratio improved markedly: "[A]t the end of fiscal year 1971, Alabama had the worst patient-to-staff ratio of any state in the region, and a ratio almost double that of the average for all states in the country. By the end of fiscal year 1974, the situation had improved to the extent that Alabama's patient-to-staff ratio was better than the average of five other states in the region and almost equal to the national average." Communities around the state were remarkably quiescent as patients came out the hospital doors. Partly that is because patients were being discharged all along before the suit was filed, partly because "the ex-patients had become so institutionalized at Bryce that now that they have been released, they rarely venture out into the community." Many went to nursing homes. Many others resumed their lives. Within the institutions, "the quality of care available . . . has improved dramatically."[31]

Despite these changes, it is foolish to suppose that courts must or can direct the rehabilitation of mental health policy in the United States. *Wyatt* v. *Stickney* illustrates one prong of the attack: litigation as a catalyst. The courts can serve as a publicist for reform in areas of the most pressing need. Unless state legislatures choose to stand or fall on total defiance (which they have not done) the effect of judicial intervention is to force state policy makers to begin to address areas that for too long have remained in darkness. In states like Alabama, where the deficiencies were palpable, judicial activism has led to some necessary changes relatively quickly. But no declaration of the "right to treatment" will produce institutional results that satisfy critics because, as *Wyatt* shows, institutions do not respond automatically to decrees even where they are quite clear.* Results can only be measured in years and probably decades, but that is true of any social change. Only as new people with commitment to new ideas take on the leadership of institutions will the institutional behavior begin to change. Where there is an underlying constitutional value at stake, the courts can help to open up those institutions to the people who really count.

Due Process in the Schools: A Remedy in Search of a Problem

Perhaps no other single institution has been the defendant in so many diverse lawsuits as the public school. It was the target of the most explosive case of the century, *Brown* v. *Board of Education*. It remains at the center of a corrosive national domestic issue: court-ordered busing. Teachers have filed suits against schools for interfering with their lifestyles. Students have taken to

---

* Judge Johnson's order forbade the use of "seclusion rooms" at Partlow, but three years later there were reports, according to the HRC, that they were still in use. ("The *Wyatt* Case: Implementation of a Judicial Decree Ordering Institutional Change," 84 *Yale Law Journal*, 1975, p. 1359.)

court for a declaration of their political rights during the school day. Flag sa-
lutes and prayers have been deleted from the curriculum at the hands of judicial editors, and forty years later the language in *Supreme Court Reports* an-
nouncing those decisions still sears. The handicapped have sought entrance to
schools through the courthouse. Questions of punishment, of testing, of the
languages that can or must be used are increasingly litigated. So too is the tangled issue of public school financing.[32]

That there have been and continue to be so many suits involving schools is
not surprising. In them children consume a significant portion of their lives
for a dozen years, and they are intimately tied to the aspirations of individuals, community, and the whole society. It is only to be expected that those
who wield power over students will be challenged as the law affecting the rest
of society evolves. The problem is whether judicial intervention in school activities threatens a state's power to define its educational purposes and to undertake them.

No single answer is possible since schools touch so many concerns of so
many people. The claim of overreaching must be grounded in some statutory
or constitutional provision alleged to have been violated. No case is won on
the plaintiff's premise that he doesn't like what the school board is doing,
therefore the court should order it to mend its ways. And most of the legal
theories do not call for an affirmative decree or a restructuring of the school's
business. Decisions upholding First Amendment rights of students and teachers do not lay down rules for schools to follow, as courts have for hospital and
prison administrations. That is not because there is a difference between
schools and prisons but because there is a difference between First Amendment and Eighth Amendment claims. The First Amendment cases do not
deal with affirmative duties. They are prohibitory: You may not, the courts
tell the school administrators, prohibit a student from wearing a black arm-
band, fire a teacher who has an unorthodox lifestyle, or permit prayers in the
school. The decisions do not require guidelines from the courts, though the
wise school administrator will adopt guidelines for the schools.

The line between the prohibitory and affirmative case is thin, however,
and can be breached whenever the claim involves an obligation of the government act. Consider *Goss* v. *Lopez*, a 1975 case in which the Supreme
Court, splitting its vote 5 to 4, held that the due process clause protects students facing suspension from school.[33]

The case grew out of student unrest in the Columbus, Ohio, schools in early
1971 in which dozens of students were suspended temporarily for periods of
up to ten days. The students had no notice of the charges against them prior
to the suspensions, nor were they given the opportunity to defend themselves.
State law permitted school principals to expel students for violation of school

rules or to suspend them for periods of up to ten days. The law required any principal who expelled or suspended a student to notify the parents. But only the parents of expelled students were given the opportunity to appeal to the board of education and to appear before board members personally to speak. No similar provision governed the case of suspensions. The Columbus school system had not provided principals with any guidelines. Nine students brought a class action suit on behalf of all suspended students. Most had engaged in obviously disruptive acts for which suspension was clearly warranted. One student, for example, began demonstrating in the school auditorium while a class was in progress. But the conduct of some was in doubt. School files were kept on some of the suspensions, including copies of letters to parents, but they were silent about many others. The plaintiff who gave the case its name, Dwight Lopez, was suspended for having participated in a lunchroom disturbance in which school property was damaged. At the trial of the class action, he denied any involvement in the melee.

The Fourteenth Amendment declares that no person may be deprived of life, liberty, or property without due process of law. This means, in the most obvious type of case, that a person may not be convicted of a crime, be sent to jail, or otherwise punished unless a hearing is first held (the Sixth Amendment spells out particular procedures that must be observed). Strictly speaking, suspension from school is not punishment in the criminal sense. It does not deprive a student of liberty, rather it restores it to him. And a seat in a classroom is an unlikely form of property.

Over the years, however, the Supreme Court has read the due process clause to apply to a host of actions by the government that have a significant direct impact on a particular person's life—for example, withdrawal of certain types of government benefits. Thus the Court has ruled that states may not terminate a recipient's right to continue receiving a welfare check without first holding a hearing to determine eligibility.[34] Parole may not be revoked without affording a hearing to the parolee.[35] So, too, does the due process clause apply "where a person's good name, reputation, honor, or integrity is at stake because of what the government is doing to him." The aim is to ensure that the government acts with cause and not arbitrarily.

Writing for the bare majority, Justice Byron R. White said the same reasoning applied in *Goss*. It is no answer that the students suffered no "severe detriment or grievous loss," as the school officials argued. "The total exclusion from the education process for more than a trivial period, and certainly if the suspension is for 10 days, is a serious event in the life of the suspended child."

To conclude that due process applies to disciplinary suspensions does not end the inquiry, for "the question remains what process is due." Here is where the constitutional conclusion calls forth the affirmative decree. A laborious hearing could defeat the purpose of suspension. Justice White conceded that

> our schools are vast and complex. Some modicum of discipline and order is essential if the educational function is to be performed. Events calling for discipline are frequent occurrences and sometimes require immediate, effective action.... The prospect of imposing elaborate hearing requirements in every suspension case is viewed with great concern, and many school authorities may well prefer the untrammeled power to act unilaterally, unhampered by rules about notice and hearing.

Such was Justice Lewis F. Powell, Jr.'s fear when he spoke for the four dissenters. He saw a ten-day suspension as relatively trivial. In view of the growing number of suspensions taking place across the country° "if hearings were required for a substantial percentage of short-term suspensions, school authorities would have time to do little else." Justice Powell also worried about the impact of the decision on the "normal teacher-pupil relationship [that] is an ongoing relationship, one in which the teacher must occupy many roles—educator, adviser, friend and, at times, parent-substitute. It is rarely adversary in nature except with respect to the chronically disruptive or insubordinate pupil whom the teacher must be free to discipline without frustrating formalities."°° Justice Powell, it should be noted, was for many years chairman of the Richmond, Virginia, school board.

Because of the majority's own concerns and the fears of the dissenters the actual holding of the majority was narrow. The Court held that the school must give the student "oral or written notice of the charges against him and, if he denies them, an explanation of the evidence the authorities have and an opportunity to present his side of the story." The notice need not be delayed:

> In the great majority of cases the disciplinarian may informally discuss the alleged misconduct with the students minutes after it has occurred.... In being given an opportunity to explain his version of the facts at this discussion, the student [must] first be told what he is accused of doing and what the basis of the accusation is.... [W]e do not believe that we have imposed procedures on school disciplinarians which are inappropriate in a classroom setting. Instead we have imposed requirements which are, if anything, less than a fair-minded school principal would impose upon himself in order to avoid unfair suspensions.

Justice White noted that one of the schools affected had had an informal procedure "remarkably similar" to that which the Court was mandating, and the

---

° Ten percent of junior and senior high school students in certain states were suspended one or more times in 1972–73, and in absolute terms the number of suspended students was large: 20,000 students in New York City, 14,600 in Cleveland.

°° This seems to be a curious misconception of the case, since principals, not teachers, are the only officials permitted to suspend or expel.

Columbus school system, in the wake of the litigation, had promulgated a local rule requiring principals to "provide at least as much as the constitutional
minimum which we have described." This local rule was announced before
the case was argued.

What appears to be a dramatic expansion of rights is, as previously seen, a
case of courts following the practices of those they judge. That is not to say
that nothing new is gained thereby: but for the litigation, no such procedures
would likely have been forthcoming. Nevertheless, that the procedures are
those devised by the school authorities themselves suggests that the rule will
not cripple school administrators or negate the possibility of efficient management of schools. The Court explicitly refrained from a full-bodied construction of the due process clause that would have afforded "the student the
opportunity to secure counsel, to confront and cross-examine witnesses supporting the charge or to call his own witnesses to verify his version of the incident." Some process is due, but not much, just enough to put a principal's
mind on what he is doing for at least a few minutes. Will it make a difference? Since 1975, school suspensions nationally have declined some 30 percent,[36] but whether the hearings themselves or fear of suit or a decline in disturbances has reduced principals' reliance on such discipline is unclear.

By itself, the decision promises little intervention by courts. But that does
not end the inquiry. The Court did more than simply announce a rule applicable to temporary suspensions from school. It also declared a general doctrine—or more accurately, a new twist in a general doctrine whose contours
remain wrinkled: that any school decision with serious consequences for a student may be subject to judicial review. The floodgates may open. Again, the
worry is Powell's:

Teachers and other school authorities . . . must decide, for example, how to grade the
student's work, whether a student passes or fails a course, whether he is to be promoted, whether he is required to take certain subjects, whether he may be excluded from
interscholastic athletics or other extracurricular activities, whether he may be removed
from one school and sent to another, whether he may be bused long distances when
available schools are nearby, and whether he should be placed in a "general," "vocational," or "college preparatory" track.
    In these and many similar situations claims of impairment of one's educational enti-
tlement identical in principle to those before the Court today can be asserted with
equal or greater justification. Likewise, in many of these situations, the pupil can advance the same types of speculative and subjective injury given critical weight in this
case. . . .
    It hardly need be said that if a student, as a result of a day's suspension, suffers "a
blow" to his "self-esteem," "feels powerless," views "teachers with resentment," or
feels "stigmatized by his teachers," identical psychological harm will flow from many
other routine and necessary school decisions. The student who is given a failing grade,
who is not promoted, who is excluded from certain extracurricular activities, who is

assigned to a school reserved for children of less than average ability, or who is placed in the "vocational" rather than the "college preparatory" track, is unlikely to suffer any less psychological injury than if he were suspended for a day for a relatively minor infraction.

Justice Powell's concern is that courts not be burdened with every case in which a claim can plausibly be pressed that harm similar to the psychological trauma of suspension may be suffered.°

A tenable distinction can be drawn between the suspension case and Justice Powell's parade of horrors. In the case at hand, due process was invoked for discipline—punishment. Traditionally, due process has required a hearing whenever it is necessary to ascertain whether the conduct actually occurred for which the punishment is meted out. But the majority's decision does not permit courts to hear an appeal or to assess whether a given punishment fits the offense—ten days instead of two. The question of fairness is procedural, not substantive. In the situations that Justice Powell envisions, due process has not been a traditional adjunct nor do the teacher's decisions imply punishment. These matters are at the core of the school's mission and are uniquely within the school's competence. In the case of allegedly faulty grading, there is no directly applicable standard: The Constitution does not proclaim a right to pass or a right to graduate.

The danger is that courts are equal to the task: Due process is a remedy constantly in search of a harm. Substantive benefits, arbitrarily denied, seem to cry out for restoration. Suppose the student receives a failing grade for rejecting a teacher's sexual advances?

That courts can make distinctions does not mean that they will. Five years after *Goss* v. *Lopez*, however, the courts have not imposed a due process requirement on action beyond discipline. The concern remains a fear, not a reality.

Fear itself can be disruptive and disabling, though. Like so many others, teachers and school administrators become apprehensive and therefore less confident and efficient in the face of a perception that much of what they do is subject to judicial second-guessing. They fear not so much that they will have to go through some procedure to demonstrate they are right but that a court will decide by its own reasoning that they are wrong. In other words, the problem of a decision like *Goss* is that the locus of decision-making power will be shifted. The schools will no longer possess it; the courts, or more likely, their experts, will. This shift, if it occurs, would necessarily reflect a change in

° The narrowly drawn *Tinker* v. *Des Moines Independent Community School District* (393 U.S. 503 [1969]) decision, in which the Court declared the First Amendment right of students to wear black armbands to protest the Vietnam War led, Justice Powell asserted, to "literally hundreds of cases by school children alleging violation of their constitutional rights . . . a flood of litigation."

the underlying legal principle: toward a substantive, rather than a procedural, rationale. The courts would entertain claims that teachers wrongly judged the evidence (test scores, essays, class participation) rather than, as in *Goss*, that they failed to garner the evidence at all.

This would be a dubious enterprise. To keep the courthouse open for appropriate cases does not mean that judges must hear every claim that a teacher graded a paper wrongly. For one thing, courts know no more about algebraic equations or symbolism in Shakespeare than do the teachers to whom the state has assigned the duty of judging student work. Where objective matters are concerned (a precise mathematical answer) it is unlikely that a teacher would persist against his professional ethic of striving for the truth in the face of demonstrable evidence that he was wrong. Students have been known to point to errors in a teacher's grading key, and teachers have been known to concede gracefully. Subjective errors, precisely because they are more difficult to assess, properly belong with those who have the professional competence to do so. Both kinds of errors are endemic to an enterprise like education, as all of life contains its measure of error. In athletic contests, referees make mistakes, too, but when instant replay reveals them, the referees are not overruled. Total redress cannot be. The very attempt would commit some other, probably greater harm: The football game would be subject to innumerable interruptions and could never be played out. The teacher would, as Justice Powell suggested, spend all his time justifying rather than teaching. And in the end we would have no greater objective guarantee that errors would stand corrected. Judges might well—undoubtedly would—make worse ones.

So a rush to the courtrooms to rectify claimed classroom errors by teachers ought to be discouraged. But it also ought to be understood, should it ever come to pass. It might represent cynicism at its worst: that there are no standards, that if you lose in one forum, keep on going, that the only acceptable solution is one in which "I" am the winner and my antagonist (for example, the teacher) is the loser. But it could also represent what seems to account for much litigation elsewhere: a fundamental distrust for those in authority. The courts cannot solve this problem, nor is it their mission to do so. Trust can be promised and trust can be earned, but it cannot be ordered.

In education, as in medicine, a vicious spiral of distrust may not be attributable solely to either the institution or the citizen, yet the burden of acting to restore trust, rightly or wrongly, lies more with the former. That is because it is organized and the consumers of the service are less so, because the institution holds the levers of power and the citizen does not. In education, however, it is true that citizens elect school boards and parents can have considerable influence in the schools through parent-teacher associations. Nevertheless, to insist that every disagreement over a decision with possible injurious consequences should wind up in court is to lessen the incentive these institutions possess to solve their own problems.

Courts are not the only institutions capable of refined judgment. That they are thought to be, perhaps because at least in principle and often in practice they sit as neutral adjudicators, accounts for the desire of litigants to prefer their judgment. This is simply another way of saying that people go to court because they distrust others. Going to court and the resulting weakened incentive of primary institutions to do their jobs reinforce one another. By the same token, the courts may be able to help break down that mutually destructive habit of thought by prodding the institution in the first instance to rethink its procedures, as *Goss* did. In turn the school may become more receptive to reconsidering its relationship with the immediate consumers and the larger public and, thus, may begin to repair the essential tissue of trust.

This is a long process. In the short run, fears of administrators and teachers that courts will in fact intervene in their daily activities ought not be discounted, however unfounded or unprovable. This apprehension, which may, as in the doctor-patient relationship, cause teachers to view their students antagonistically and provoke the spiral of distrust, is inherent in every aspect of a common law legal system. Broadly phrased legal standards invite litigation, and even emphatic statements about the necessity for leaving decision-making where the law and custom lodge it, with teachers, prison administrators, doctors, cannot deter forever every litigant. All discretion can somewhere be abused. A responsible legal system will keep open the avenue of redress without having to prevent every conceivable abuse by erecting a costly preventive machinery. A legal system is ultimately efficient when it permits claims to arise on an ad hoc basis and does not freeze a regulatory mechanism into place in the forlorn hope that uncertainties can be avoided. Over time, these uncertainties tend to disappear or become more certain, as the courts articulate case by case what the criteria for judicial involvement, and noninvolvement, will be.

Here is an important lesson for the administrator. Winning a case does not end the matter. We do not live in an either-or system: Either the courts order me to do it or I need not. Judicial abstention places the onus on the administrator, where he has argued it should be, but his action is not predetermined by the court's ruling. The determination that one is legally free to be arbitrary scarcely compels one to be so. This is a lesson that has not yet been learned. Until it is taught and absorbed, social distrust will remain rampant.

Equality and the Open-ended Remedy

Not all constitutional values can be comfortably contained. One that is especially troubling is the great equal-protection-of-the-law guarantee of the Fourteenth Amendment, binding on all the states.° Many institutions have been affected by litigation testing the meaning of this provision. But it was in the context of education that the decision was handed down that changed the face of modern litigation.

Brown v. *Board of Education* dealt with an issue that can be simply put: May a state racially segregate the public schools? For fifty-eight years, the Constitution was taken to permit enforced segregation as long as the facilities for each group were in fact equal. "Separate but equal" had been the law of the land since 1896, when the Supreme Court in the infamous *Plessy* v. *Ferguson* decision opined that "enforced segregation of the two faces stamps the colored race with a badge of inferiority . . . not by reason of anything found in the act, but solely because the colored race chooses to put that construction upon it."[37] From the standpoint of social justice, the decision was a travesty; from the standpoint of social policy it condemned blacks to a position of permanent inequality and inferiority. *Plessy* was wrong.

The question was, What to do about it? *Plessy*'s reasoning and a legion of formally and informally sanctioned practices meant that the political process was closed as an avenue of change. Had there been no provision in the Constitution speaking to formal equality before the law, as there was not until after the Civil War, one could bemoan the historic oversight and brood on the possibility that an enlightened humanity would one day become a majority force inclined to legislate a common decency. But there *was* a provision, and it continued to lure the constitutional litigators.

The easiest attack was against the claimed equality. Surely *equal* must mean something. Yet by the twentieth century, it had become

a ghost word, a balm for the nation's conscience, a token of the law's hollow symmetry and logic, but quite irrelevant insofar as the Negro was concerned. Signs of inequality sprouted everywhere. In the park was the separate water fountain that happened not to work; at the back of every restaurant was the black carry-out line; in the theatre was the Jim Crow balcony, unmaintained, because "they'd trash it up anyhow." Nor was there a separate-but-equal election to which blacks might be consigned when excluded from the white one.[38]

° No explicit constitutional guarantee of equality binds the federal government, but the Supreme Court has interpreted the Fifth Amendment's due process guarantee as doing so. (Bolling v. Sharpe, 347 U.S. 497 [1954].)

In the South, where segregation was the way of life, the per capita spending on schooling for black and white was grossly unequal. In time some of these inequalities were recognized in court and branded unconstitutional: Where there was only a white law school, the Court ordered blacks admitted. White-only primaries and racially restrictive land covenants were inherently unequal because no alternatives were possible for blacks.

John W. Davis, former presidential candidate, senior partner in a major New York law firm, and the greatest appellate advocate of his age, urged the Supreme Court to decide *Brown* in accordance with *Plessy*'s understanding: If southern segregation laws doomed black children to inferior schools, the remedy was to order the states to raise the standards of those schools.[39] Genuine equality of the separate schools should remain the desideratum. The Court, of course, did not view it that way. The sole holding in *Brown* in 1954 was that segregated schools are "inherently unequal."

Because the Court spoke in the blandest tones and cited several works of contemporary sociology as justification for a somewhat different conclusion—namely, that segregation harmed Negro school children—many of the Court's supporters have uneasily viewed *Brown* as an exercise in necessary political statesmanship but not as a reasoned judicial opinion. In their view the Court acted correctly only because it reached the right result. To process-oriented jurisprudes, the justices failed their appointed office because they neglected to reach a result through reasoned elaboration. Granted that they *said* separation is inherently unequal, but how did they know it be so? Ought the Court rely on research that may turn out to have ill-founded conclusions based on dubious social science? Is it permissible to jettison the institutional modus operandi whenever, in the opinion of at least five justices, there is a compelling moral duty to inveigh against evil? Is this not a prescription for judicial usurpation, if not tyranny?[40]

That *Brown* should have been intellectually troubling—and that it can continue to trouble—is testament to the power of a slogan to cloud men's minds. No great feat of imagination is required to see that "equal protection of the law" can more sensibly be taken to mean that legal distinctions based on race are impermissible. Why go to the trouble of demonstrating harm, when the constitutional term gives a right not to be legally discriminated against, harmed or not? For the Constitution, in other words, the harm *is* the discrimination.

From the perspective of "neutral" constitutional principles, emphasis on the importance of the benefit provided is beside the point. What mattered was the unequal conferring of a positive social benefit—public education. Segregation denied black individuals the opportunity to mingle with those of the dominant culture in the public schools. In other words, enforced segregation violates the Fourteenth Amendment not because it is more harmful to one group than to another but because it is inherently unequal. No amount of money spent on black schools and black teachers can compensate for the missing element.

There is no need to belabor the obvious or to defend a settled constitutional principle. The consequence of constitutional terms of art is that sooner or later the courts will insist that phrases like *equal protection* be morally suffused.

Striking down segregation in public education may appear on the surface no more a call for an affirmative decree than similar decisions voiding, say, miscegenation laws. No flexible or discretionary decree is necessary to implement a judicial ruling that race cannot be a factor in the granting of a marriage license. The city clerk can simply be ordered to dispense one or the court can overlook the absence of a license. But terminating unlawful segregation is not so simple. There is no obvious, ministerial course to be followed if massive resistance is the school district's answer to the constitutional rule, and that is why *Brown* was only a beginning.

A judicially imposed remedy does not follow logically and clearly from a definition of the unlawful injury. Consistent with a ruling against enforced segregation, a court could lay down a plan for integration, complete with every administrative detail, or it could rest content with pronouncing the constitutional rule and hope that the local authorities would act thereafter without regard to race. The Supreme Court opted in 1954 for the latter approach, declaring that school districts must move toward desegregation "with all deliberate speed"—a standard that permitted the South to seek "gradualism with infinity as the deadline."[41]

The story of the next quarter century, from 1955 to the present, is too well known to bear repeating. Certain stops along the way are, however, worth noting. For fifteen years, the Court was silent on remedial issues. Implementation of desegregation decrees was left to the lower courts, and in communities with unsympathetic judges, progress toward desegregation was nil. Many courts hewed to a distinction between desegregation and integration. The Supreme Court, they said, would not allow forced segregation, but it had not mandated an affirmative policy of integration. Massive resistance, evasion, tokenism, death, and destruction were the result.

In the mid-1960s, Judge J. Minor Wisdom of the Fifth Circuit, which oversees the federal bench in the Deep South, "transformed the face of desegregation law."[42] He held that school boards had a duty to integrate. This was a major change of focus. An individual school child could speak in traditional litigation terms when arguing that a law that kept her out of a white school unconstitutionally discriminated. But the litigant's plea in a suit demanding integration was decidedly untraditional. Now not merely repeal of a law was sought. Redress for the black community as a "collective entity" became the crux of the matter. The remedial decree Judge Wisdom framed was therefore dramatically affirmative: It dealt with advertising of school openings, transportation, assignment, treatment of students within the school, remedial learning programs, school construction sites, and faculty and staff hiring and assignment. In 1968 the Supreme Court finally caught up, overthrew the vague and unworkable "all deliberate speed" standard, and began to impose affirmative duties on school officials to end dual school systems everywhere.[43] Those who object to the affirmative decrees that followed should thus reflect that for nearly fifteen years school systems had had the leeway to act responsibly and had failed to do so, even when prodded by federal district courts.

Was the Supreme Court's strategy a success or failure? Though school integration was still more hope than reality when the justices decided finally to set stricter standards, the political climate had changed enormously. Southern gradualism had been proved bankrupt, politically and morally. Two major civil rights bills had become federal law, one guaranteeing equal rights in a wide range of private activities and the other creating an effective means of registering black voters. In a very few years, the impact of this electoral change was felt throughout the South. More intangibly, by the early 1970s, few would be willing publicly to espouse American apartheid. In political terms, if not in social and economic terms, blacks had made enormous strides since 1954. A fiduciary respect for all persons on the part of state and local government was spreading.

At the same time, the affirmative goal, the ending of separate school systems for black and white, had not been achieved. Staring at fifteen years of ignoble resistance by local officials, the courts began to focus their energies on imaginative remedial orders. In 1969, for example, Judge Frank Johnson ordered the Montgomery, Alabama, schools to assign teachers to the schools by racial ratios: two blacks for every three whites, the ratio of teachers in the entire district. What had begun from one perspective as a policy of constitutional color blindness now required rigid racial quotas.[44]

The busing controversy began in earnest when the Supreme Court approved a busing plan for the Charlotte-Mecklenburg, Virginia, school system, which comprised 84,000 students (24,000 of them black) in more than 100 schools. The plan had largely been devised by an expert witness and called for start-up costs of at least $1 million and an annual budget of $532,000. The plan was held to be necessary to integrate the 14,000 black students who had been attending all black schools and who rarely saw a white teacher.

In 1977, the Supreme Court started along still another path in upholding a district court order mandating a variety of remedial programs within the Detroit schools, including removal of "racial, ethnic, and cultural bias" from school tests.[45] These programs were not original with the judge. They were devised within the school board itself, and the court order specifically left policing of their content to the board. Nevertheless, this decision puts the federal courts in the business of approving, and perhaps ultimately monitoring, programs to remedy the effects of past discrimination in the schools.

Still other judicial policies aimed at school equality began to take shape during the 1970s. One is entirely a phenomenon of the state courts: the equalization of school expenditures within each state. In 1972, the Supreme Court rejected the opportunity to rule that every state is obligated to do away with the local property tax system as the means of financing public schools.[46] The prospect of upsetting a long-established method of financing schools was too much for the Supreme Court, but many state courts, beginning with California in 1971, have entertained the same arguments and held that the disparities in financing violate the equal protection clauses of the state constitutions. Alternatively, the New Jersey Supreme Court has struck down that state's financing system by loosely interpreting a state constitutional provision "for the maintenance and support of a thorough and efficient system of free public schools."[47]

The purpose of this sketchy summary of the wondrously variegated litigation concerning equality in American schools is to point out how fundamentally different the realm of a court is when it seeks to advance equality through affirmative decrees—different, that is, from the kinds of affirmative decrees establishing minimum standards. The reason for this difference is that *equality* is a seductive term of no fixed meaning, when viewed from the perspective of redressing past inequality. Achieving an equal society, which appears to be the tendency of so many of the recent court decisions, is a polycentric problem of infinite complexity.

For one thing, the question is, Who is being made equal to whom? Each student to every other student? Blacks as a collective entity to whites as a collective entity? And if this latter conception of equality is the preferred one, are blacks and whites to be absolutely equal or only in proportion to their numbers in the total population? By what principle may one of these conceptions be chosen over another? A decision barring compulsory racial segregation can without much effort be derived from constitutional principles, but a positive application of equal protection threatens a host of other values that can only dimly be asserted against the radiation of judicially fostered equality. The original impulse was to root out official racism, but what is sacrificed are values not rooted—at least not rooted entirely—in racism. Neighborhood schools, for example, are feared lost to the insatiable demands of a master plan for numerical balance. For many communities, which long used busing as a means of perpetuating segregation,° judicial busing orders may be the only means of undoing a system of school districts designed from a racial motive. But this is not necessarily the case; neighborhood schooling is unquestionably a value that need not have racial overtones. Similarly, while it may be plausible to interpret constitutional guarantees of equality as requiring a minimum expenditure in each school district in a state or even a fundamentally new way of financing school expenditures, it is unclear how a court can preclude a particular community from deciding to tax itself to spend more on the education of its children than that required as a legislatively or judicially mandated minimum. And although various means of testing students, both for placement purposes and to certify how well they have mastered the subjects, may be racially biased, it is not unequivocal that every test in which minorities or the poor score at the low end of the grading scale are without a valid purpose or serve that purpose badly. The state should remain entitled to measure scholastic and intellectual performance.

An abstract notion of equality presents no discernible means of limiting the remedies that can be adopted nor the persons and institutions who can be brought within their embrace. This is so even though the particular lawsuit seeks on its surface a specific end. It is not necessary to plead for general social equality to gain, in logic, a radical social restructuring.

Unlike the establishment of minimum standards for prisons or mental hospitals, the creation of a society based on equality of all persons is open-ended. The right to treatment is not declared for all but only for those who are incarcerated. Equality, when underwritten in affirmative decrees, is a pseudostandard. Though the aim—to integrate public schools—be relatively discrete, the attempt ultimately tangles up other important aspects of community life. Schools are racially segregated not only because they were commanded by law to be. In most urban areas they are segregated because neighborhoods are segregated. Housing patterns may themselves be the result of unconstitutional restrictions on the living patterns of blacks and on the jobs that they might hold, but nonlegal, cultural factors are at work as well. These may trace to racial prejudice, but that is scarcely a condition like compulsory segregation that courts can attack. Nevertheless, if courts can order busing, and the rezon-

° The most extreme case on record was that of a black schoolboy in White Sulphur Springs, West Virginia, who was forced to travel 108 miles a day, though he lived but 4 blocks from the neighborhood school. During the period of state-fostered private academies, buses regularly took a sizable segment of the white school population beyond their neighborhood boundaries. (J. Harvie Wilkinson, *From Brown to Bakke, The Supreme Court and School Integration* [New York: Oxford University Press, 1979], p. 136.)

ing of school districts, why cannot they under general equity powers prohibit white flight, strictly supervise all aspects of community budgets, rearrange housing patterns, close down all private schools (whether or not maintained with state funds), and strictly censor the content of the school curriculum, among other things—all to foster the eventual integration of neighborhood schools? Though they have not gone that far, some courts have evidenced an intent to level disparities not necessarily fostered by the state and not necessarily irrational.[48] The siren song of equal protection is seductive, and private values, unless separately grounded in the Constitution as a brake against judges romantically inclined to achieve total redress, must often succumb.

The sum of judicial actions suggests that the courts are aiming at a larger accomplishment than formal equality before the law: the establishment of a racially harmonious society. Such a task is clearly too large for the courts to carry out unaided. A unified society does not await the resolution of individual disputes or of problems that will yield to rational solution, such as more money objectively spent, better tests, or the like. Rather, the goal remains unfulfilled because it clashes with the realities of the human condition. Judicial attempts to overcome human obstinancy by recourse to what is at best a subterfuge, an ill-defined and changeable rule of substantive equality, cannot work in a market-oriented, politically open society where end results are not determined as a matter of right. Cries of outrage against the court are not uttered solely by those who continue as open or closet racists, though they may shout the loudest. Other voices, too, are heard bemoaning the blind alley into which the search for a fiduciary ethic has strayed. Requiring a school board to treat all children in an objectively equal manner, by forbidding compulsory segregation, is within the judicial competence because it implants a fiduciary standard in a constitutional command. The discord that attends judicial attempts to enforce this rule, which inevitably judges must do by resorting to subjective standards, is understandable as the reaction of communities to the realization that they have lost the power to determine a significant aspect of their own lives.

That said, we must understand that we—or our ancestors—brought this on ourselves. However incompetent the courts ultimately may prove to be in their direction of school policies, they are not acting irrationally. However arbitrary a particular decree may seem, judicial orders in a larger sense are far from capricious. What the courts have imposed upon the white majority is a sweeping historical vicarious liability: Affirmative action has become the ultimate modern expression of an instinct that lies buried deep in the common law judicial mind. Minority descendants are held to have been injured by the ancestors of the majority, whose descendants in turn must pay the remedial price. The affirmative decree is new, but it represents a qualitative change in the relation between courts and government agencies. As such it has no natural or self-evident stopping point, which is at once its virtue and its defect.

Affirming the Affirmative Decree

Critics maintain that courts are ill-equipped to set social policy. In a searching look at the way courts go about their business, Donald Horowitz has assembled a broad list of institutional defects. Courts seek reductionist solutions: They examine critical issues through the eyes of specific parties, and they focus on rights rather than costs. A rights orientation precludes adjustment and compromise. Finding that a litigant may claim a right, a court cannot then easily disregard it because of competing interests. The "judge cannot frame his issues in terms of more health care versus less prison reform."[49] In locating the existence of a right, courts are guided by what Horowitz calls "every-last-case" reasoning rather than "run-of-the-case" reasoning,[50] meaning that the specific case does not by itself inform judges whether it is representative or unique, whether what occurred was typical or aberrational and likely to be an extreme one, especially where public interest attorneys are following a litigation strategy intended to secure broad new rights.

In making decisions, the courts are handicapped as novices in policy issues and by the difficulty of garnering social facts: recurrent patterns of behavior on which policy must be based. There is "no assurance that the judge has correctly formulated the structure of incentives: his logic and the logic of the actors affected by rules of law may begin from different premises."[51]° After the case is concluded, there is no provision for policy review and no feedback, except to the extent that discrete cases subsequently come to court in the aftermath of policy decisions. When the policies involved are constitutional, there is no easy way for legislatures or administrative agencies to seek relief from

° For example, the Supreme Court has declared as a constitutional policy that unlawfully seized evidence must be excluded from criminal trials. This policy has been justified as a deterrent to unconstitutional police conduct. Exclusion of the evidence may result in acquittal, which presumably defeats the purpose of the seizure and thus makes the police conduct self-defeating. In fact police may not be primarily interested in conviction but in harassment, exerting power, being a presence "on the street," and the continued seizure of evidence under unlawful circumstances may facilitate plea bargains and thus never come to later judicial attention. (Donald L. Horowitz, *The Courts and Social Policy* [Washington, D.C.: The Brookings Institution, 1976], Ch. 6.)

the unintended consequences of judicial policy decisions. By contrast, the political organs of government have flexible tools, account for effects beyond the purview of litigants, and can create supple responses to broad problems.

All this does not settle the issue. The question is not whether courts do badly at directing social policy in their handling of institutional reform cases but whether we are better or worse off because of their presence. There can be no definitive answer to the question, nor can we essay our condition at the present time, with all its confusions and ambiguities, and hope to understand what the courts have wrought. We can assess the judicial system only by looking back to see where we have come from. From this perspective we can recall the petty brutality of the police station, the more pervasive brutality of the prison and the mental hospital, and the shameful conditions of black schooling to appreciate how far, despite our present problems, we have advanced.

The very involvement of courts in the social policy process is testament to the lack of involvement by others. Legislatures and administrative agencies may be better equipped to resolve social and political issues, but they frequently fail to do so, especially where these issues have touched deep constitutional nerves. The rise of institutional litigation is a response to the spread of governmental bodies from which the public has increasingly become insulated and over which there is only nominally the possibility of democratic control. Those who are incarcerated, treated, educated are explicitly excluded from management, and the public at large is rarely organized to demand that government power be tempered by responsibility. The public cannot control administrators, except in the most general way by forcing broad policy declarations from a reluctant legislature. The only hope of those affected is through the directional probe of a court.

Justice Felix Frankfurter frequently appealed to his brethren on the Supreme Court to refrain from hearing a case or declaring new rights so that the political agencies of government would be understood as the final repositories of power and so that the people could direct their energies at forcing their representatives to do their work. Democracy does not work well where courts frequently find ways of making legal or constitutional issues out of matters that could be resolved in political ways, he argued.

The analysis is not necessarily sound. A sensitive enough historical study might well demonstrate that the evidence points in the other direction: that only through judicial involvement do the other branches of government eventually begin to function. Legislators and administrators cave in to political pressure as they must, because they know that the courts will rescue them and the republic. "One sometimes suspects," Louis Henkin has said, that in the area of internal security laws, "many in Congress are pleased to have the

Court save them from follies which they deem politically necessary."[52] An identical statement could be made of many areas of national life in which legislators prefer the punt to the fourth-down play. Their motivation could be one of responsible concern (by framing legislation at its outer permissible boundaries one can knowingly test the extent of congressional power) or of utter cynicism. F. Edward Hebert, longtime congressman from Louisiana, advised the federal government in 1967 to induct vocal antiwar demonstrators into the army. "Let's forget the First Amendment," he said; "I know this [prosecution] would be rescinded by the Supreme Court but at least the effort should be made. It would show the American people that the Justice Department and Congress were trying to clean up this rat-infested area." Stung by the predictable criticism, Hebert amplified, "It's not that I love the First Amendment less; it's that I love my country more."[53] In times of turmoil, in times of bitter divisiveness, or in times of moral bankruptcy when none dare breach the obtuseness of conventional wisdom, policy makers may excuse their failure not only to act sensibly but to act at all.

Judicial intervention in social policy has come hand in hand with the growth in the legislative and administrative web of government. In a society that relies primarily on private ordering, there are few roots from which broad judicial policy initiatives can grow. Environmental policy is perhaps the clearest recent example. No general common law principle is available to private litigants to call a halt to the externalities that a system of private ordering produces: A homeowner can protest the despoliation of his backyard by a neighbor who constantly burns trash, but there is no abstract right of redress for pollution caused by the operation of motor vehicles throughout the country. Creative lawyers can concoct fanciful theories to attempt to overcome this "deficiency" in the legal system. Professor Christopher D. Stone once proposed that courts adjudicate the rights of natural objects. Trees should have standing to protest environmental degradation, their arguments to be presented by court-appointed lawyers.[54] The courts have not accepted this theory. Both politically and jurisprudentially, only the legislature can initiate an environmental policy. But when government begins to displace private ordering, the courts can be energized, because the Constitution is a preexisting legal policy for controlling governmental actions. Constitutional standards are the means by which courts can impose a fiduciary ethic on society, even when—especially when—the government fails to act.

When the courts rule, their decisions are rarely final, rarely definitive, rarely immune from negotiation. To the contrary, judicial decisions awaken the political branches of government from their slumbers. The effect of most court decisions is thus to activate, not to enervate, democratic government. Perhaps only through such prodding will legislature and executives regain the trust that is essential if they are to govern. Courts do not wish to hold jurisdiction or act as routine supervisors over institutions better governed by others. In 1970 the Supreme Court approved Judge James B. McMillan's busing plan for Charlotte, Virginia. In 1974 a new school board was elected, pledged to carry out guidelines and policies that represented a "clean break with the essentially 'reluctant' attitude which dominated Board action for many years." One year later, the board having stuck to the plan and experiencing a lessening of tensions, Judge McMillan returned "constitutional operation of the schools to the Board."[55] This is the pattern to which institutional reform cases tend.

Chapter 6

The Erosion of Immunity: Who Cannot Be Sued?

Governmental Immunity

A modern history of law would be largely a chronicling of the increasing vulnerability of individuals, corporations, and public institutions to lawsuits. Few significant activities have ever been immune from judicial writs. Even the First Amendment, which provides personal autonomy for thought and expression, has not put an end to suits against the press. To the contrary, despite a judicial policy of guarding the press against the "chilling effect" of litigation, lawsuits abound to test the permeability of the First Amendment's shield.

In only one area of human conduct has a general immunity been traditionally conceded: the immunity of governmental employees and governmental entities from liability in damage suits for harmful acts that would put any private defendant in judicial trouble. Today, however, this traditional immunity is fast disappearing. The newest targets of the litigious society are officials and the public treasuries. Courts by no means have worked alone to lower the barriers to litigation. Legislatures as well as courts have scraped away the walls of immunity.

Because the king was the source of all law—and because the early judges were his direct and politically sensitive agents—suits against the crown were forbidden from the early days of English jurisprudence. "The King can do no legal wrong" was the legal liturgy, solemnly intoned down the centuries. The ruling doctrine was known as "sovereign immunity." But by the time "government" became a significant factor that impinged in innumerable ways on the lives of the citizenry, the king was no longer the locus of all governmental action. The power of the state was exercised through a myriad of agents, departments, and political entities, none of whom were sovereign in the sense of the reigning monarch. Nevertheless, the immunity of the king was transferred in effect to all branches of government in a 1788 English case. One Russell damaged his wagon on a bridge that needed repairs. He sued all male inhabitants of the County of Devon (then unincorporated) because the county concededly had the legal obligation to maintain the bridge in working order. The court dismissed the suit for seven reasons:

1. The suit was without precedent.
2. Neither law nor reason supports it.
3. A strong legal presumption holds that what has not been done before cannot be done.
4. To permit the suit would lead to "an infinity of actions."
5. There was no county fund from which the claim could be paid.
6. Only the legislature should impose this kind of liability
7. "It is better that an individual should sustain an injury than that the public should suffer an inconvenience."[1]

The doctrine was imported in America in 1812 by the Supreme Judicial Court of Massachusetts. Mower's horse was killed when it fell in a hole on Leicester bridge. Mower argued that the Devon case was not applicable since the town of Leicester was not only incorporated but also had a fund to pay any judgment. Hidebound, the Massachusetts court ignored the important differences between the cases and stated as a binding rule of common law that towns cannot be liable for neglect of bridges.[2] Once planted on American soil, the doctrine of sovereign immunity took root, spread westward and just grew into the American rule. "Nothing seems more clear than that this immunity of the King from the jurisdiction of the King's courts was purely personal. How it came to be applied in the United States of America, where the prerogative is unknown, is one of the mysteries of legal evolution."[3]

During the next century and a half, the doctrine of sovereign immunity was dogma riddled with inconsistent exceptions. Proprietary hospitals could be sued for torts of its agents, but municipal hospitals were immune, although in California, city hospitals were suable whereas county hospitals were not.[4] Beginning in the 1950s the state courts began to abolish the judge-made rules of municipal immunity for the negligence of public officials. By 1980 thirty-three state courts had rejected complete sovereign immunity and many state legislatures had enacted limiting statutes, so that only five states (Georgia, Maryland, Mississippi, South Carolina, and South Dakota) retain anything resembling total immunity for all acts of government.[5]

In 1946 Congress enacted the Federal Tort Claims Act, for the first time permitting a wide range of suits against the government. Most common acts of negligence committed by public employees were included. But the law excepted significant categories of conduct. Intentional torts—assault, battery, false arrest and imprisonment, malicious prosecution, and misrepresentation, among others—were excluded, but in 1974 certain intentional torts of law enforcement officers were made subject to the act. Also excluded from coverage are all acts of government employees in furtherance of official policy established by statute or regulation, whether or not the statute or regulation is valid, and all consequences of "discretionary" functions.

The judicial and legislative retrenchments of sovereign immunity left large pockets of immunity and many unanswered questions. Municipalities and local governments can be sued in state courts if sovereign immunity has been abolished by their states. But if immunity remains a fixture in state law, can a private litigant seek redress in federal court? Can local or state officials be sued personally for damages? If municipal governments may be hauled into federal courts to circumvent state restrictions on suits, are they liable only for harms caused by their explicit policies or can they also be made to stand in for the injurious acts of public employees, even if those acts do not further express or imply public policy?

During the 1970s, the Supreme Court began to shrink further the domain of sovereign immunity by answering many of these questions in such a way as to permit plaintiffs to go forward with their suits. This the court accomplished by resorting primarily to two legal theories, one a reinterpretation of a nineteenth century civil rights act and the other a novel construction of the Bill of Rights.

THE LIABILITY OF PUBLIC OFFICIALS

Sovereign immunity protects the public treasuries. By its terms, it is not a doctrine that protects public officials, for as individuals they have never been sovereign in their own right. Nevertheless, until the 1960s, government employees performing official business have had a comparable immunity. The reason for protecting government employees from liability for actions carried out in the line of duty was cogently stated by Learned Hand. Sovereign immunity, he said, is not designed to protect the guilty, for if it were possible in practice to confine such complaints to the guilty, it would be monstrous to deny recovery. The justification for [immunizing officials] is that it is impossible to know whether the claim is well founded until the case has been tried, and that to submit all officials, the innocent as well as the guilty, to the burden of a trial and to the inevitable danger of its outcome, would dampen the ardor of all but the most resolute, or the most irresponsible, in the unflinching discharge of their duties. . . . In this instance it has been thought in the end better to leave unredressed the wrongs done by dishonest officers than to subject those who try to do their duty to the constant dread of retaliation.[6]

As an elementary justification of the basic common law rule, Hand's statement is probably still valid. Over the years, the courts have zealously guarded this principle, one federal appellate court going so far as to say that the secretary of the treasury cannot be brought to account even for "arbitrary, wanton, capricious, illegal, malicious, oppressive, and contemptuous" actions.[7]

In 1959 the Supreme Court affirmed this principle in a case in which federal employees claimed that they had been libeled by their superior. The bare 5 to 4 majority concluded that a federal official may not be sued for common law torts if the claimed injury was the result of his exercising discretion conferred by law in the carrying out of public policy.[8] Where there is a measurable standard of conduct and the act does not further public policy, no immunity is conferred. Under this ruling, therefore, a postal truck driver cannot escape liability for causing an accident on the road; nor, given the Federal Tort Claims Act, can the government. (An irony of the case is worth noting: it took the plaintiff a jury trial, an appeal to the United States Court of Appeals and to the Supreme Court, a remand to the court of appeals, and a further and final appeal to the Supreme Court to establish his right to be free from suit.)

The case immunized federal officials, but it did not preclude suits against state and local officials. In a case two years later the Court sounded a theme that would be played increasingly during the next two decades. Immediately, it presaged a vast extension of liability of municipal employees. The 1961 case grew out of a predawn raid in 1958 in Chicago by thirteen city police officers, led by one Pape, who burst into the home of Monroe, his wife, and their six children. They were routed from their beds and forced to stand naked in the living room while the officers "ransacked" each room, emptying drawers and ripping mattress covers. Monroe was struck with a flashlight, Mrs. Monroe was pushed, the children were hit and kicked and verbally abused. Monroe was then carted off to the police station, held for ten hours, interrogated about an alleged two-day-old murder, and finally released without any charges of any sort ever being preferred against him or his family. The police had neither search nor arrest warrants.

Monroe sued the police and the city of Chicago in federal court, under a provision of the Civil Rights Act of 1871, now known as Section 1983, which reads as follows:

Every person who, under color of any statute, ordinance, regulation, custom, or usage, of any State or Territory, subjects, or causes to be subjected, any citizen of the United States or other person within the jurisdiction thereof to the deprivation of any rights, privileges, or immunities secured by the Constitution and laws, shall be liable to the party injured in an action at law, suit in equity, or other proper proceeding for redress.

This was the first provision in a statute directed against the Ku Klux Klan and official state violence toward emancipated slaves. Since Congress does not have constitutional power to legislate criminal law generally, it could not directly outlaw lynching, assault, and mayhem. Under the Fourteenth Amendment, however, it could provide an avenue of civil redress for those whose federal constitutional rights were abridged. This Congress did by providing civil relief (and, in another section, criminal penalties) against those who exercised or purported to exercise state power to interfere with a citizen's legal rights. But Section 1983 was rarely invoked, and in time it became virtually a dead letter.

In *Monroe* v. *Pape* the Supreme Court wrestled with the question whether city police could be sued under Section 1983 and concluded that they can be.[9] The Civil Rights Act is "meant to give a remedy to parties deprived of constitutional rights, privileges, and immunities by an official's abuse of his position." The Court thus opened the federal courts to complaints against state officials, complaints that could not be brought if the wrongdoers were employed by the federal government.

In a lengthy dissent, Justice Frankfurter argued, among other things, that since the police misconduct was illegal under Illinois law, it did not fit within Section 1983, which requires conduct "under color of law." Moreover, he said, Illinois would apparently provide the Monroes with a remedy. His position was, in essence, that the Monroes should have gone to the state courts first; if those courts should clothe the police with immunity, then the plaintiffs could have sued in the federal courts under Section 1983. But the only indication that the state of Illinois would have vindicated the Monroes was a *federal* court opinion saying so, in effect nothing more than a *guess* by the United States Court of Appeals in Chicago that the state courts would have resisted the pressure that the extreme sensitivity of the interest at stake would exert. The majority's response is understandable: Section 1983 is an independent federal right; the plaintiffs need not exhaust money and patience making what might well turn out to be a fruitless trip to the state bench. As for "color of law," the issue is not whether the conduct itself was lawful but whether it was incident to the performance of a recognized official function. The defendants were not impostors but police.

The *Monroe* decision revivified Section 1983. Now, twenty years later, it has become the most popular civil rights provision in the federal plaintiff's lexicon, "the fountainhead of the torrent of civil rights litigation of the last 17 years," commented Justice William Rehnquist in 1978. In 1960 only 280 civil rights cases were filed in federal courts in the whole country. The data then were not broken down into separate categories as they are today. The comparable figure for 1980, which includes many non-Section 1983 cases such as voting, jobs, public accommodations, welfare, and prisoner suits, was 25,341. Of these, excluding prisoner petitions, 7,213 were Section 1983 complaints.[10]

The single largest category of Section 1983 cases is that of prisoner suits. "For state prisoners, eating, sleeping, dressing, washing, working and playing are all done under the watchful eye of the State. . . . What for a private citizen would be a dispute with his landlord, with his employer, with his tailor, with his neighbor, or with his banker becomes, for the prisoner, a dispute with the State." [11] But the nature of the disputes is not necessarily benign: Most prisoners seek redress for inadequate medical care, property loss or damage, interference with access to courts, and brutality. By contrast, a close study of 664 prisoner suits in five federal districts from 1975 through June of 1977, showed that racial discrimination complaints exceeded 5 percent of the total in only one district. In 1966, when the Administrative Office of the United States Courts first compiled the statistic, there were 218 prisoner suits filed throughout the country. Fourteen years later, in 1980, that number had grown to 12,397.[12]

Although Section 1983 does not include federal officials, in 1971 the Supreme Court paved the way for damage claims against federal officers in *Bivens* v. *Six Unknown Agents of the Federal Bureau of Narcotics*.[13] The story was essentially the same as in *Monroe*. Federal agents arrived at Bivens's home in 1965 without warrants. Bivens was arrested and manacled in view of his wife and children, and the agents threatened to arrest the entire family; they then "searched the apartment from stem to stern." Bivens sought damages for the agents' violation of his Fourth Amendment rights against unlawful search. Over strong dissents, the Supreme Court upheld the right to sue for damages resulting from "constitutional torts."

Monroe and *Bivens* worked a fundamental reversal of the time-honored principle of immunity. Nevertheless, they raised more questions than they answered and therefore necessitated clarifying litigation that continues to this day. Two of the most important questions unanswered by these seminal cases are: (1) What kinds of injuries are redressable? (2) How much immunity does the public official have who causes a redressable injury? By 1980 these questions had no definitive answers; even the treatise writer asks more questions than he can answer.[14]

Particular injuries cognizable in actions under either Section 1983 against state and local officials or the Constitution itself against federal officials emerge case by case, but not always seemingly consistently. Three are worth noting. The first involved libel. A police chief circulated a list with photographs of Active Shoplifters, compiled from police reports. The plaintiff had once been arrested for shoplifting but not convicted; even so, his picture and name were included on the list. The Supreme Court dismissed his suit, holding that Section 1983 provided no recourse under the circumstances. Not every wrong committed by a state official is a deprivation of constitutional rights, a predicate necessary for proceeding under Section 1983. No specific constitutional guarantee protects a person against libel.[15] (Other cases suggest the difficulty with this approach: The injury that flows from a particular libel might cause the plaintiff to lose his job, a "property" interest protected by the due process clause, hence actionable under Section 1983.)

The second case concerned deprivation of a woman's right against sex discrimination. The official was Louisiana Congressman Otto Passman, who discharged a female assistant because he preferred a man to understudy his administrative assistant. The Supreme Court said this kind of discrimination is a constitutional tort like the wrong of breaking and entering in *Bivens*.[16] From these cases, Professor Kenneth Culp Davis has concluded that "most deliberate torts against the physical person or against a property interest are now likely to be" redressable in federal court.[17]

The third case revolved around the constitutionally based procedural right to a hearing. After an audit, the Commodity Exchange Authority of the United States Department of Agriculture instituted a proceeding to revoke or suspend the license of a registered futures merchant, Arthur N. Economou and Company, for willful failure to maintain minimum financial requirements. But the federal agency failed to give the company notice in the form of a customary warning letter. The suspended license was restored after a court ruled that the procedure had been unlawful. Economou then sued a variety of officials for $32 million, alleging several types of illegalities. Although the case is muddled, the Supreme Court did unequivocally rule that a constitutionally defective hearing can give rise to a lawsuit against federal officers.[18]

In *Bivens*, the majority opinion concluded by noting that the Court had not decided whether or not narcotics agents are immune from liability by virtue of their official position. This might sound strange to those untutored in the fine distinctions that consume so much of the lawyer's vital energy. Was that not the very issue? Only in part. The threshold question, which the Supreme

Court and many lower courts have been struggling to answer, is whether the challenged act can give rise to a lawsuit at all. Is it, in other words, an unlawful wrong? Only if it is must the courts weigh the degree to which public officials are immune from suit.

The doctrine that is emerging, for both federal and nonfederal officials, is one of *qualified* immunity. No longer is a deliberate, willful infringement of a person's rights protected by a blanket immunity. What counts, the courts say, is whether the officials have conducted themselves in good faith. Thus in *Economou*, the Supreme Court said:

> Federal officials will not be liable for mere mistakes in judgment whether the mistake is one of fact or one of law. But we see no substantial basis for holding . . . that executive officers generally may with impunity discharge their duties in a way that is known to them to violate the United States Constitution or in a manner that they should know transgresses a clearly established constitutional rule.

The Court announced a similar rule of qualified immunity in 1974 for state and local officials sued under Section 1983. The cases grew out of the disturbances at Kent State University. The parents of one of the students who died sued the governor of Ohio, officers in the National Guard, and the president of the university. The lower courts dismissed the suit on the ground that the defendants were absolutely immune. The Supreme Court reversed, holding that "in varying scope, a qualified immunity is available to officers of the executive branch of government." The variations depended on responsibilities of the officeholder and "all the circumstances as they reasonably appeared at the time." These, "coupled with good-faith belief," may exonerate an official.[19] Again, the exact extent of the immunity remains cloudy. In a suit against members of a local school board, the Supreme Court the following year seemed to narrow immunity still further. The board expelled some high school students for three months without affording them a hearing as required under *Goss* v. *Lopez*. The Court seemed to suggest that officials who have their heads stuck in the sand cannot be characterized as acting in good faith. It is not enough for a board member to act "sincerely and with a belief that he is doing right"; "ignorance or disregard of settled, indisputable law" is no more justifiable than "actual malice," the Court said.[20]

How "settled" and "indisputable" a constitutional standard must be for officials to be subject to monetary damages for failure to know and abide by it is a perplexing problem. What is not dreamed of today may be on the horizon tomorrow and may become a bulwark of civil liberties the day after that, especially in a system that does not prohibit to judges the use of adverbs to clinch any argument. The judicial development of the past decade seems to stand the purpose of immunity on its head. Immunity, the courts continue to intone, is intended to forestall the fear that causes public officials to hesitate to carry out public duties. Arguably, public officials will have nothing to fear so long as the principle of absolute immunity remains firm. Weaken the rule and the principle itself may be lost.

There is evidence that the fear is real. In 1977 Attorney General Griffin B. Bell spoke of the

current crisis of confidence among federal law enforcement and intelligence personnel caused by the explosion of civil damage actions against them. . . . Every one of these suits, regardless of how lacking in merit, carries a potential of monetary loss. . . . An official who gets caught up in such a case is in for the agony of prolonged uncertainty about whether he might lose his life's savings or his home. He, and his family, must endure that agony even if he ultimately is exonerated.[21]

Bell was arguing for statutory changes that would immunize the agents and substitute the United States government as the sole defendant.

Bell echoed many who point to the worries of law enforcement officials. In testimony before Congress in 1977, John Greacen, an American Bar Association spokesman, said, "The Bar is quite encouraged by FBI Director [Clarence] Kelley's opinion that law enforcement zeal is, in fact, affected by the threat of civil liability."[22] However, no officials, as yet, offer convincing empirical evidence that law enforcement is in fact being hampered by the steady stream of immunity rulings. Partly that is because it is difficult to demonstrate the fact, if it is a fact. Police and others are not likely to annouce, "Look, we would have been able to make that collar if only we didn't have to worry about being sued." But partly it is because neither the logic of the decisions nor the actual results yet give cause for undue alarm. The thrust of the cases is that *deliberately* undertaken illegal acts will put the perpetrators in jeopardy of lawsuits. That seems reasonable. Private persons who knowingly break the law generally stand in danger of going to jail, and this prospect is not at all a consequence of the relaxation of immunity. Moreover, few suits to date have left the defendants financially troubled. *Bivens* itself was settled for a minor sum, and no appellate court has yet sustained a money judgment in favor of a victim of federal law enforcement illegality, though there have been some large settlements.

THE IMMUNITY OF GOVERNMENT

Few doctors who are subject to suit for malpractice have discontinued their professional careers. They have purchased insurance and perhaps become a bit more cautious. So with public officials. Though the research remains to be undertaken, we may doubt that the erosion of immunity has made public employees appreciably more cautious about doing what they honestly believe needs to be done. Perhaps they consult their lawyers more; indeed, they ought to. Not only is it wise to know what the law is, it is also prudent, for proof of consultation will generally support a good-faith defense. Furthermore, like most officers of private corporations, public employees are generally indemnified for judgments they must pay, and their legal bills are gnerally covered. Officer Pape, who lost the damage suit initiated against him by the Monroes for his unlawful invasion of their apartment in Chicago, was luckier than most people brought to court for breaking and entering. The city, which was immune from suit for his violation of the Monroes' rights, paid the judgment and ultimately retired him with honors.[23] This proclaims louder than the denials of any lawyer's brief that the break-in was at least officially condoned and more likely was official policy of the government itself. Why not, then, hold the city liable?

The Supreme Court was emphatic in its 1961 decision in *Monroe* v. *Pape* that municipal governments were immune from suit under Section 1983. The Court reasoned that the post-Civil War Congress did not intend the word *person* to include cities or other governmental units. Thus, unless sovereign immunity was dissolved by the states themselves, there was no remedy for an aggrieved person seeking a defendant somewhat more solvent than the usually judgment-proof police officer. Since *the government* is nothing more than a name for that collection of people who are its agents and employees, the same ones who carry out "its" policies, the distinction may seem and ultimately was found to be odd. In 1978 the Court reassessed its position, and after a lengthy analysis of the legislative history of Section 1983 did a *volteface*; henceforth, cities and local governments are persons suable in federal court for violations of constitutional rights.[24]

Whenever the allegation is that the wrong furthered "a policy statement, ordinance, regulation, or decision officially adopted and promulgated by that body's officers," a Section 1983 suit can go forward. Nor is that all. Local governments may also be sued for constitutional violations embodied in custom, "even though such a custom has not received formal approval through the body's official decision-making channels." The Court drew the line at vicarious liability, however. Neither a simple act of negligence nor an unauthorized violation of constitutional rights by the police or other agent can be imputed to the public treasury.

The Court reserved decision on the extent of a government's immunity. It reached this question in April 1980 in a convoluted case concerning the failure of the city of Independence, Missouri, to give proper notice and a hearing prior to discharging its chief of police. Two months after the discharge, the Supreme Court in unrelated cases had declared that a public employee "allegedly stigmatized in the course of his discharge" is entitled to a name-clearing hearing. The lower courts in the Independence case concluded that since there was no way by which the officials of Independence could have known of this constitutional right, they were entitled personally to a limited good-faith immunity from suit. This immunity, the courts said, should be extended to the city itself. "The City of Independence should not be charged with predicting the future course of constitutional law."

The Supreme Court disagreed. There having been no tradition in common law of immunity for municipal corporations, the Court refused to read into Section 1983 any immunity at all. It concluded that a municipality may not assert even the good faith of its officials when sued under the Civil Rights Act for a constitutional violation. The Court summed up the current state of the law:

The innocent individual who is harmed by an abuse of governmental authority is assured that he will be compensated for his injury. The offending official, so long as he conducts himself in good faith, may go about his business secure in the knowledge that a qualified immunity will protect him from personal liability for damages that are more appropriately chargeable to the populace as a whole. And the public will be forced to bear only the costs of injury inflicted by the "execution of a government's policy or custom, whether made by its lawmakers or by those whose edicts or acts may fairly be said to represent official policy."[25]

The financial impact of these and related decisions handed down by the Supreme Court in seven governmental immunity cases during the spring of 1980[26] is difficult to predict. Where there is palpable personal injury caused by an act that can be characterized as a constitutional violation, damages can be substantial. A Virginia inmate, paralyzed when state prison authorities injected him with heavy doses of an antipsychotic drug, settled out of court for $518,000. The gist of the prisoner's complaint was that administering the drug amounted to a cruel and unusual punishment in violation of the Eighth Amendment, a claim upheld in numerous decisions.[27]

In state courts where ordinary negligence suits against municipalities are permitted, local governments have experienced an insurance crisis similar to that of manufacturers and physicians. A study of claims against sixteen California cities showed a 200 percent increase in general liability claims paid between 1970 and 1975. During this period, the average losses of small cities went from $5,000 to $11,674 and those of large cities climbed from $39,322 to $162,367 (though one very large suit inflated this last figure; the 1974 statistic was $84,367). Total awards against the state of California showed similar growth, from $32,000 in 1964 to $426,000 in 1970 to $1.9 million in 1975.[28] Occasionally, the effect of damage awards can be devastating. The city of Cashion, Oklahoma, declared bankruptcy when it was handed a judgment of

$150,000, a sum larger than the town's annual budget.[29] Not every suit against government claims physical injury. Searches and seizures, denial of voting rights, police harassment, school suspensions, and the like may result in mental distress or conviction of crime, consequences on which it is difficult to place a monetary value. Courts are reluctant to impose large speculative damages. For that reason, some statutes explicitly provide for civil fines. For example, the cost of unlawful wiretapping is $100 a day or $2,000, whichever is larger. There have been proposals to amend the Federal Tort Claims Act to provide a statutory floor and ceiling for recovery of damages resulting from constitutional violations by federal employees. One current proposal, not yet enacted, would permit $100 a day damages for continuing violations, in no event to exceed $15,000 per individual and $1 million in a class action.[30] Courts have also occasionally found reasons to impose damages that, though arbitrary, are more than merely nominal. Thus Judge Jack B. Weinstein in the class action against the Central Intelligence Agency for opening Americans' mail charged the agency $1,000 for each person whose mail was opened.[31]

Similarly, given an egregious enough set of circumstances, the courts will not be reluctant to approve large settlements for mental anguish. Perhaps the most prominent current wave of cases is that seeking damages for discriminatory strip searches. Police departments in a number of cities have been in the habit of routinely stripping and searching women arrested on virtually any charge. In numerous cases, the policy can only be called irrational. Among the allegations pending in 1980: In Chicago, a high school girl was stripped and searched "after being found in a corridor without a pass." A Missouri woman was strip-searched when she was arrested for failure to pay a $5 parking ticket. A party of campers at Devil's Lake State Park in Wisconsin were awakened at 2 A.M. one night by police who told them they had bunked down in an unauthorized area; some of the men were patted down, but one of the women was taken into a tent, stripped, and subjected to a ten-minute "cavity" search. The courts are beginning to hold these searches unconstitutional, and the Supreme Court's April 1980 ruling that municipal governments cannot rely on a good-faith defense means, potentially, that cities and counties may find they have large damage bills. Thus a settlement in Chicago of an ACLU suit on behalf of 191 women for $70,000 may go to court; attorneys predict far higher sums if cases go to juries.[32]

Physical injuries and mental anguish sustained under aggravated circumstances fit within conventional tort damage principles. The Supreme Court has ruled that these principles are the standards to be applied, and for a host of Section 1983 cases, they will be stingy.[33] A wide range of constitutional violations will ultimately result in judgments of small cost to the defendants (ex cluding legal fees which will increasingly be borne by the government), unless plaintiffs become discouraged and cease bringing suits altogether.

But not every case of municipal liability is likely to result in large payouts.

Since the Court's decision in 1978 that tort standards are the applicable ones in damage suits, courts around the country have allowed only nominal damages (often one dollar) in nonphysical constitutional violation cases. In the 1978 case, high school students were suspended for twenty days without the requisite hearing. The United States Court of Appeals had said that "substantial non-punitive damages were permissible in cases proving violation of procedural rights, even if it could be shown that with a hearing the same suspension order would have been made." The Supreme Court unanimously reversed. In a proper case, Justice Lewis Powell said, a plaintiff who *proves* that the lack of a hearing caused him actual emotional distress might recover substantial damages. This is an ancient tort remedy. However, "where a deprivation is justified but procedures are deficient, whatever distress a person feels may be attributable to the justified deprivation rather than to deficiencies in procedure." Unless the students could show that a hearing would have led school authorities not to suspend them, their damages must be limited to one dollar each. Other constitutional violations justifying only nominal damages include:

discriminatory failures to enter into good faith labor negotiations, denial of the right to a speedy appeal, confinement of a prisoner in a "Behavior Adjustment Unit" without full procedural due process, an unconstitutional refusal to allow an expelled student to call his accusing teacher as a witness, termination of supplemental food benefits for four-year-old children without due process, and the illegal impoundment of an automobile for nearly two weeks.[34]

The refusal to permit damages in these cases suggests that the relaxation of governmental immunities will not likely bankrupt municipal treasuries on the whim of a jury. True redress for significant harms, however, is now available to citizens as it is to consumers. The cost of tortious conduct will be borne, in the main, by government through indemnity statutes, not by employees, just as private employees are rarely billed for the injuries they cause.

IMMUNITY FOR JUDGES

Lest the courts be credited with a dispassionate and rational regard for the public welfare, some note should be made of the one area in which the Supreme Court persists in maintaining absolute immunity—immunity for judges.

The key modern case began in July 1971 when an Indiana woman presented Judge Harold D. Stump of DeKalb County circuit court with a "Petition to Have Tubal Ligation Performed on Minor and Indemnity Agreement." The mother said under oath that her fifteen-year-old daughter was "somewhat retarded," though she had been promoted each year in the public school. The daughter had begun dating and on occasion had stayed out all night. In view of her behavior and mental capacity, the daughter would be best served, the mother declared, if she underwent a tubal ligation "to prevent unfortunate circumstances." The mother further stated that she would indemnify the doctor who would perform the operation against any legal judgment he might suffer. Judge Stump approved the petition the same day. Informed that she needed her appendix removed, the daughter entered the hospital six days later, and the operation was done.

Two years later she married. Unable to conceive, she consulted doctors and learned for the first time what had happened. She and her husband filed suit in federal court against her mother, the doctor, the hospital, and Judge Stump. The district court dismissed the suit against the judge, citing Supreme Court precedents stretching back to 1872.[35] The United States Court of Appeals reversed. Judge Stump forfeited his immunity, that court declared, because he acted completely outside his jurisdiction and because he failed "to comply with elementary principles of procedural due process." Indiana law provided for sterilization of certain institutionalized people, but the law required approval by an administrative body prior to judicial review. Otherwise the law was silent about the need for judicial approval of sterilization for anyone else. The state law did provide that parents may consent to and arrange surgery on minors.

The Supreme Court reversed, holding Judge Stump absolutely immune from suit.[36] In the majority opinion, Justice Byron White said that what Judge Stump did was within his jurisdiction. The controversy revolved around the meaning of a *judicial act*. The majority ruled that Judge Stump's approval of the petition was a judicial act because approving petitions "is a function normally performed by a judge" and because "the parties . . . dealt with the judge in his judicial capacity." Had it been otherwise, the mother would never have submitted the petition to him.

Dissenting, Justice Potter Stewart declared that "a judge is not free, like a loose cannon, to inflict indiscriminate damage whenever he announces that he is acting in his judicial capacity." That the mother supposed she was dealing with a judge properly performing his duties "can safely be assumed . . . but false illusions as to a judge's power can hardly convert a judge's response to those illusions into a judicial act. . . . [A] judge's approval of a mother's petition to lock her daughter in the attic would hardly be a judicial act simply because the mother had submitted her petition to the judge in his official capacity." Did the judge have the power to ratify the mother's decision? "[W]hen a parent decides to call a physician to care for his sick child or arranges to have a surgeon remove his child's tonsils, he does not, 'normally' or otherwise, need to seek the approval of a judge."

In the 1872 case that established the doctrine of absolute immunity for judges, the Court asserted as "a general principle of the highest importance to the proper administration of justice that a judicial officer, in exercising the authority vested in him, [should] be free to act upon his own convictions, without apprehension of personal consequences to himself." But, as Justice Lewis Powell pointed out in a separate dissent, the Court's determination that individual harm should be subordinated to the public interest in an independent judiciary is acceptable only when the judicial system itself provides a means for protecting individual rights. In the 1872 case, the judge's asserted error was subject to correction on appeal. Not so in the case of Judge Stump. The daughter was unrepresented, had no notice, could not appeal. Judge Stump was truly a "loose cannon." And the consequences of his shot were not amenable to subsequent redress. If there is reason to be cynical about the process of judicial interpretation, this is the point. Immunity from suit has tended to disappear as people have begun to recognize that the power to injure must be tempered with responsibility in exercising it. That responsibility ought to extend to judges, who after all wield a power that grows more potent in the litigious society.

Autonomy and Immunity

In assessing the tendency of immunity doctrine, it is important to bear in mind that actual *injury* is not the criterion of liability. The erosion of governmental immunity does not mean that every act of government is subject to judicial second-guessing. There remains a significant area of conduct for which government is not answerable in court. Its protection lies in what might be termed "substantive immunity." This rule will not necessarily lead a court to dismiss a suit out of hand, as the older rule of immunity did. But it will defeat any reasonable expectation of recovery.

Substantive immunity protects the exercise of legitimate discretion in the performance of public functions, as the Supreme Court unanimously underscored in a 1980 decision. The case arose when a California parole board decided to release Richard Thomas, who was convicted of attempted rape in the

assault of two women in Tecolote Canyon in San Diego. He had been committed to a state mental hospital as a "mentally disordered sex offender not
amenable to treatment" and then sent to prison for a term of one to twenty
years. His sentencing carried a recommendation that he not be paroled. Five
years later, with the knowledge that he was likely to commit another violent
crime, the parole officers released him to the care of his mother. Five months
after his release, he detoured through Tecolote Canyon on his way to a ther-
apy session and knifed a fifteen-year-old girl to death. Her "family heard that
just weeks before the murder, Thomas had told authorities he feared what he
might do. He was afraid he might lose control." [37] Charging that the parole
authorities' decision was reckless, willful, wanton, and malicious, the girl's
parents sued for actual and punitive damages of $2 million. A California stat-
ute bars any suit against the government or its employees for injuries resulting
from parole determinations. The state courts ruled that this law provided the
parole authorities with absolute immunity. They rejected the contention that
the law violated due process and Section 1983. The Supreme Court affirmed
the dismissal of the suit. The state did not kill the victim, the Court declared;
the parolee did.

> The statute neither authorized nor immunized the deliberate killing of any human be-
> ing. It is not the equivalent of a death penalty statute which expressly authorizes state
> agents to take a person's life. . . . [T]he basic risk that repeat offenses may occur is al-
> ways present in any parole system. A legislative decision that has an incremental im-
> pact on the probability that death will result in any given situation—such as setting
> the speed limit at 55 miles per hour instead of 45—cannot be characterized as state ac-
> tion depriving a person of life just because it may set in motion a chain of events that
> ultimately leads to the random death of an innocent bystander. [38]

An opposite conclusion in the parole case would have paved the way for
total redress by the judiciary. For the implication would have been that all
decisions of government are subject to reassessment in court, according to
standards that could easily evade or ignore the fiscal and regulatory
responsibilities of the legislature and executive. The inquiry would proceed
from the failure of the government to provide for the safety of citizens,
whether the failure stemmed from action or inaction. The parole case involved a decision to do something that turned out to have incorporated a mistaken assessment of the risk. But the case would have been little different if
the family of the victim had charged a city police force with negligence in
failing to deploy its men so that murder was not deterred or if the family had
attempted to hold the city council liable for failure to appropriate enough
funds to build a larger force. This contention is not entirely whimsical. It has
been seriously proposed. Ralph Nader argued in congressional testimony in
1969 that citizens should be allowed to sue government officials who fail to

protect public safety and welfare. Within the decade the claim was being pressed seriously in lawsuits around the country. Although most of these involved the claim that the police had a special reason to guard either the person or the place and negligently failed to do so, some made a more general claim. Thus Renee Katz, a promising eighteen-year-old flutist whose hand was severed (and subsequently reattached) when she was hurled onto the subway tracks in Manhattan, sued New York City in 1979 for $10 million on the theory that the city was negligent in failing to station policemen in the subway.[39]

Virtually any human misconduct can be blamed on some other human failure: to detect, to warn, to deter, to educate. These failures are inherent in the scarcity of resources, time, and knowledge. The proper allocation of a community's resources is a question of ultimate social preference—guns or butter, policemen or teachers or welfare benefits. A legal rule giving the courts authority to consider the reasonableness of these delicate balances would commit not merely the most important decisions to judges; it would commit every decision to them. The declaration of affirmative duties quickly turns courts into quasi-managers. Each decision breeds the need for another decision because the answer to one question raises many others. A woman is murdered: Was it reasonable for the city to pay out millions for parades when it could have trained and deployed more policemen? A building is razed by fire: Would it not have been more sensible to hold teachers' salaries to a more modest level to make room in the budget for a few extra fire fighters? And would not all these problems be alleviated by raising taxes and spending more money; why should the people be left with so much disposable income when they only fritter it away on inconsequential pleasures?

Since discretion is unavoidable, the fundamental question is where discretion should be lodged. A rule that brought every discretionary act of government before the courts would lodge the ultimate discretion with the judges. Had the Supreme Court approved this rule, criticism that courts overreach themselves would be warranted, and nothing less than a constitutional amendment would have been necessary to preserve the historical foundations of American government. But a rule that would permit every inaction to be called into question is not operative. Where no overarching legal standard is applicable, the government retains its autonomy—not from the people but from the courts—in the formulation and execution of public policy.

Similar considerations apply to two other types of suits that have generated headlines in recent days: damage claims by former students against schools and by children against parents. That the charges are for "educational" and "parental" malpractice only clouds the issue by raising a semantic confusion with true professional malpractice. Understanding the nature of discretion

committed to institutions other than courts should make clear why these bo-
gus forms of malpractice are not likely to develop into full-fledged areas of
litigation.

A New York high school graduate who could read with only fourth-grade
ability charged his public school district with a failure to educate him. Despite his diploma, he claimed he lacked "even the rudimentary ability to
comprehend written English." He sought $500,000 in damages. The courts
dismissed the complaint.

To entertain a cause of action for "educational malpractice" [the state's highest court
said] would require the courts not merely to make judgments as to the validity of
broad educational policies—a course we have unalteringly eschewed in the past—but,
more importantly, to sit in review of the day-to-day implementation of these policies.
Recognition in the courts of this cause of action would constitute blatant interference
with the responsibility for the administration of the public school system lodged by the
Constitution and statute in school administrative agencies.[40]

The decision, though grounded on the constitutional allocation of authority
for making educational decisions, seems intuitively correct also because the
service schools perform is not passive. It depends, for success, on the motiva-
tions of the alleged victim. No clear standard is available to assess the relative
contributions of student and teachers to the student's inability to read. Moreover, unlike the "right to treatment" cases, what is here argued for is a right
to a result, a "right to education." In the mental health litigation, no one
pressed on the court the claim that the plaintiffs were entitled to a cure.

It would be too much to conclude, however, that schools must always be
immune from the consequences of mistaken decisions within their sphere of
expertise. A school that mistakenly, and negligently, assigned a six-year-old
boy to classes for the mentally retarded ought to be answerable for the incal-
culable injury committed in condemning him to a life of ignorance. This
point has eluded the New York Court of Appeals, which dismissed just this
claim in 1979 on the strength of the decision quoted in part above.[41] The distinction may be difficult to draw in some cases but here it was plain: Though
there is no general right to an education (as opposed to a right to attend
school), there is a right to be free of "affirmative acts of misfeasance."* A
negligent misclassification can be actionable without any serious threat to the
autonomy of schools to carry out their educational mission.

* The child was tested in 1957 and determined to be retarded on the basis of an IQ score of 74.
But the examining psychologist recommended reevaluation within two years because the boy's
speech defect made assessment of his mental acuity difficult. The school forgot to do so for
twelve years. Readministered in 1969, the test showed that the then eighteen-year-old had an IQ
of 94, which would have been more than sufficient to place him in normal classes. By then it was
too late.

A similar distinction can be made in the so-called parental malpractice cases, of which the most notorious is the suit, ultimately dismissed, of the twenty-four-year-old Colorado man who sought $350,000 from his parents for neglecting his clothing, food, shelter, and psychological needs while he was growing up.[42] The claim was not that he was forced into the woods and abandoned, like the Wild Child of Aveyron, but that the degree of care was insufficient. It is safe to predict that other such suits will similarly be dismissed because the courts will conclude that parents retain discretion to raise children according to their various criteria. Whether to raise or raze a child's religious consciousness, whether to encourage development in a stern or permissive home, whether to indulge cravings for junk food or to regulate the diet strictly, whether to live in the country or the city are questions at the heart of value creation. No law requires that the formation of character and of values in children be left with the family because until recently this was an unquestioned social norm. Law that permits government intervention into family affairs is tailored to situations in which the family has already been ruptured— in cases of physical abuse of the child, for example. To be sure, courts could alter fundamentally the family relationship by allowing the question of children's rights against parents to be raised in open court. But a legal determination that questions may be voiced is no guide to their answer. For the courts to encourage conflicts to be aired in a public forum would be an empty formalism, unless the judicial preference for total redress were to be the rule applied. This would hold that any change in position to which a child objects is perforce a compensable injury. For that very reason such a rule would be the reductio ad absurdum of litigation conducted in the absence of socially accepted or legislatively mandated standards.°

Substantive immunity recognizes a large zone of autonomy within which institutions other than courts are free to make their own determinations, but it does not automatically require the dismissal of a lawsuit that charges lapses not grounded in standardless norms, as did the old rule of governmental immunity. If there is thus always a chance that government officials or others with clearly defined roles will be prey to a lawsuit, it is unlikely that they will lose or need to spend a great deal in defending themselves in cases in which legal standards are absent and the criteria for constructing them are hopelessly multiple and irreducible.

°One of the few successful suits against parents was that of a teenage Minnesota girl who persuaded a court to interpret a custody statute so that she could remain with relatives rather than be taken by her parents on a three-year trip around the world. This was not, it should be emphasized, a parental malpractice action, and it has not apparently been duplicated elsewhere. (In the Matter of the Welfare of L.A.G., Hennepin County Dist. Ct., Juvenile Div., Minn., August 11, 1972; discussed in Lori B. Andrews, "Families and the Law: When Kids Take Parents to Court," *Parents Magazine*, May 1980, p. 81.)

The Immunity of Litigants and Lawyers

One final type of immunity is worth a brief mention: the legal immunity of litigants and lawyers for the very act of suing. The legal system itself can be the source of considerable harm. Indeed, that is the principal message of litigation's public critics. We do not permit a man with a grudge to invade his enemy's home, to rummage through his private papers, to call him away from his daily routine to answer to a personal attack. Yet these otherwise tortious acts are legitimized if the invader is armed with legal papers in the form of a complaint, a document easy to prepare and file with a court clerk. If the litigant is wrong about his claim, there is little, if anything, that the defendant can do to recover for his injuries—loss of time, wages, opportunities, or reputation, which are normally recoverable when defendants wrongly harm plaintiffs.

In theory, there is a remedy for abuse of the legal process—a lawsuit for the tort of "malicious prosecution."[43] Some physicians held out the hope during the mid-1970s that they could deter medical malpractice litigation by charging patients and their attorneys with the costs of litigation and the damage to professional reputation whenever the patient lost the suit. In practice, the hope has been proved forlorn. Of the two-hundred-odd suits by doctors against patients since 1975, in only one has the doctor prevailed all the way through the appeal. The remedy of a countersuit will almost always be unavailing because the doctor must show something more than failure of the original suit. The requisite standard is one of actual malice: that the original plaintiff, knowing he had no case, sued the defendant out of spite and with an intent to injure. Not surprisingly, this is a nearly impossible burden to overcome since it is the rare case in which a plaintiff knows the claim to be false but pursues it cold-bloodedly nonetheless.° There is certainly no evidence that the typical medical malpractice suit is a fabrication from its inception.[44]

There is no reason to expect judges to welcome the argument that the narrow conception of malicious prosecution is an injustice that should itself be redressed. Nor is a legislative overriding of the general rule any more likely to be forthcoming. The legitimacy of a lawsuit does not rest on its outcome. Most actions are settled. Most of the remainder present difficult problems of proof. Many assert new rights that courts may be induced to accept. Permit-

---

°The New York Court of Appeals ruled in late 1978 that a physician had no legal claim against a lawyer who named him in a malpractice action even though the physician had had no connection with the deceased patient. The patient's chart carried the doctor's name, erroneously, as chief cardiologist; the hospital had failed to remove the doctor's name as chief cardiologist after he ceased such duties. The decision is overly protective of lawyers. (*Drago* v. *Buonagurio*, 46 N.Y. 2d 778, 413 N.Y.S. 2d 910, 386 N.E. 2d 821 [1978].)

ting countersuits for failure to succeed in these cases is too drastic a remedy for the narrow problem of frivolous suits. And a radical change might not reduce litigiousness but only change its character: Fighting fire with fire may feed the general conflagration. Redress for injuries that the legal system creates should be sought not in attempts to undermine the major avenue of redress open to all of us in this injury-prone world but in reform of the lawsuit itself—in the mechanics of suing.

Chapter 7

Reflections on Litigiousness: Limits and Lessons

The Adversary System

WHAT does litigation accomplish? The answer is threefold. It can provide recompense for injuries that have already occurred. It can deter future harms, known and unknown. The knowledge that suits can exact a heavy monetary toll tends to reform some kinds of behavior (product design, medical practice). Where the consequences of proposed conduct are unknown but are potentially harmful, as in the area of environmental concerns, litigation can focus attention on the issue and force decision makers to investigate and assess before acting blindly. Finally, litigation can be instrumental in terminating ongoing harms or at least in reforming institutional systems that tend to perpetuate them.

That much modern litigation has succeeded in prompting far-reaching reform seems to confirm the validity and vitality of what lies at the core of the litigious society: the adversary system ("the greatest legal engine ever invented for the discovery of truth," said the legal scholar John H. Wigmore[1]). To lawyers, who have been chiefly responsible for the design of our government, the adversary ethic is due unblinking loyalty. Adversariness is the poetry in the heart of democracy. Our liberties depend on its Versus: the right to challenge in court anyone whose activities may harm us and to call on independent lawyers for aid to help pursue our cause.

For certain kinds of problems, an adversary system is inescapable. A society with a strong commitment to political freedom will want to ensure, at a minimum, a means of deterring oppression by government. The adversary approach to criminal prosecutions clearly does so. By putting the state to an extreme burden of proof and by guaranteeing defendants access to fiercely independent lawyers, we can in general prevent the state from imprisoning those whom it distrusts or fears. Similarly, a competitive society will look to the forms of trial as the best means of enforcing compliance with contractual commitments and of deterring fraud. An adversary system, in other words, seems to mesh nicely with adversary behavior.

Not every form of human activity is necessarily adversary, however. The parent's role is not normally to oppose the child. The doctor's intent is to help, not to injure. But the growing desire for redress of injuries prompts us more and more to search for the wrongdoer. That search leads us with increasing frequency to view conduct and relationships as conflicting that not so long ago were unhesitatingly accepted as altruistic and benign.

To see conflict where no one perceived it before has become the trademark of our times. Anyone who now promises to act in the best interest of another would have enormous difficulty in sustaining the position. The list of those whose claims would no longer be accepted includes psychiatrists, wardens, deans, teachers, social workers, husbands, university presidents, and research scientists.[2]

As new adversaries are discovered, it seems only natural to extend the legal model—the fact-finding inquiry—to those who seek shelter from the blows of others. The adversary system has spread in two ways. It is becoming the dominant mode of decision making in institutions whose actions directly affect others. Thus schools must provide students with a hearing before discipline is imposed. Welfare agencies may not terminate welfare payments without holding a hearing. Administrative agencies generally are being forced to act like courts. Even purely private activities are being pressed to adopt judicial forms. A former customer sued a power company on the grounds that the utility terminated her electricity for nonpayment of a bill without first having listened to her story. The basis of the argument was that the company, as a public utility, was required to provide service. Hence, it was essentially a public agency required by the Fourteenth Amendment to hold a hearing before depriving a customer of a valuable benefit. The Supreme Court was not impressed and held that the utility was not a public instrumentality, and that there was no right to a hearing.[3] However, there is nothing to prevent a legislature or an administrative body that oversees private companies from mandating a hearing.

At the same time that the notion of a hearing is spreading to nonjudicial institutions,° it is also being adopted by courts as a means of overseeing potentially every private decision. A New York State intermediary appellate court ruled that it is for the courts, not physicians or families to decide whether or not to remove life-sustaining machinery from terminally ill comatose patients. The case arose when the nieces, nephews, and religious superior of Brother Joseph Charles Fox asked a hospital to turn off a respirator that was keeping him alive. Brother Fox, aged eighty-three, had gone into a coma during an operation in the hospital. But the doctor and hospital refused to remove the respirator, saying they wanted a court order. The trial judge issued such an order, but the district attorney appealed, arguing that there could never be such a right. The appellate court ruled that it might be proper to terminate life-sustaining treatment but that the decision could only be made by a court in each case. At the hearing the court would be obliged to take testimony from the family, the physician, the hospital (through a committee of three doctors), a court-appointed guardian, and the state attorney general or district attorney, who in turn would have the right "to have examinations conducted by physicians of their own choosing."[4]

This seems more process than is due and the form unsuited to the problem. Presumably the hospital, doctor, and family would independently consider the merits of termination. Adding a guardian and the district attorney suggests that the court wishes adversary representation. But what will these representatives be adverse to, unless it is necessary that in the discharge of their duties they must consistently argue that the machines remain hooked up? And if they routinely make that argument, the court may dispense with them altogether, taking judicial notice of the general principle that doctors should continue to treat as long as there is life. If there were evidence of collusion between medical staff and family to terminate the life of a patient who might conceivably recover, or if there were evidence that hospitals were requiring that machines be left running in order to collect exorbitant fees from families, then the legislature might wish to impose a hearing (though not necessarily in court). But no such evidence was apparent in New York, where the court seems to have arrogated to itself the power to sit as referee among experts, a task under the circumstances it is ill suited to perform. Not every inquiry needs to be adversary in nature, nor does every serious decision need to be made in an adversary proceeding.

°Not every hearing pressed on these institutions is necessarily adversary. In *Goss*, for example, the Supreme Court did not require school authorities to permit students to appear with lawyers, much less did it require the school to provide lawyers.

Important and as effective as the adversary system can be, it is not without a deleterious side. It can be a hugely inefficient means of uncovering facts; its relentless formalities and ceaseless opportunities for splitting hairs are time consuming and expensive. It is not available therefore to everyone, and if it is the only system for obtaining redress then justice cannot be done. For that reason, it may mislead us as a society into supposing that its availability is a guarantee of safety. Litigation is not a panacea; social policies are not necessarily carried out merely because there is an avenue open to some. Suing is an inefficient means of securing systemic compliance with a general policy.[5] (A recent study of the Freedom of Information Act, for example, showed that despite the broad right of citizens to sue federal agencies for a range of documents, the law has been largely ineffective in making public what government wants to keep secret.[6])

Litigation depends too much on individual willingness to enforce the law; a victory of principle in one case is no guarantee that the loser will abide by the law in an identical but unrelated transaction. If the history of race litigation teaches nothing else, it teaches that.

Moreover, like every other human system, litigation is subject to regular abuse. The limitations of semantics, the fallibility of memory, the will to prevaricate, all contribute to unpredictability. The outcome is never certain, and litigation is therefore frequently an exercise in anguish and futility. As a mechanism to instill in people a fiduciary regard for others, it can be effective. But for all that it does not often treat well those who are ensnared in it. Litigation, and especially the trial itself, can be unremittingly harsh. Lawyers are often adversaries not only of each other but of their clients; some kinds of litigation are prolonged (and even initiated) solely to ensure the lawyers sufficient billable hours to earn a decent or even a handsome living. The process can be psychologically harmful, hurting self-esteem as well as pocketbook. Other modes of resolving disputes and solving problems bear scrutiny.

Alternatives to Litigation

Six methods of eliminating or reducing courtroom litigation are known. The first is to redefine the subject in dispute so that legal machinery for resolving differences becomes unnecessary. The second is to replace the trial with a mechanism that automatically gives the injured party relief. The third is to remove from the trier's jurisdiction certain issues that relate to the dispute.

Fourth, disputes can be shifted to other forums. Fifth, the mixture of incentives that currently bring people to court can be changed; barriers to litigation can be installed in their place. Finally, the underlying causes of litigation can be treated, removing the need to go to court.[7]

The first approach involves basic political and social choices. The second, third, and fourth methods comprise what is coming to be known as "civil diversion," an approach to removing civil disputes from court in order to secure speedier and less expensive justice, relieve the workload of the courts, and reach more precise and correct determinations in complex matters.

Civil diversion assumes that there is an underlying dispute; it accepts harm and the ensuing litigiousness as a fact of modern life and asks what can be done to resolve the dispute more efficiently. The first alternative does not. It begins with the opposite assumption: that some claims should be rejected out of hand and that people should be free to act regardless of whom they harm or what they do. Since this alternative runs counter to the deepest temper of our time, it seems an unlikely approach.

There is some historical precedent for it, however. During the nineteenth century the court reports were full of suits charging the tort of "alienation of affection." Included in this tort was the wooing of another person's spouse, and, by extension, of one's fiance. The harm was, of course, the destruction of the family, the loss of companionship, personal unhappiness. A different moral climate has swept away most of this tort, though it survives in one form in many states—the loss of consortium (or, as the law less circumspectly but no less delicately calls it, "conjugal" companionship) arising out of automobile or other accidents. One could imagine a legal regime in a sexually permissive society that accepted every act of adultery, every divorce and remarriage, every transfer of live-in friend from one home to another as the subject of a damage suit. But it makes more sense to consider affection, love, and companionship part of the autonomous realm in which the state ought not intrude. One who cannot retain the affection of another should not look to the courts for balm. (Had not most states statutorily abolished the tort, who knows? In time the Supreme Court might have rendered these suits unconstitutional by noting how they conflict with the First Amendment's guarantee of freedom of association, much as the Court made libel suits more difficult to win by placing them within that amendment's protective mantle.)

Finding other areas of needless litigation depends on a social assessment of values, and it seems unlikely that in the age of redress legislatures can or should be persuaded to label lawful what in truth is harmful. Those who hope for a sweeping repeal of the antitrust laws or of the tort of malpractice are not likely to find their wishes gratified.

By contrast, the civil diversion approach refuses to ignore the harm but seeks to redress it by some means other than those currently employed in the civil trial court. One approach is to substitute a mechanism that gives automatic relief, eliminating the fact-finding inquiry altogether. No-fault automobile insurance is one example of this approach, though in practice it is far from automatic across the entire range of accidents. But the principle is sound: By eliminating the inquiry into fault, the remaining issues simplify the recovery mechanism sufficiently so that in many cases no formal hearing is necessary. A police report will verify the occurrence, and a mechanic's report will verify the damage. The insurance company need only pay the repair costs. As it is presently structured, no-fault insurance does not provide complete relief outside the courtroom since above a certain threshold, usually fairly low, suits for medical costs, wage loss, property damage, and pain and suffering are still viable. At best, no-fault automobile insurance at present is, in Professor Earl Johnson's words, "semi-automatic."[8] Universal no-fault is unlikely to replace the traditional personal injury suit. Nevertheless, if automobile no-fault could be perfected, a significant proportion of lawsuits (perhaps as much as one-third nationwide) now clogging the civil courts could be removed.

Another inquiry that could be removed from the courtroom is probate. The probate of most wills does not involve a dispute, yet a court's approval must still be sought before the assets can be distributed. Plans permitting independent administration of small estates, free of court supervision, are beginning to reduce the number of matters that come before judges.

A second way to divert civil disputes is to eliminate certain issues that the trier may entertain. One common example is the movement toward no-fault divorces. Accept the premise that divorce is a personal decision between husband and wife; then whenever both agree, no sound reason exists for the state in effect to be the adverse party. (In the absence of no-fault, the frequent effect of the need for adversary proceedings is to compel the parties to perjure themselves in order to show that fault occurred and that one party is therefore entitled to relief against the other.)

Elimination of issues such as fault does not necessarily remove the matter from court. It may indeed increase the number of cases that come to court. The rate of filings for divorce in some states went up immediately after no-fault laws were enacted (in New Jersey, the divorce docket climbed by 70 percent within the first year after a no-fault ground was adopted[9]). This increase is of course partly artificial; some people no doubt waited to take advantage of the more liberal law. But some increase should be expected; the reason the law was enacted was to make it easier for people to obtain a divorce. The savings that result are in the time and resources devoted to the judicial proceeding.

Issue elimination helps plaintiffs. For that reason it is not likely to appeal to those who are likely to remain defendants. The century-long movement toward strict liability and the adoption of such presumptions as res ipsa loquitur represent the desire of judges to make it easier for plaintiffs to prove cases. [On occasion, issue elimination can hurt a class of plaintiffs. For example, summary eviction procedures entitle landlords to seek quick ouster of tenants who have not paid their rent. Under these procedures only the issue of payment will be heard. That there are valid reasons for withholding rent cannot be contested at the summary proceeding, and tenants must go to regular court, often an alternative they cannot afford. By eliminating a self-help remedy (withholding rent), these statutes may reduce the number of some kinds of lawsuits, but the result will be inequitable, and the numbers of other lawsuits (summary eviction) may increase.[10]]

The third approach to civil diversion, and the one from which the name is derived, is the shifting of disputes from courts to other forums for resolution. The primary alternatives are arbitration and mediation. Neither of these concepts is new; in the labor field, for instance, arbitration and mediation of grievances is decades old. But interest grew during the 1970s for adopting these mechanisms to resolve a wider range of disputes. In particular, bar groups and government have focused on the resolution of minor disputes through neighborhood centers that provide for voluntary settlement of grievances.[11] Many of these disputes involve matters that might otherwise wind up in police court: neighbors angry at each other over barking dogs, physical abuse in families, and the like. When these disputes do arrive in criminal courts, they are frequently dismissed because of the crush of more important business. The judge may admonish the defendant and threaten him with punishment if he disturbs the peace again, but the threat is not often taken seriously. As a consequence, "neighborhood tensions haven't been reduced, and relationships haven't been improved. At best, a shaky truce may have been ordered."[12]

Many cities have begun to establish dispute resolution centers; by 1979 they were operating on an experimental basis in more than 100 cities across the country.[13] Their number will doubtless grow during the 1980s, partly through funding authorized by the Dispute Resolution Act, which President Jimmy Carter signed into law in February 1980.[14] These programs (called, variously, neighborhood justice centers or community mediation centers) seek to resolve minor criminal matters, landlord-tenant disputes, and consumer complaints and to prevent them from arising in the future.

As important and useful as these procedures may prove to be, they do not presage the end of litigiousness. To the contrary, as Attorney General Edward H. Levi has pointed out, "[t]he very availability of alternate dispute resolution mechanisms may result in more disputes to be processed, if not by the courts, then at least by governmental institutions."[15] Most of the current programs deal with minor matters, as they are intended to, and will not necessarily have a significant impact on the many types of lawsuits considered here. Large damage claims are not likely to be arbitrated voluntarily although some states are beginning to mandate nonbinding arbitration in damage suits. Medical malpractice panels are the most prevalent, but ordinary personal injury and even commercial claims are beginning to be referred initially to arbitration.

Although the option of suing in court is retained, the success of many arbitrations and sanctions against pursuing a lawsuit and failing (the forfeiture of a bond or the necessity of paying the other party's attorneys' fees) do represent a means of truly diverting cases from courts. To those concerned with judicial administration, these alternatives may be crucial. They may also be crucial to litigants waiting for judges to call up their cases, now backlogged for twenty or thirty months. But these alternatives may not result in a net decrease in litigation, since freeing the court calendars of petty matters may provide an incentive to others to seek judicial resolution of disputes that now are settled for lack of court time. Similarly, large social issues will not quickly disappear from the courtroom, though even here there have been attempts, some successful, to mediate communitywide disputes over such problems as low-cost housing development and school integration. Success, however, may breed more takers.

As helpful as many of the alternatives to traditional litigation may be, critics would not likely agree that litigiousness had ended if minor disputes, civil and criminal, wound up outside the courts, no matter how beneficial that would be to the individual parties—and to all of us. The significant problem of the side effects (for example, the cost of litigation, the delays) remains, and independent efforts to reduce the litigants' injuries are still required.

Toward Legislative Control of the Lawsuit

Much is made of the function that courts perform in checking the other two branches of government. Much less is written of control over the judiciary. Partly because legal procedures are assumed to be matters best left to experts, the courts are largely in control of the legal process. Changes in the vital procedural rules that govern access to courts and the handling and disposition of cases have for decades been considered the province of judges. The federal rules are the handiwork of a committee of lawyers and judges appointed by the judiciary and ratified by the Supreme Court. Though Congress has the inherent power to write these rules, it does not, reserving to itself the never-exercised power to veto. This is unfortunate. In a litigious society, the conduct of litigation is no less important than its objects. From a judicial perspective, courtroom procedures are necessary to do justice in each case. They do not necessarily reflect a valuation that the aggregate effects are socially beneficial. That is for Congress and the state legislatures to do.

One aim of legislative control would be to reduce the number of frivolous lawsuits filed out of spite or to extort a settlement out of a defendant who cannot stand the cost of full-scale litigation. Legislation to deal with this problem would need to change those "institutional arrangements," in the words of Professor Maurice Rosenberg, "that tend to make lawsuits in this country easy to maintain and tolerable to lose."[16] Most of these arrangements are financial: the growth in funding alternatives outside the plaintiffs' pocketbooks. Contingent fees, statutes providing for recovery of attorneys' fees from losing defendants, public funding, private grants to public interest law firms make it possible to bring suits that would not otherwise wind up in court. But these financial arrangements prompt a great deal of meritorious litigation, so terminating them or reducing their effectiveness would eliminate much good.

Little is known about the frivolous suit. Because frivolousness is judgmental, it is not reflected in court statistics. The first priority of legislative intervention, therefore, ought to be to engage in a detailed study of the problem's scope. If some classes of statutory rights lead to more extortionate than meritorious litigation, substantial modifications in the right perhaps should be made.

A more commonly proposed solution is to change from the so-called American rule to the English rule for awarding attorneys' fees. It is a widely respected convention in the United States that each party, win or lose, must bear the cost of his own attorney, a feature of civil procedure said to be "unique in the common law world."[17] In England and her other former colonies, the winning party is entitled to recover his legal costs, including attorneys' fees. As a practical matter, these rarely come to the total costs and account for varying proportions of the attorneys' charges. But in the United States, only by virtue of certain statutes (for example, the federal antitrust and employment discrimination laws) is there any fee-shifting at all, and then only from the losing defendant to the winning plaintiff. Shifting fees from losing plaintiffs to winning defendants is so rare that it is fair to say it does not happen.

There is considerable controversy over the effects of a change, easily accomplished by statute, in the American rule. The conventional wisdom is that a change would deter many plaintiffs with a meritorious claim because their meager finances will not make sensible the risk of having to pay the opposing party if the case is at all close. "The reality," says Professor Rosenberg, "is more varied and the circumstances more subtle than those assumed."[18] According to his analysis, the effect would depend on whether the plaintiff were well-to-do, indigent, or of moderate means, and on whether the suit were brought by a lawyer expecting a contingent fee or a payment for time and trouble no matter the outcome. The wealthy plaintiff might be encouraged to risk losing if by winning he could do so at no cost. The unsuccessful indigent plaintiff paying under a contingent fee arrangement might lose nothing beyond the expectation of recovering his damages. For the person of moderate means, the effect will depend on the nature of the suit and the method of calculating the attorney's fee.

If a change were to be negotiated through Congress, it must be based on evidence not yet assembled. The drafter should not lose sight of the goal: to deter frivolous litigation, not to stir up still more or dampen the incentive to bring meritorious cases. Nevertheless, it seems reasonable to examine proposals that would award attorneys' fees in situations less compelling than those preferred in malicious prosecution suits. At least in money damage suits the plaintiff ought to be charged with the burden of acting in accordance with some standard of reasonableness. There is no apparent reason for permitting the lawsuit to be a source of unredressable harm. A well-tailored statute could give the power to judges to award attorneys' fees to plaintiff or defendant in the proper case.

The statute ought not restrict the fee-shifting to transfers from plaintiff to defendant, as has been recently proposed. Stung at paying more than $5,000 to win dismissal of a patently frivolous libel suit, Steven Brill, editor of the monthly *American Lawyer*, has suggested that the loser, if a plaintiff, should pay the winner's total legal costs in all civil suits. "If the plaintiff wins, he or she would get the judgment but not the costs, because the goal here is to deter and compensate for bad suits, not to intimidate defendants or to encourage still more litigation by making it viable for a plaintiff seeking to 'make a point' with a small-dollar suit to get the defendant to pay for his or her having brought it." This position is untenable. The social goal cannot be only to deter bad suits but also to deter harmful and wrongful acts. On Brill's reasoning, any winner is entitled to compensation for costs; why should an injured plaintiff have to pay for justice to be done? If investigation shows that a significant number of minor cases are brought which have a low cap on recoveries (as in truth-in-lending cases, for example) but in which attorneys' fees are recoverable, a limitation on the fee, which many courts impose, can prevent the litigation from being an exercise of benefit only to the attorneys.[19]

The frivolous suit is the lesser of the problems posed by modern litigation. The larger problem is the harm that it causes all parties in meritorious suits. These harms include the length and cost of preparation and trial and the prospect that the jury or judge will hand down judgments or remedies bearing no relation to the act complained of.

"Litigation costs have become intolerable, and they cause a lengthening shadow over the basic fairness or our legal system," Justice Lewis Powell has written.[20] The problem stems largely, though not solely, from the culture of lawyers. A lawyer paid by the hour, as most attorneys are,° has an incentive, subconscious perhaps, to drag out proceedings.† Lawyers uniformly deny this propensity in public and admit to it (in the behavior of colleagues) in private. The penchant for working long hours is not simply financially rooted; it is also part of the lawyer's training and tradition. Especially is this so in the federal courts in which "discovery" procedures (by which attorneys can obtain documents and testimony by deposition from witnesses and the adversary prior to trial) are broad and loosely supervised. As Arthur Liman, a prominent federal practitioner in New York has put it:

Discovery has become a narcotic for members of our profession. Some litigating lawyers consider themselves almost professionally derelict if they do not ask for every document they can think of, formulate every interrogatory that arouses their curiosity in four different forms—even if they already have full knowledge of the answers—and notice the deposition of every possible witness, no matter how trivial or cumulative his role. While some of this excess may be a deliberate strategy to bludgeon an adversary into a settlement, much is the result of insecurity or habit by responsible members of the bar who believe that their clients' interests require that no stone be left unturned in the discovery stage.[21]

Rampant discovery is theoretically subject to control by federal judges, yet few have time or inclination to become involved in the exceedingly tedious game. In 1980, after nearly four years of discussion by various committees concerned with refining the discovery rules, the United States Supreme Court ordered pip-squeak changes that will have little practical effect.[22] Congress ought to search for a nuanced means of limiting discovery abuse.

Legislation can also attack the problem of the overreaching remedy. One aspect concerns damages. Since there is no way to quantify physical pain or mental suffering, defendants fear limitless exposure and argue for limitations on or abolition of such awards. From the perspective of the seriously injured,

---

°Generally speaking, only personal injury cases and certain tasks of predictable dimensions, like drafting a will or conveying title to real property, are handled on an other than hourly basis.

†A celebrated example of the lawyer's penchant for delay was the twelve-year battle at the Food and Drug Administration over a labeling regulation defining "peanut butter" as a substance containing at least 90 percent peanuts. The hearing transcript was more than 24,000 pages long, and the lawyers managed to come up with 75,000 pages of documents. (Mark J. Green, *The Other Government* [New York: Grossman, 1975], p. 138.)

abolition is unfair: Who doubts the very real suffering endured by the paraplegic victim of an unsafe automobile or the deformed child born to a mother who was prescribed harmful medicines? Occasional attempts to abolish pain and suffering in certain classes of cases—for example, medical malpractice—are probably consigned to the fate of unconstitutional statutes for violating principles of equal protection and fundamental fairness.[23] But a statute that spells out limitations on pain and suffering for all classes of injuries would probably pass constitutional scrutiny.

It should be noted that the philosophy of total redress has not yet infused the remedy for pain and suffering. It is a peculiarity of the common law system that pain and suffering awards are almost exclusively limited to cases of physical injury. In the larger sense, this is an anomaly, for there are any number of situations in which defendants cause plaintiffs mental anguish for which no recovery is possible. The tenant who is wrongly forced out of his dwelling may seek no sum for his troubles; the party suing for breach of contract may not recover for the many anxieties that attend his legal attempt to enforce his contractual rights. This anomaly occurred because until relatively recently the common law refused to recognize purely mental suffering. Only when it accompanied physical injury was it includable in a jury's verdict. Within the past two decades, however, courts have begun to recognize claims for certain types of psychic injuries—for the most part, those stemming from situations that could have led to physical injury but happened instead to result in fright. It is possible to foresee the day courts will permit recoveries for nontortious suffering, such as that occurring when a contract is breached. The wisdom of such a trend, should it materialize, is open to question. Anxiety attends every legal action and should be accepted as one of the ordinary hazards of life. If courts do approve the principle, however, it is within the legislative power to annul it.

Legislative bodies also have the power to shape the remedies in institutional cases. Where the remedy a court orders is clearly open-ended, it is within the constitutional oversight of Congress to withdraw the jurisdiction of the courts to hand down and enforce it. This is a situation of some delicacy; currently pending in Congress, for example, is a bill that would deprive the federal courts of the power to prevent schools from requiring children to say prayers. Obviously, Congress could seriously distort constitutional values by unwise and even flippant legislative stays directed against the courts, but the power is there.

This cursory review by no means exhausts the difficulties that attend the trial process, but this is not the place even for summary. Within the democratic context, the courts are not autonomous and their word need not be accepted as final.

Democracy and the Courts

That courts are nonmajoritarian institutions in a democratic land has worried millions of words out of the commentators over the nearly two hundred years of our existençe as a constitutional republic. Laws are to be made by representative legislatures, not by unelected judges, according to the usual critique. Yet for two centuries we have endured as a nation that more than any other must be described as democratic in form and operation. This is no paradox. It is the consequence of slippery words.

What is majoritarian? The American political process has always been infinitely more subtle than the blunt concept of majority rule would suggest. We have never relied on a simplistic notion of majority rule. The President is not popularly elected, the people do not vote on policy questions or legislation (except occasionally in state referendums), and even significant votes in Congress are subject to a minority veto.

Moreover, the specific task of legislation is rarely a considered or conscious majority process. Few members of Congress are sent there by constituents with instructions to take particular positions on pending bills or to introduce new ones. No member of Congress has instructions on the entire range of matters brought before that "grand inquest of the Nation." Nor do members of Congress have the knowledge, stamina, or time to think through the mass of legislation that flows through the Capitol Hill corridors each year. They are dependent on their staff and experts, when they choose to rely on anyone at all.

Majority rule is further weakened by parliamentary rules. Legislation firmly supported by a solid majority of the American public, at least insofar as opinion polls can determine, can be blocked by an adamant-enough minority. Many bills can disappear in committee rooms. Not every failure of Congress to legislate is a policy decision by a majority that there ought to be no law.

The reality is that Congress ratifies what it conceives to be public opinion, formed through word of mouth, newspapers, books, periodicals, radio and television broadcasts. This kind of opinion does not deal in detail. In brokering the compromise that enables legislation to be enacted, Congress (and the state legislatures generally) resort to fuzzy language and ambiguous standards. Only by making it seem as though most people got what they came for can congressmen escape the fury of their constituents. Like every other aspect of the political process, legislation is an attempt to pass the buck.

It may also be an attempt to pass the time. New York State legislators, for instance, found themselves in such a hurry to end their session in June 1980 that they voted pell-mell on bills they had not read at the rate of one every thirty seconds.[24] But even when time is available, it is not often used to ease the intellectual and political burdens that broad and ill-defined statutes put on courts.

An example is the Age Discrimination Act of 1975, which Professor Peter H. Schuck has picked apart in a corruscating article. The act purports to prohibit age-based discrimination in programs receiving federal assistance. In fact, the act undercuts the force of its initial premise through broad exceptions. These exclude from coverage all activities and programs in which, by some other law, age criteria are permitted to condition benefits or participation. The net is "a law based largely upon conflicting premises" without any authoritative guidelines for the courts to follow. After tracing the many perplexities that the statute creates, Schuck concludes that

Congress performed few of the conventional policy-making functions for which it is thought to be admirably designed: it failed to specify the problem; it gathered little information; it failed to articulate and weigh competing values or reduce them to operational terms; it considered no alternatives; and it declined to make hard choices. Having neglected to define the problem, Congress designed a legislative solution that, by reason of its singular indeterminacy, seemed consistent with any number of possible problem definitions.

Because the act permits private litigation to test its provisions, the courts will inevitably be drawn into complex social disputes, a prospect Schuck finds troubling:

Whether [an administrative] agency is determining the extent to which it should target CETA [Comprehensive Employment and Training Act] job-training funds on teenagers or senior citizens, which mix of services Community Mental Health Centers should provide, what age groups an adoption agency should concentrate on placing, or what the office hours of a local social service agency should be, the agency will be confronting problems [not readily solved under the act].

When these choices are passed on to the courts, they will likely fail, Schuck believes.

Without decision rules to look to, without a methodology for identifying appropriate criteria or assigning them appropriate weights, courts will be cast adrift on a sea of discretion. . . . When this comes to pass, and the judiciary has been duly denounced as "imperial," it will be well to recall that in this case, at least, its crown, like that offered to Shakespeare's Caesar, was neither requested nor usurped but was pressed upon it by politicians at the Capitol.[25]

The Age Discrimination Act may be an extreme example, but historically legislation has always deferred to the courts and the executive for the detailed resolution of social problems. Legislation declares generalities; testing is in the hands of individuals.

For a long time, however, those hands have been mainly official. The enforcement of law was left to prosecutors and the executive agencies, and the tradition was that few laws, no matter the struggle for their enactment, were enforced. Prosecutorial discretion and underfunding have combined to prevent the general policies embedded in legislation from taking effect. This is not a novel thought and should not be surprising. Americans relish freedom and want to walk the line of legality. Appeals to the spirit of the law are regularly met with defiance, privately and publicly.

These are political facts over which the majority has little control. Prosecutorial discretion is not amenable to popular control, except under the most aggravated circumstances. The massive delegation of rule-making authority to administrative agencies is likewise beyond public control.

Except through litigation. To create rights it is necessary for large groups of people to coalesce and advocate before the legislature. But the refinement of right cannot successfully be left to that same process. An open society has many ways of giving voice to claims, demands, and pleas. The courts are the agency to which we commit the task of working out the meaning of great truths, only dimly perceived and inchoately expressed at passage. Laws are sent out orphans into the world, and they are judged not by their creators but by outsiders, sometimes overly suspicious of the wayward child, sometimes overly sympathetic to the lost child. It would be useful for the parents to acknowledge that they are still around and participate in the shaping of their offsprings' behavior, but it is unlikely that they will.

At least some of the unhappiness over the litigious tendencies of various groups in recent years springs from the realization that through the courts laws are being enforced. During the 1960s and 1970s, Congress began to entrust enforcement to private parties (and the courts stretched statutes to permit this, without significant reversal by Congress), thus upsetting the tacit compromise between grand declaration of legal principle and silent failure to enforce.

Legislation is an attempt to muddle through the storms of political conflict; suing is an attempt to clarify the generalities. Legislatures can avoid reason and argument; they can fail to explain; they can refuse to act. Not so the courts. They are there to give answers. Litigation is society's way of tying up loose ends.

The point can be overstressed. It is possible that litigiousness may result from the unwillingness of people to accept compromise solutions. Given the wherewithal to continue the fight, there is no reason to accept what Congress has declared. But it seems more likely that litigants seek out courts as the last resort because they perceive that the government has broken down. This possibility strongly suggests that the most salient cure to an overabundance of litigation is reform of government.

In short, if courts are antimajoritarian, the answer is to seek ways to build up majoritarian institutions responsive to the felt needs of the people. The answer to private enforcement of the laws is public enforcement. Whether this is possible in an age that lacks consensus is problematical.

But no matter how responsive the government is to the will of the public, judicial review and interpretation will remain a fixture. The political question is whether judicial decisions foreclose action by democratic institutions. The answer is that they do not seem to do so, even in the one area in which the courts claim a superiority of judgment: the arena of constitutional interpretation.

The most important antimajoritarian strand in the American political process is the constitutional concept of limited government. The Constitution cherishes the rights of minorities and directs Congress (and state legislatures) to resist the pressure of popular sentiment in the protected spheres of private liberty and public equality. In a society that adheres to a regime of constitutional limitations on the power of government, courts inescapably must serve as policymakers—though not, to be sure, as the sole source of policy. The objection to judges staying the hand of government for constitutional reasons has been explored at length in countless articles and books of varying complexity.[26] They can be summed up in a single sentence: "But the judges aren't elected!" The rejoinder may be phrased equally tersely: "And they never were."

The controversies in which the judges have been the most roundly condemned for overreaching—racial equality, reapportionment, prison and mental hospital reform—are precisely those areas in which the institutional breakdown was the greatest. If it was overreaction, the judicial response was directed to vast wrongs.

Constitutional litigation has served to open up the democratic process, not to foreclose it. The lawsuit focuses attention, garners publicity, stirs anger, hope, reform. As Leonard W. Levy, one of our finest legal historians, has written:

Taking the long view again, an historian may confidently assert that there has never been a single case of judicial review in favor of the Bill of Rights hurtful in any way to the democratic process, popular responsibility, or the moral sense of the community. The cases proving that judicial review has stunted the growth of the people or had undemocratic effects are those in which the Court checked statutory efforts, federal and state, to defend minorities or the underprivileged, but never those in which the Court has defended against legislatures, minorities, or the underprivileged or the unpopular. . . . [V]alidation by the Court of legislation adversely affecting civil liberties ends debate without stimulating the democratic process; judicial review can promote the debate and the process.[27]

All that said, a note of caution is in order. Judges are not disembodied spirits. They are human beings, subject to the temptations of power and history that seduce all officeholders. There is a culture of judges, a tradition that impels decisions that will be noticed. Judges may read widely and watch demonstrations on television and even recall the hurly-burly days when they practiced law in the real world, but as judges they inhabit a more circumscribed realm. For reasons of propriety and time their world is described by the legal community and within that community by those who comment professionally on what they do. Both for reasons of professional pride and for hopes (shared by every worker) of advancement in career, it is desirable for a judge to demonstrate a special quality, not merely to bear up well under the onslaught of a burdensome case load which requires sensitive judgments in essentially boring cases but to be creative. As Paul D. Carrington has noted, "a court that wants to receive the notice of law reviews or scholars or to be the object of attention in classrooms can achieve recognition only by writing opinions that advance the law."[28] That judges wish to win recognition and esteem is understandable, but it is not a justification for overbroad decisions.°

Nevertheless, the argument has been pressed that because the federal judiciary is independent and because its process is such that all decisions are subject to public accountability in a higher court (excluding the Supreme Court, of course), it is "the only institution capable of achieving, over time, the solid, stable, workable accountability of public and private power that the safety

---

°Consider this notice in the Class of 1932 section of the *Harvard Law School Bulletin*'s Alumni News (1977):

Hon. Donald R. Wright retired as Chief Justice of California after having served in that capacity for almost seven years. Chief Justice Wright was first appointed to the Municipal Court in Pasadena by former Governor Earl Warren and thereafter in 1961 he was elected to the Superior Court of Los Angeles County. In 1968 he was appointed to the Court of Appeals and in 1970, former Governor Ronald Reagan appointed Judge Wright as Chief Justice. During his tenure on the State Supreme Court Chief Justice Wright wrote over 250 opinions, including *People v. Anderson*, the first opinion in the United States outlawing capital punishment. (*Harvard Law School Bulletin*, Spring 1977, p. 46.)

No one writes in that he has resisted for the umpteenth time the judicial temptation to declare capital punishment unconstitutional.

and happiness of the country require." Assuming, for the sake of argument, that the statement just quoted is both meaningful and correct, it does not follow, as Morton Mintz and Jerry Cohen, the authors of the statement (and as proponents of the Bumpers amendment), propose, that the courts should be given an explicit legislative function to perform.

In *Power, Inc.*, Mintz, a widely respected investigative reporter for the *Washington Post*, and Cohen, a Washington lawyer and former chief counsel to the Senate Antitrust and Monopoly Subcommittee, suggested that the antidote to the catalog of horrors crowding the pages of their book is a constitutional amendment vastly enlarging the jurisdiction of federal courts. The amendment would give standing to citizens to go to court with claims "challenging any act or conduct of a person which act or conduct threatens to cause or is causing substantial harm to the safety or happiness of a consequential number of people." Leaving aside the vagueness of "substantial" and "consequential" (a problem of judgment with which courts currently grapple daily), we ought to be concerned about the notion that courts should have conferred upon them so much substantive power. For Mintz and Cohen define "happiness" as "the rights of citizens to fundamental justice, fundamental liberties, fundamental fairness, and the perpetuation and protection of environmental quality." In turn, "fundamental justice" is defined to include "the principles of 'distributive justice' to the extent that any governmental entity, by legislation or otherwise, establishes barriers or lessens the opportunities of citizens to share in the entitlements, wealth, and resources of the United States on an equitable basis."[29]

This proposal is perhaps the most striking manifestation of the belief that because courts have successfully intervened in great public affairs in the past we ought therefore as a society to yield plenary power to them over all the rest. As proposed, the amendment is without standards. Tutored by training and tradition to resist the appearance of legislating, judges would in short order repair to the only possible standard: total redress. In time the claim of harm would be its own best proof, though it would take an adroit Supreme Court to conform the inevitable and opposite judgments of two different lower courts—one holding that the existence of laws prohibiting abortion causes substantial harm to both the safety and happiness of women, the other that the abolition of such laws causes substantial harm to the safety and happiness of the unborn. As important as litigation is in a constitutional and democratic republic, it shares with every other institution the crucial requirement that its authority be limited.

Toward a Restoration of Trust

We have not become more litigious because the technical barriers to lawsuits have come down. Those barriers have come down because we have sought ways to sue. Litigiousness is not a legal but a social phenomenon. It is born of a breakdown in community, a breakdown that exacerbates and is exacerbated by the growth of law. A society that is law saturated inclines toward the belief that in the absence of declared law anything goes. No restraints of common prudence, instinctive morality, or reflected ethics need deter or function. What is not declared unlawful is perforce permissible. But ethics and moral sense are not coextensive with law. They are at once broader and narrower. A law may be immoral and worth disobeying. An act may not be unlawful to do yet surely to be shunned. But until there is a consensus on fundamental principles, the trust that is essential to a self-ordering community cannot be.

In many ways, the courts have become the final repositories of social trust, and they have sought to discharge their duty by holding accountable those whose trust was not merited. They have also sought, more cautiously, to restructure institutions to make them more worthy of trust. Courts can help raise consciousness and over time reform human conduct from the inside out, so that people feel inclined rather than compelled to do good.

But litigation is not an ideal means of building community: its procedures and its impact do much to sow mistrust, and its limited successes may blind us to the need for reforms that lie outside the ceaseless cycle of plaintiff and defendant. As long as people are being harmed by human activities, litigation remains at best a short-term answer.

But even if reforms take hold in industrial and medical practice, in the approach of governmental decisions to environmental concerns, in the delivery of essential services, the mutual trust that eliminates suing may remain elusive. That is because the growing complexity of our life and the spread of specialist knowledge is making each of us more and more illiterate about the way the world works.

The educational level of the public is crucial to its ability to accept an ethos that will change constantly as technology changes. Critical to the development of an ethos is the individual's understanding of the effects his actions have on others. These effects are much harder to appreciate in today's world than they were in an era of small manufacturing and face-to-face dealing. An insight into allocative economics, an understanding of the political process, and even a general technological literacy would have to be as accessible to many educated people as income tax rules, football strategy, and stock market literacy are now.[30]

Unless we can learn to appreciate the limits of technology and nature, we are condemned to our suspicions of those around us.

°   °   °

Pockmarked beggars, weak with hunger and half-blind, wandering the by-ways of an overpopulated land that cannot yield a subsistence to most of its inhabitants, do not file lawsuits when they trip in an unpaved street. But in our affluent society, the window shopper with an eye on a jewelry display may seek recompense for a bruised knee, anguish, and loss of services caused by a stumble on a cracked sidewalk.

It is by no means apparent that her freedom to do so is an affront to beggars everywhere. Nevertheless, it is sobering to consider how the industrial revolution in its modern form has bequeathed us a vision of life far removed from that known to all the rest of humanity.

We reject harm and ill-being as the natural estate of the species. We live in a cocoon of health and happiness. Who is unhappy is ill: Mental depression is something to be cured; economic depression something to be guarded against. For a vast part of the American populace, daily life is outside nature, no longer subject to the old vagaries. The common enemies of man—war, famine, disease, and poverty—are vanquished, or ought to be. When they occur they are viewed as anomalies, perturbations of the social order, obstacles that need quick removal to restore the norm.

That is the vision, and when reality is perceived as not squaring with that vision, the rational mind seeks causes and culprits. In our world those culprits can only be other people and their institutions. It is inadmissible to say that the injuries that befall us, caused indirectly if not prompted by other people, are part of the natural order. We cannot see, or do not wish to admit, that no society can ever rid itself of everything that could conceivably be called ill-being, because humans remain subject to an often perverse and parsimonious nature, which imposes limits on everything at which we aim. That we filter our lives through social and political institutions to shield us from the worst of nature "red in tooth and claw," cannot alter a fundamental aspect of any world: that resources are always scarce because men and women will always be capable of wanting more than is possible from all the arrangements in a society at one time.

Those who do not partake of that more or better, lacking understanding, will always be able to claim that they are being badly served. Harm and injury are easily enough located. That they are destined to accompany us gives no comfort. In a society that takes for granted what to any other age would be considered beyond utopia, each harm, every source of ill-being, cries out for redress.

Distinguishing between acts of God and acts within our power to control is no simple matter. We may take for our coda the Case of the Insufficient Vasectomy. The facts were mundane. After their seventh child was born, a Minnesota couple decided the family should grow no larger. The father consulted a doctor and accepted the recommendation that he undergo a vasectomy. Despite the operation, however, the wife again became pregnant, and following delivery of the eighth child, the unhappy parents sued the surgeon and his medical clinic. They sought damages for pain and suffering during pregnancy, pre- and postnatal medical expenses, and the cost of raising and educating the child. The Minnesota Supreme Court held in 1977 that the parents could recover such damages and costs.[31]

The case seems a sport. Surely the critics of litigiousness are correct in their perception that the desire for total redress places impossible burdens on those who undertake serious and significant duties. No medical procedure is foolproof: Is it sensible for a doctor to be held responsible for the consequences of a couple's sexual desire? And is it sound public policy to saddle the child with the knowledge that he is being supported by someone else because his existence is an accident? In an address to the American Family Institute, Justice William H. Rehnquist deplored this case as an example of the increasing "commitment to the adversary process which, in my view, cannot but endanger even further the vitality of the family as an institution in our society."[32]

But if we take a closer look, the picture changes. As was true of the other topics examined in previous chapters, what is easy to deplore in the abstract becomes more difficult to condemn when the particulars are uncovered. This was not a case in which the doctor foolishly guaranteed success, bungled the operation, or neglected to inform his patient of all medical consequences. The case turned, rather, on a specific act of negligence.

The couple was advised that until the husband's production of sperm was halted, sexual relations must cease or contraception must be employed. Several weeks after the operation, the doctor told the husband that test results were "negative." The doctor did not request that the husband return for further tests nor disclose the need for further contraception. In fact, however, the tests results were not negative and the husband was still some weeks away from being completely sterile. Therein lay the negligence and the claim for damages.

Moreover, the consequence for the physician was not as stark as a casual statement of the case makes it out to be. Full financial responsibility for eighteen years of the child's life was not charged to the physician's bank account.

The Minnesota Supreme Court declared that the cost of raising the child must be offset "by the value of the child's aid, comfort, and society which will benefit the parents for the duration of their lives." In the actual event, the jury had awarded the couple a total of $19,500—as damages for pain and suffering, for medical expenses, and for raising the child. The court remanded the case for retrial on the issue of damages because the jury had not been instructed to consider the benefits the child would bring to his family.

We can all agree that total redress cannot be. But at the same time we must resist the beguiling simplicity of characterizations that do not quite fit. Though it appears so at first glance, the vasectomy case is not one of total redress, as indeed few cases are.

As a primary mode of allocating what is one's due in an open, nontraditional, market society, where there is no other authoritative allocation, litigation can be intrusive and even jarring when it upsets settled expectations. But it is the primary alternative to the more expensive and pervasive regulatory approach that sets artificial rules, demands reports and forms, and subjects individual enterprise to nettlesome rigidities. If it is sometimes undemocratic, it is also a bulwark against the rise of an undemocratic, administrative state. If our system of litigation leads to the filing of some frivolous complaints, it also lends itself handily to the airing of serious social problems that too easily can be branded nonmeritorious until their facts are laid out and the nay-sayers are made to squirm under a warranted and withering cross-examination.

The system of litigation cannot be judged from single decisions. It must be examined over time. In any one field, any given judicial declaration may be wrong, perhaps egregiously so. But no social institution can guard against all mistakes. The question we ought to ask is whether the mistakes tend to perpetuate or whether they are corrected over time. The answer must be sought on a two-way street. For litigation is a method of correcting mistakes as well as a device for making them. To condemn litigiousness because it may overreach, without at the same time condemning the flaws and faults of those whose activities stand in need of correction, is to commit what might aptly be termed the Canine Fallacy, after the lesson Sherlock Holmes taught of the dog that did not bark in the night. How much that goes *right* does so because our legal system stands ready, albeit imperfectly, to provide redress to those who are wronged? How much would go wrong if that right were impaired? How many more lawsuits would need to be brought—and how much more regulation would need to be imposed—if the process of litigation were impeded by too drastic a set of restraints?

"The result we reach today," the Minnesota Supreme Court said, "is at best a mortal attempt to do justice in an imperfect world." The same can be said for much of the modern litigation that we have examined. That we are un-comfortable with it, that it poses acute dilemmas, ethical and otherwise, is not a sufficient cause to condemn it. Until the day when our institutions can be trusted to serve us as fiduciaries and when we can be educated to understand the limitations of the world we have constructed, litigation will remain the hallmark of a free and just society.

Notes

CHAPTER 1

1. Jerome Carcopino, *Daily Life in Ancient Rome* (New Haven: Yale University Press, 1940), pp. 186–7.

2. *New York Times*, February 27, 1976, p. 35.

3. 64 *A.B.A.J.* 961 (1978).

4. Berman v. Allan, 80 N.J. 421, 404 A.2d 8 (1979).

5. *Newsweek*, January 10, 1977, p. 42.

6. *Business Week*, June 6, 1977, p. 58.

7. *New York Times*, October 20, 1977, p. B3.

8. *Student Lawyer*, May 1979, p. 14.

9. *National Law Journal*, July 16, 1979, pp. 1, 14.

10. *New York Times*, March 31, 1978, p. A14.

11. *Journal of Insurance*, September/October, 1978, p. 24.

12. Goldwater v. Carter, 617 F.2d 697 (D.C. Cir. 1979), appeal dismissed, 444 U.S. 996 (1979).

13. John H. Barton, "Behind the Legal Explosion," 27 *Stanford L. Rev.* 567 (1975); Maurice Rosenberg, "Contemporary Litigation in the United States," in Harry W. Jones, ed., *Legal Institutions Today: English and American Approaches Compared* (Chicago: American Bar Association, 1977), p. 152. See also Bayless Manning, "Hyperlexis: Our National Disease," 71 *N.W.U.L. Rev.* 767 (1977); Laurence H. Tribe, "Too Much Law, Too Little Justice," *The Atlantic*, July 1979, p. 25; "Too Much Law?" *Newsweek*, January 10, 1977, p. 42; "Those °°°° Lawyers," *Time*, April 10, 1978, p. 56; "The Rights Explosion: Splintering America?" *U.S. News and World*

Report, October 31, 1977, p. 29; Maurice Rosenberg, "Let's Everybody Litigate," 50 *Tex. L. Rev.* 1349 (1972).

14. The effort to collect systematic litigation statistics only began in the late 1970s, and data bases that currently exist are thin. Perhaps the most comprehensive effort on the state level is the compilation now being undertaken by the National Center for State Courts (NCSC) in Williamsburg, Virginia. The 5 million calculation is for all suits, including criminal prosecutions (where felony sentences can be awarded), in courts of general jurisdiction. The figure thus omits such cases as appear in probate court, specialized housing courts (landlord-tenant disputes), et cetera. If all courts are included, the number of lawsuits in the U.S. jumps to 12 million (1976 data). This figure is "a little on the high side," according to staff member Mary Elsner [personal interview, July 3, 1980], because it is based on population figures in each state and assumes the same behavior patterns in small states that exist in the larger ones that keep better statistics. But it is unlikely that there is as much litigation per capita in Montana or Wyoming as in New York or California.

Since 1978 NCSC, together with the Conference of State Court Administrators, has been gathering national data on state courts and trying to settle on uniform terminology, which requires answers to such questions as, What is a case? Under the State Judicial Information System Project, NCSC plans to conduct quality control audits on the data supplied and also to offer assistance to states in collecting their data. The effort is just underway. Another project to gather and analyze civil trial data is being undertaken by the Institute for Civil Justice, formed in early 1980 by the Rand Corporation, the Santa Monica, California, think-tank. See *National Law Journal,* March 17, 1980, p. 4.

15. Barton, "Behind the Legal Explosion"; personal interview with Mary Elsner of the National Center for State Courts, July 3, 1980.

16. Personal interview with Professor Earl W. Johnson, October 19, 1978.

17. See Burton A. Weisbrod in collaboration with Joel F. Handler and Neil K. Komesar, *Public Interest Law, An Economic and Institutional Analysis* (Berkeley: University of California Press, 1978), pp. 81, 88–9.

18. *National Law Journal,* October 22, 1979, p. 39.

19. *Time,* April 10, 1978, p. 56.

20. "Will Lawyering Strangle Democratic Capitalism?" *Regulation,* March/April 1978, p. 15.

21. "Litigation-Prone Society," 78 *N.Y.S. J. of Medicine* 658, 661 (1978).

22. *New York Times,* June 9, 1978, p. A8.

23. Nathan Glazer, "Toward an Imperial Judiciary?" *The Public Interest,* vol. 41, Fall 1975, p. 118.

24. Lewis Mumford, *Technics and Human Development: The Myth of the Machine,* vol. 1 (New York: Harcourt Brace Jovanovich, Harvest, 1967), p. 68.

25. The oft-quoted phrase is that of Justice Oliver Wendell Holmes, dissenting, in Southern Pacific Co. v. Jensen, 224 U.S. 205 (1917).

26. The story of how the common law withstood the onslaught of reformers is retold in Jethro K. Lieberman, *Milestones! 200 Years of American Law* (New York and St. Paul, Minn.: Oxford University Press and West Publishing Co., 1976), chap. 1.

27. Lawrence M. Friedman, *A History of American Law* (New York: Simon and Schuster, 1975), pp. 20–21.

28. Timothy Dwight quoted in Maxwell Bloomfield, *American Lawyers in a Changing Society, 1776–1876* (Cambridge: Harvard University Press, 1976), pp. 39–40.

29. Charles Warren, *A History of the American Bar* (Boston: Little, Brown, 1912), p. 214.

30. Warren, p. 215.

31. Letter of Charles Jared Ingersoll, December 1803, quoted in Warren, p. 211.

32. H. St. John Crevecoeur quoted in Warren, p. 217.

33. Bloomfield, p. 54.

34. Alexis de Tocqueville, *Democracy in America,* ed. J. P. Mayer and Max Lerner, trans. George Lawrence (New York: Harper and Row, 1966), p. 248.

35. Marbury v. Madison, 1 Cr. (5 U.S.) 137 (1803).

36. Henry Steele Commager, *The American Mind* (New Haven: Yale University Press, 1950), p. 362.

37. Robert H. Jackson, *The Struggle for Judicial Supremacy* (New York: Vintage, 1941), p. 101; Norman v. Baltimore & Ohio R.R., 294 U.S. 240 (1935).

38. A.L.A. Schechter Poultry Corp. v. United States, 295 U.S. 495 (1935).

39. See Carol Weisbrod, *The Boundaries of Utopia* (New York: Pantheon, 1980).

40. Commager, p. 362.

41. Morton J. Horwitz, *The Transformation of American Law, 1780–1860* (Cambridge: Harvard University Press, 1977), pp. 255–6.

42. Charles Rembar, *The Law of the Land* (New York: Simon and Schuster, 1980), p. 227.

43. See Marlene Adler Mark, "The Prince of Torts," *New Times*, September 4, 1978, p. 29; *Washington Post*, April 24, 1978, p. A18.

44. See, for example, United Mine Workers v. Illinois State Bar Association, 389 U.S. 217 (1967).

45. Sindell v. Abbott Laboratories, Inc., 163 Cal. Rptr. 132, 607 P.2d 924 (1980); James S. Granelli, "Novel Tort Theory Upheld," *National Law Journal*, April 7, 1980, p. 3.

46. Robert Nozick, *Anarchy, State, and Utopia* (New York: Basic Books, 1974), p. ix.

47. Sir Henry Maine, *Ancient Law* (New York: Dutton, Everyman's Library, 1917), p. 100.

48. Friedrich Kessler and Grant Gilmore, *Contracts, Cases and Materials*, 2d ed. (Boston: Little, Brown, 1970), p. 1118.

49. See Allen Buchanan, "Medical Paternalism," 7 *Philosophy and Public Affairs* 370 (1978).

50. Milton Friedman, *Capitalism and Freedom* (Chicago: University of Chicago Press, 1962), p. 156.

51. Norbert Wiener, *The Human Use of Human Beings* (New York: Doubleday, Anchor Books, 1954), p. 110.

52. The argument is explored at length in Duncan Kennedy, "Form and Substance in Private Law Adjudication," 89 *Harv. L. Rev.* 1685 (1976).

53. Weisbrod, *Public Interest Law*, p. 10.

54. See e.g., Moss v. FPC, 502 F. 2d 461 (D.C. Cir. 1974); "Congressional Access to the Federal Courts," 90 *Harv. L. Rev.* 1632 (1977).

55. Lon L. Fuller, "The Forms and Limits of Adjudication," 92 *Harv. L. Rev.* 353 (1978).

56. Fuller, "Forms and Limits," pp. 394–95.

57. Melvin A. Eisenberg, "Participation, Responsiveness, and the Consultative Process," 92 *Harv. L. Rev.* 410, 425 (1978).

58. Fuller, "Forms and Limits," pp. 397–98.

59. See Hoyt Gimlin, ed., *The Rights Revolution* (Washington, D.C.: Congressional Quarterly, 1978).

60. *New York Times,* July 6, 1980, p. E6. See also "Enforcing the Right to an 'Appropriate' Education," 92 *Harv. L. Rev.* 1103 (1978).

61. Abram Chayes, "The Role of the Judge in Public Law Litigation," 89 *Harv. L. Rev.* 1281, 1282–83 (1976).

CHAPTER 2

1. U.S., Congress, House, Committee on Small Business, *Hearings Before the Subcommittee on Capital Investment and Business Opportunities*, 95th Cong., 1st sess., June 6, 1977, p. 279.

2. *Time*, April 10, 1978, p. 56.

3. See, for example, *Time*, September 12, 1977, p. 2.

4. Personal interview with Victor E. Schwartz, director of the Interagency Task Force on Product Liability, November 28, 1978. See also U.S., Congress, Senate, Select Committee on Small Business, *Impact on Product Liability*, 94th Cong., 2d sess., pt. 1 (1976), p. 614.

5. See *Business Insurance*, November 13, 1978, p. 12; "A New Way to Pay the Injured," *Business Week*, October 29, 1979, table p. 98; *Verdict Reports*, vol. 16 (Solon, Ohio: Jury Verdict Research, Inc.), September 4, 1979; "Current Award Trends," in *Injury Valuation Reports*, vol. 2A, no. 211 (Solon, Ohio: Jury Verdict Research, Inc., 1978), p. 5; Larry Bodine, "Million-Dollar Jury Awards," *National Law Journal*, June 18, 1979, pp. 1, 12–13.

6. "The Costly Aftermath of the Swine Flu Scare," *Business Week*, May 19, 1980, p. 124H; *New York Times*, November 21, 1979, p. A16.

7. Lawrence M. Friedman, *A History of American Law* (New York: Simon and Schuster, 1973), p. 261.

8. Morton J. Horwitz, *The Transformation of American Law, 1780–1860* (Cambridge: Harvard University Press, 1977), pp. 86–87.

9. Holmes quoted in Mark deWolfe Howe, ed., *The Common Law* (Boston: Little, Brown, 1963), p. 76.

10. Horwitz, p. 99.

11. Ryan v. New York Central R. R. Co., 35 N.Y. 210 (1866).

12. William Prosser, Handbook on the Law of Torts 3rd ed. (St. Paul, Minn.: West Publishing Co., 1964), p. 924.

13. Friedman, p. 422.

14. Friedman, p. 424.

15. See, for example, Steven Kelman, "Regulation by the Numbers—A Report on the Consumer Product Safety Commission," *The Public Interest*, no. 36, Summer 1974, p. 83.

16. See Duncan Kennedy, "Form and Substance in Private Law Adjudication," 89 *Harv. L. Rev.* 1685 (1976).

17. MacPherson v. Buick Motor Co., 217 N.Y. 382, 111 N.E. 1050 (1916).

18. Friedman, pt. 3, chap. 6, and G. Edward White, *Tort Law in America* (New York: Oxford University Press, 1980).

19. Henningsen v. Bloomfield Motors, Inc., 32 N.J. 358, 161 A.2d 69 (1960); Greenman v. Yuba Power Products, 59 Cal. 2d 57 (1963).

20. California Citizens' Commission on Tort Reform, *Righting the Liability Balance*, 1977, p. 123.

21. Personal interview with Victor E. Schwartz, November 5, 1979.

22. James A. Henderson, Jr., "Judicial Review of Manufacturers' Conscious Design Choices: The Limits of Adjudication," 73 *Col. L. Rev.* 1531, 1540, 1541 (1973).

23. Henderson, "Judicial Review," p. 1558.

24. A. D. Twerski, A. S. Weinstein, W. A. Donaher, H. R. Piehler, "The Use and Abuse of Warnings in Product Liability—Design Defect Litigation Comes of Age," 61 *Cornell L. Rev.* 495, 526 (1976).

25. See Richard A. Epstein, "Products Liability: The Gathering Storm," *Regulation*, September/October 1977, p. 18.

26. LeBoeuf v. Goodyear Tire and Rubber Co., 451 F. Supp. 253 (W. D. La. 1978).

27. Moran v. Faberge, Inc., 273 Md. 538, 332 A.2d 11 (1975).

28. Dawson v. Chrysler Corp., 49 L. W. 2200 (3d Cir. 1980).

29. Barker v. Lull Engineering, 143 Cal. Rptr. 225, 573 P.2d 443 (1978).

30. See *New York Times*, July 17, 1979, p. C13.

31. U.S., Department of Commerce, Interagency Task Force on Product Liability, 1977, *Legal Study*, vol. 3, pp. 11, 23. See, generally, Anita Johnson, "Behind the Hype on Products Liability," 14 *ABA Forum* 317 (1978).

32. California Citizens' Commission, p. 111.

33. California Citizens' Commission, pp. 102–4.

34. California Citizens' Commission, pp. 136–37.

35. Personal interview with Victor E. Schwartz, November 5, 1979. Interagency Task Force on Product Liability, *Final Report*, 1977, p. V–18.

36. Jeffrey O'Connell, *The Lawsuit Lottery* (New York: The Free Press, 1979), p. 179.

37. Interagency Task Force, *Final Report*, p. V–17.

38. Interagency *Task Force*, Final Report, p. V–17.

39. U.S., Congress, House, Committee on Small Business, *Product Liability Insurance*, 95th Cong., 2d sess., 1978, H. Rept. no. 95–97, p. 6; *Product Liability Insurance*, p. 34.

40. See "The Devils in the Product Liability Laws," *Business Week*, February 12, 1979, p. 72.

41. *Business Week*, May 19, 1980, p. 124H.

42. "CBS Reports. See You in Court," aired July 9, 1980.

43. "The Devils in the Product Liability Laws," p. 72; National Commission on Product Safety, *Final Report* (Washington, D.C.: Government Printing Office, 1970), p. 68.

44. Duke Power Co. v. Carolina Environmental Study Group, Inc., 438 U.S. 59 (1978).

45. See Robert E. Keeton and Jeffrey O'Connell, *Basic Protection for the Automobile Victim* (Boston: Little, Brown, 1965).

46. O'Connell, chap. 8 and references cited.

47. California Citizens' Commission, p. 43; O'Connell, p. 179.

48. California Citizens' Commission, p. 123.

49. "The Devils in the Product Liability Laws," p. 77.

50. Insurance Services Office, *Product Liability Closed Claim Survey: A Technical Analysis of Survey Results* (New York: 1977), p. 60; *Highlights of Technical Analysis*, p. 5.

51. See Jane C. Kronick, "Community Responsibility for Accident Victims," *Hastings Center Report*, October 1979, pp. 11ff. and references cited.

52. O'Connell, chaps. 10, 11.

53. McCormack v. Hankscraft Co., 278 Minn. 322, 154 N.W.2d 488 (1967); see "Impact on Product Liability," p. 1613; Ford Motor Co. v. Zahn, 265 F. 2d 729 (8th Cir. 1959); see Anita Johnson, "Products Liability 'Reform': A Hazard to Consumers," 56 *U.N.C.L. Rev.* 677, 684–85 (1978).

54. The T. J. Hooper, 60 F.2d 737 (2d. Cir. 1932).

55. National Commission on Product Safety, *Final Report* (Washington, D.C.: Government Printing Office, 1970), p. 48, quoted in Johnson, p. 682.

56. Johnson, p. 682, citing U.S., Congress, Senate, Judiciary Committee, *Voluntary Industrial Standards: Hearings Before the Subcommittee on Antitrust and Monopoly*, 94th Cong., 1st sess., 1975, p. 63.

57. See, for example, "FAA Is Often Accused of Laxity and Delays in Its Air-Safety Role," *Wall Street Journal*, November 12, 1979, p. 1.

58. Interagency Task Force, *Legal Study*, vol. 4, p. 148, n. 10; see Interagency Task Force, *Final Report*, p. vii–38.

59. O'Connell, pp. 64–65.

60. Personal interview with Paul D. Rheingold, December 11, 1978.

61. U.S., Department of Commerce, Model Uniform Product Liability Act, Sec. 104, 44 *Federal Register* 62721, October 31, 1979.

62. Twerski, p. 515.

63. Twerski, quoted in "The Devils in the Product Liability Laws," p. 77.

64. "The Rise of the Corporate Risk Manager," *Business Week*, October 27, 1980, p. 190H.

65. "The Devils in the Product Liability Laws," p. 78.

CHAPTER 3

1. *Business Insurance*, April 17, 1980, p. 2.

2. Robert E. Cartwright, "Medical Malpractice: A Trial Lawyer's View," in *Legislator's Guide to the Medical Malpractice Issue* (Washington, D.C.: Georgetown University Health Policy Center, 1976), p. 61.

3. *Trial Magazine*, May/June 1975, p. 2.

4. *Business Insurance*, June 2, 1975, p. 4.

5. Statistics cited in John Guinther, *The Malpractitioners* (Garden City: Doubleday, Anchor Press, 1978), p. 18.

6. Guinther, p. 227.

7. U.S., Department of Heath, Education, and Welfare, *Trends Affecting the U.S. Health Care System*, no. HRA 76–14503, prepared by Cambridge Research Institute (Washington, D.C.: Government Printing Office, 1975), p. 40; many of the statistics from this report are cited and interpreted in Guinther, pp. 125–27, 225–31.

8. Guinther, pp. 227–28.

9. Guinther, pp. 227–28.

10. Guinther, p. 206.

11. U.S., Department of Health, Education, and Welfare, *Report of the Secretary's Commission on Medical Malpractice* (Washington, D.C.: Government Printing Office, 1973), app., p. 55.

12. Guinther, p. 122.

13. *Report on Medical Malpractice*, p. 62.

14. *Trends Affecting U.S. Health Care*, p. 89.

15. See Sylvia Law and Steven Polan, *Pain and Profit: The Politics of Malpractice* (New York: Harper and Row, 1978), pp. 102ff.

16. Zebarth v. Swedish Hospital Medical Center, 81 Wash. 2d 12, 499 P.2d 1 (1972); Younger v. Webster, 9 Wash. App. 87, 510 P.2d 1182 (1973).

17. Anderson v. Somberg, 67 N.J. 291, 338 A.2d 1, cert. denied, 423 U.S. 929 (1975).

18. Law and Polan, p. 106.

19. Law and Polan, pp. 97ff.

20. Martin L. Gross, *The Doctors* (New York: Random House, 1966), p. 120.

21. Naccarato v. Grob, 384 Mich. 248, 180 N.W. 2d 788 (1970); Brune v. Belinkoff, 354 Mass. 201, 235 N.E. 2d 793 (1968).

22. The Kalmowitz case is discussed in Jeffrey O'Connell, *The Lawsuit Lottery* (New York: Free Press, 1979), chap. 1.

23. Lawrence K. Altman, "A Dilemma for Doctors, Patients, and the Courts," *New York Times*, April 27, 1975, pp. 1, 42.

24. O'Connell, p. 6.

25. O'Connell, chap. 1.

26. Helling v. Carey, 83 Wash. 2d 514, 519 P.2d 981 (1974).

27. Richard A. Epstein, "Medical Malpractice: The Case for Contract," 1976 *A.B.F. Res. J.* 87, 113.

28. Epstein, p. 102.

29. See M. W. Reder, "Medical Malpractice: An Economist's View," 1976 *A.B.F. Res. J.* 511, 535ff.

30. Epstein, p. 97.

31. Epstein, p. 109.

32. Washington appellate court declaring *Helling* interred is Gates v. Jensen, 20 Wash. App. 81, 579 P.2d 374 (1978); see Note, 51 *Wash. L. Rev.* 167 (1975), suggesting that Helling is still valid. Other Washington cases: Meeks v. Marx, 15 Wash. App. 571, 550 P. 2d 1158 (1976); Swanson v. Brigham, 18 Wash. App. 647, 571 P.2d 217 (1977). Only other cases are: Hood v. Phillips, 537 S.W. 2d 291 (Civ. App. Tex. 1977); Barton v. Owen, 71 Cal. App. 3d 484, 139 Cal. Rptr. 494 (1977); Truman v. Thomas, 155 Cal. Rptr. 752 (Ct. App. Cal. 1979).

33. See Law and Polan, pp. 106ff.

34. Louise Lander, *Defective Medicine* (New York: Farrar, Straus & Giroux, 1978), p. 120.

35. Guinther, p. 173.

36. *Report on Medical Malpractice*, app., p. 13.

37. The Employers of Wausau case is discussed in Guinther, p. 182.

38. Lander, p. 113.

39. Lander, p. 116.

40. Guinther, p. 193.

41. The Argonaut story is told in Guinther, pp. 176–78, and Lander, pp. 118–20.

42. Guinther, p. 196.

43. Guinther, pp. 196–97.

44. Guinther, p. 188.

45. Personal interview with Peter H. Foley, July 7, 1980.

46. Guinther, pp. 196–97.

47. Guinther, p. 22.

48. Lander, p. 136.

49. Lander, p. 138.

50. See *New York Times*, five-part series on incompetent doctors, January 26–30, 1976, esp., January 27, p. 24.

51. *New York Times*, January 28, 1976, p. 17.

52. *Report on Medical Malpractice*, p. 55.

53. Guinther, pp. 137–38.

54. *New York Times*, January 27, 1976, p. 24.

55. *Malpractice Claims* (Milwaukee: National Association of Insurance Commissioners, 1976), pp. 65–69; summarized in Guinther, p. 9.

56. *Trends Affecting U.S. Health Care*, p. 223.

57. Lander, p. 143.

58. *Malpractice Claims*, pp. 15, 101.

59. *Malpractice Claims*, p. 103.

60. For summary of changes, see Guinther, pp. 242–43; Lander, chap. 11.

61. Law and Polan, p. 113.

62. *Malpractice Claims*, pp. 92–93.

63. See David M. Margolick, "Mediation Isn't Cure for Patients' Claims," *National Law Journal*, February 4, 1980, p. 1; Mattos v. Thompson, 49 *L.W.* 2249 (Pa. S.C. 1980).

64. Law and Polan, p. 116.

65. Law and Polan, p. 117.

66. *Report on Medical Malpractice,* p. 16; Law and Polan, 117.
67. Statistics cited in Guinther, pp. 121–22.
68. On patient anger, see Lander, chap. 1.
69. Quoted in Lander, p. 140.
70. Lander, p. 141.
71. Law and Polan, pp. 32–34; Guinther, pp. 144–47.
72. Spencer Kimball, "Unfinished Business in Insurance Regulation," 4 *Wisc. L. Rev.* 1019 (1969).
73. Quoted in Lander, p. 34.

CHAPTER 4

1. "Public Interest Law," *Wall Street Journal,* December 17, 1979, p. 24.
2. Wilderness Society v. Morton, 479 F.2d 842 (D.C. Cir. 1973); See David M. Trubek, "Environmental Defense, I: Introduction to Interest Group Advocacy in Complex Disputes," in Burton A. Weisbrod, in collaboration with Joel F. Handler and Neil K. Komesar, *Public Interest Law, An Economic and Institutional Analysis* (Berkeley: University of California Press, 1978), chap. 7.
3. "Nuclear Nemesis," *Wall Street Journal,* March 10, 1978, p. 1.
4. Committee on Pollution, National Academy of Sciences: National Research Council, *Waste Management and Control—Report to Federal Council for Science and Technology* (1966), pp. 3–10; quoted in Frank P. Grad, *Environmental Law,* vol. 1, 2nd ed. (New York: Matthew Bender, 1978), pp. 1–8.
5. Judge Friendly quoted in Trubek, p. 170, fn. 88.
6. Trubek, p. 172.
7. Calvert Cliffs' Coordinating Committee v. Atomic Energy Commission, 449 F.2d 1109, 1111 (D.C. Cir. 1971), cert. denied, 404 U.S. 942 (1972).
8. Trubek, p. 173.
9. William O. Doub, "Technological Regulation and Environmental Law," 26 *Administrative L. Rev.* 191, 193 (1974).
10. Trubek, p. 177.
11. NRDC v. Morton, 458 F.2d 827 (D.C. Cir. 1972). See Trubek, pp. 174–75.
12. Trubek, pp. 174–75.
13. NRDC v. Morton, 458 F.2d 827 (D.C. Cir. 1972).
14. John N. Nassikas, "Energy, the Environment, and the Administrative Process," 26 *Administrative L. Rev.* 165, 175–76 (1974).
15. Environmental Defense Fund v. Froelke, 473 F.2d 346 (8th Cir. 1972); see discussion in Weisbrod, *Public Interest Law,* chap. 8.
16. J. Skelly Wright, "New Judicial Requisites for Informal Rulemaking: Implications for the Environmental Impact Statement Process," 77 *Administrative L. Rev.* 59, 62 (1977).
17. Seacoast Anti-Pollution League v. Costle, 572 F.2d 872 (1st Cir. 1978), cert. denied, Public Service Co. of New Hampshire v. Seacoast Anti-Pollution League, 439 U.S. 824 (1978), appeal after remand 597 F.2d 306 (1st Cir. 1979).
18. *Wall Street Journal,* February 24, 1978, p. 10.
19. Natural Resources Defense Council v. Nuclear Regulatory Commission, 547 F.2d 633, 653 (D.C. Cir. 1976).
20. Vermont Yankee Nuclear Power Corp. v. Natural Resources Defense Council, 435 U.S. 519 (1978); see also "Vermont Yankee Nuclear Power Corp. v. Natural Resources Defense Council, Inc.: Three Perspectives," 91 *Harv. L. Rev.* 1805 (1978).
21. Nicholas A. Robinson, "Judicial-Review Constraints in U.S. Courts," *New York Law Journal,* September 25, 1979, pp. 1–2.
22. John B. Oakes, "Saving the Web of Life," *New York Times,* December 28, 1979, p. A27. For an argument against delay, see Eugene Bardach and Lucian Pugliaresi, "The Environmental-Impact Statement vs. the Real World," *The Public Interest,* vol. 49, Fall 1977, pp. 22–38.
23. *Wall Street Journal,* June 9, 1978, pp. 1, 20.
24. For the Bumpers amendment and the Senate debate, see *Congressional Record,* September 7, 1979, S12145ff.

CHAPTER 5

1. Alexander Bickel, *The Supreme Court and the Idea of Progress* (New Haven: Yale University Press, 1978), p. 134.

2. Nathan Glazer, "Towards an Imperial Judiciary?" *The Public Interest*, vol. 41, Fall 1975, p. 118.

3. Plessy v. Ferguson, 163 U.S. 537 (1896).

4. Brown, 347 U.S. 483 (1954).

5. Wyatt v. Stickney, 344 F. Supp. 373, 344 F. Supp. 387 (M.D. Ala. 1972), enforcing 325 F. Supp. 781, 344 F. Supp. 1341 (M.D. Ala. 1972), aff'd in part, remanded in part, decision reserved in part sub nom. Wyatt v. Aderhold, 503 F.2d 1305 (5th Cir. 1974). The case is discussed in Philip J. Leaf, "Alabama After Wyatt: PIL Intervention Into a Mental Health Services Delivery System," in Burton A. Weisbrod, in collaboration with Joel F. Handler and Neil K. Komesar, *Public Interest Law, An Economic and Institutional Analysis* (Berkeley: University of California Press, 1978), pp. 374ff.

6. 325 F.2d at 1310.

7. Frank M. Johnson, "The Constitution and the Federal Judge," 54 *Tex. L. Rev.* 903, 909 (1976).

8. "The *Wyatt* Case: Implementation of a Judicial Decree Ordering Institutional Change," 84 *Yale L.J.* 1338, 1347 (1975).

9. The story is told in Bob Woodward and Scott Armstrong, *The Brethren* (New York: Simon and Schuster, 1979), pp. 369ff.

10. Case Comment: "Wyatt v. Stickney and the Right of Civilly-committed Mental Patients to Adequate Treatment," 86 *Harv. L. Rev.* 1282, 1288 (1973).

11. "Right of Civilly-committed Mental Patients," p. 1289.

12. Wyatt v. Aderhold, 503 F.2d, p. 1316; italics in the original.

13. Wyatt v. Aderhold, p. 1316.

14. "Right of Civilly-committed Mental Patients," p. 1283, note 105.

15. Wyatt v. Stickney, 344 F. Supp. at 1343.

16. Leaf, "Alabama After Wyatt," p. 379.

17. Wayne McCormack, "The Expansion of Federal Question Jurisdiction and the Prisoner Complaint Caseload," 1975 *Wisc. L. Rev.* 523, 536.

18. "Right of Civilly-committed Mental Patients," p. 1298.

19. Robert F. Kennedy, Jr., *Judge Frank M. Johnson* (New York: G. P. Putnam's Sons, 1978), p. 232.

20. See Judith N. Shklar, *Legalism* (Cambridge: Harvard University Press, 1964).

21. Quoted in *Boston Globe*, July 31, 1977, pp. 1, 2; quoted in *Note*, "Implementation Problems in Institutional Reform Litigation," 91 *Harv. L. Rev.* 428, 446, note 94 (1977).

22. "The *Wyatt* Case: Implementation," p. 1356.

23. "The *Wyatt* Case: Implementation," pp. 1357, 1359.

24. "The *Wyatt* Case: Implementation," pp. 1377–78.

25. "Implementation Problems," p. 451.

26. "The *Wyatt* Case: Implementation," pp. 1375–76.

27. Inmates of Suffolk County Jail v. Eisenstadt, 360 F.Supp. 767 (D. Mass. 1973), aff'd 494 F.2d 1196 (1st Cir. 1974).

28. Judge Johnson's order was in Pugh v. Locke, 406 F.Supp. 318 (M. D. Ala. 1976). The court of appeals reversed in part in 559 F.2d 283 (5th Cir. 1977). See also Newman v. Alabama, 503 F.2d 1320 (5th Cir. 1974); see Kennedy, chapter 22.

29. Leaf, "Alabama After Wyatt," p. 386.

30. Leaf, "Alabama After Wyatt," p. 387.

31. Leaf, "Alabama After Wyatt," pp. 382–85, 388, 391, 393.

32. For fuller discussion, see Tyll van Geel, *Authority to Control the School Program* (Lexington, Mass.: D. C. Heath, 1976); John C. Hogan, *The Schools, The Courts, and the Public Interest* (Lexington, Mass.: D. C. Heath, 1974).

33. Goss v. Lopez, 419 U.S. 565 (1975).

34. Goldberg v. Kelly, 397 U.S. 254 (1970).

35. Morrissey v. Brewer, 408 U.S. 471 (1972).

36. "Help! Teacher Can't Teach!" *Time*, June 16, 1980, p. 59.

37. Plessy, 163 U.S.

38. J. Harvie Wilkinson, *From Brown to Bakke, The Supreme Court and School Integration* (New York: Oxford University Press, 1979), p. 19.

39. See Richard H. Harbaugh, *Lawyer's Lawyer, The Life of John W. Davis* (New York: Oxford University Press, 1973), chap. 28.

40. See Wilkinson, pp. 31–39.

41. Wilkinson, p. 63.

42. Wilkinson, p. 111.

43. Green v. County School Board, 391 U.S. 430 (1968).

44. U.S. v. Montgomery County Bd. of Education, 289 F.Supp. 647 (M. D. Ala. 1968), aff'd 395 U.S. 225 (1969).

45. Milliken v. Bradley, 433 U.S. 267, 279 (1977).

46. San Antonio Independent School District v. Rodriguez, 411 U.S. 1 (1973).

47. Serrano v. Priest, 5 Cal. 3d 584, 96 Cal. R. 601, 487 P.2d 1241 (1971). Robinson v. Cahill, 63 N.J. 196, 306 A.2d 65 (1973), cert. denied. 414 U.S. 976 (1974).

48. See, for example, Hobson v. Hansen, 269 F.Supp. 401 (1967), aff'd sub nom. Smuch v. Hobson, 408 F.2d 175 (D.C. Cir. 1969), further relief ordered, 320 F.Supp. 409 (1970), 320 F.Supp. 720, 327 F. Supp. 844 (1971).

49. Donald L. Horowitz, *The Courts and Social Policy* (Washington, D.C.: The Brookings Institution, 1976), p. 38.

50. Horowitz, p. 32.

51. Horowitz, p. 49.

52. Quoted in Anthony Lewis, "The Supreme Court and Its Critics," 45 *Minn. L. Rev.* 305, 318 (1961).

53. *New York Times*, May 6, 1967, p. 1; May 10, 1967, p. 21.

54. Christopher D. Stone, "Should Trees Have Standing?—Toward Legal Rights for Natural Objects," 45 *S. Cal. L. Rev.* 450 (1972).

55. Wilkinson, p. 157.

CHAPTER 6

1. Russell v. The Men of Devon, 100 Eng. R. 359, 2 T.R. 667 (1788).

2. Mower v. Inhabitants of Leicester, 9 Mass. 247 (1812).

3. Edwin M. Borchard, "Government Liability in Tort," 34 *Yale L. J.* 1, 4 (1924).

4. See Justice Traynor's opinion in Muskopf v. Corning Hospital District, 55 Cal.2d 211, 11 Cal. R. 89, 359 P.2d 457 (1961).

5. Kenneth Culp Davis, *Administrative Law Treatise,* Supplement (Rochester, N.Y.: Lawyers Co-Operative Publishing Co., 1980), sec. 25, p. 203.

6. Gregoire v. Biddle, 177 F.2d 579, 581 (2d.Cir. 1949).

7. Standard Nut Margarine Co. v. Mellon, 72 F.2d 557 (D.C. Cir. 1934), cert. denied 293 U.S. 605 (1934).

8. Barr v. Matteo, 360 U.S. 564 (1959).

9. Monroe v. Pape, 365 U.S. 167 (1961).

10. 1980 Annual Report of the Director, Administrative Office of the U.S. Courts, tables C2, p. A16, and 21, p. 62; 1960 Report, table C2.

11. Presier v. Rodriguez, 411 U.S. 475, 492 (1973).

12. William Bennett Turner, "When Prisoners Sue: A Study of Prisoner Section 1983 Suits in the Federal Courts," 92 *Harv. L. Rev.* 610 (1979); 1980 Annual Report, table 21, p. 62.

13. 403 U.S. 388 (1971).

14. Davis, pp. 216–19.

15. Paul v. Davis, 424 U.S. 693 (1976).

16. Davis v. Passman, 442 U.S. 228 (1979).

17. Davis, p. 215.

18. Butz v. Economou, 438 U.S. 478 (1978).

19. Scheur v. Rhodes, 416 U.S. 232 (1974).

20. Wood v. Strickland, 420 U.S. 308 (1975).

21. Address to the American Bar Association. Judicial Administration Division, Chicago, August 8, 1977.

22. U.S., Congress, Senate, Judiciary Committee, *Federal Tort Claims Act: Statement on Proposed S.2117 Before Subcommittee on Administrative Practice and Procedures and Citizens' and Shareholders' Rights and Procedures*, 95th Cong., 2d sess., June 15, 1978. See also "Agents Affected by Fear of Future Lawsuits," 11 *Crime Control Digest*, December 26, 1977, p. 9.

23. Davis, Supplement (1976), p. 559.

24. Monell v. Department of Social Services, 436 U.S. 658 (1978).

25. Owen v. City of Independence 445 U.S. 622 (1980).

26. Martinez v. California, 444 U.S. 277 (January 15, 1980); Owen v. City of Independence, 445 U.S. 622 (April 16, 1980); Carlson v. Green, 446 U.S. 14 (April 22, 1980); Gomez v. Toledo, 100 S.Ct. 1920 (May 27, 1980); Supreme Court Virginia v. Consumers Union of the United States, Inc., 100 S.Ct. 1967 (June 2, 1980); Maher v. Gagne, 100 S.Ct. 2570 (June 25, 1980); Maine v. Thiboutot, 100 S.Ct. 2502 (June 25, 1980).

27. *New York Times*, June 1, 1980, p. A44.

28. *Professional Liability: Staff Background Paper to California Citizens' Commission on Tort Reform* (Los Angeles, 1979), p. 100.

29. "CBS Reports. See You in Court," aired July 9, 1980.

30. H. R. 2659, 96th Cong., 1st sess., 125 *Cong. Rec.* H1107 (daily ed., March 6, 1979); S. 695, 96th Cong., 1st sess., 125 *Cong. Rec.* S2919 (daily ed., March 15, 1979).

31. Birnbaum v. United States, 436 F.Supp. 967 (E.D.N.Y. 1977).

32. Joseph R. Tybor, "Strip Searches Under Fire," *National Law Journal*, May 5, 1980, pp. 1, 8–9.

33. Carey v. Piphus, 435 U.S. 247 (1978). See, generally, "Damage Awards for Constitutional Torts: A Reconsideration after *Carey* v. *Piphus*," 93 *Harv. L. Rev.* 966 (1980).

34. "Damage Awards," p. 977.

35. Stump v. Sparkman, 435 U.S. 349 (1978).

36. Bradley v. Fisher, 13 Wall. 335, 347 (1872).

37. *Washington Post*, November 5, 1979, p. A3.

38. Martinez v. California, 444 U.S. 277 (1980).

39. U.S., Congress, Senate, Commerce Committee, *Federal Railway Safety Act of 1969: Hearings Before the Subcommittee on Surface Transportation*, 91st Cong., 1st sess., 1969, p. 414. For lawsuits around the country, see Edward J. Burke, "New Relief for Victims of Crime," *National Law Journal*, October 20, 1980, p. 1; for Katz, see *National Law Journal*, July 16, 1979, p. 35. Under an analogous theory, the Attorney General of California, George Deukmejian, has sued the Los Angeles Unified School District and 32 city and county officials, charging them with failure to curb violence in the schools; the pleadings state that "it is cruel and unusual punishment to compel students to attend public schools where there is an excessive level of violence." See James S. Granelli, "A General Sees Fire," *National Law Journal*, July 7, 1980, p. 10.

40. Donohue v. Copiague Union Free School District, 47 N.Y.2d 440, 418 N.Y.S.2d 375, 391 N.E. 2d 1352 (1979).

41. Hoffman v. Board of Education, 49 N.Y.2d 121, 424 N.Y.S. 2d 376 (1979); see *New York Times*, December 18, 1979, p. B1.

42. *New York Times*, January 28, 1979, p. A33; Jacqueline Trescott, "Children vs. Parents," *Washington Post*, April 4, 1979, p. B1; Fred Barbash, "Courts Increasingly Asked to Rule on Affairs of Heart," *Washington Post*, August 18, 1980, pp. A1, 8.

43. See "Groundless Litigation and the Malicious Prosecution Debate: A Historical Analysis," 88 *Yale L. J.* 1218 (1979).

44. *Wall Street Journal*, August 15, 1980, p. 34.

CHAPTER 7

1. John H. Wigmore, *Evidence in Trials of Common Law*, vol. 3. (Boston: Little, Brown, 1923), p. 1367. See also Anne Strick, *Injustice For All* (New York: G. P. Putnam's Sons, 1977); Walter V. Schaefer, "Is the Adversary System Working in Optimal Fashion?" 70 *F.R.D.* 159 (1976); Marvin E. Frankel, *Partisan Justice* (New York: Hill and Wang, 1980).

2. David J. Rothman and Sheila M. Rothman, "The Conflict Over Children's Rights," *The Hastings Center Report*, vol. 10, June 1980, p. 9.

3. Jackson v. Metropolitan Edison Co., 419 U.S. 345 (1975).

4. Robert Blair Kaiser, "Life and Death Decisions Will Be Made, but By Whom?" *New York Times*, June 29, 1980, p. E20.

5. See, generally, Stuart A. Scheingold, *The Politics of Rights* (New Haven: Yale University Press, 1974); Jeffrey O'Connell, *Ending Insult to Injury* (Urbana: University of Illinois Press, 1975); Marc Galanter, "Why the 'Haves' Come out Ahead: Speculations on the Limits of Legal Change," 9 *L. and Soc. Rev.* 93 (1974).

6. John P. Heinz and Andrew C. Gordon, *Public Access to Information* (New Brunswick, N.J.: Transaction Books, 1980).

7. See, generally, Earl Johnson Jr., Valerie Kantor, and Elizabeth Schwartz, *Outside the Courts: A Survey of Diversion Alternatives in Civil Cases* (Denver: National Center for State Courts, 1977); Frank E. A. Sander, "Varieties of Dispute Processing," 70 *F.R.D.* 111 (1976); *Mediating Social Conflict* (New York: Ford Foundation Report, 1978); "Litigation and Dispute Processing," pts. 1, 2, in 9 *L. and Soc. Rev.*, nos. 1, 2 (Fall 1974, Winter 1975); Richard L. Abel, "A Comparative Theory of Dispute Institutions in Society," 8 *L. and Soc. Rev.* 217 (1973). "Streamlining the Justice System: Proposals and Alternatives," 11 *Loyola of Los Angeles Law Review* 485 (1978); "Business Saves Big Money with the 'Minitrial,'" *Business Week*, October 13, 1980, p. 168. See also Frank E. A. Sander and Frederick E. Snyder, *Alternative Methods of Dispute Settlement—A Selected Bibliography* (Washington, D.C.: American Bar Association Committee on Resolution of Minor Disputes, December 1979).

8. Johnson, Kantor, and Schwartz, chap. 2.

9. Johnson, Kantor, and Schwartz, p. 35.

10. Johnson, Kantor, and Schwartz, p. 8.

11. Report on the National Conference on Minor Disputes Resolution (Washington, D.C.: American Bar Association Committee on Resolution of Minor Disputes, May 1977).

12. Joseph P. Stulberg, vice president of American Arbitration Assn., quoted in *Wall Street Journal*, October 27, 1978, p. 48.

13. Daniel McGillis, "The Quiet [R]Evolution in American Dispute Settlement," *Harvard Law School Bulletin*, Winter 1980, p. 20.

14. U.S., Congress, House, Judiciary Committee, Report 96–492, pt. 2, 96th Cong., 1st sess., October 23, 1979.

15. Edward H. Levi, "The Business of Courts: A Summary and a Sense of Perspective," 70 *F.R.D.* 212, 219, (1976).

16. "Contemporary Litigation in the United States," in Harry W. Jones, ed., *Legal Institutions Today: English and American Approaches Compared* (Chicago: American Bar Association, 1977), p. 153.

17. Neil J. Williams, "Fee Shifting and Public Interest Litigation," 64 *A.B.A.J.* 850 (1978).

18. Rosenberg, p. 163.

19. "Loser Pays All," *American Lawyer*, July 1980, pp. 5, 6. On truth-in-lending, see, for example, Mirabel v. General Motors Acceptance Corp., 576 F. 2d 729 (7th Cir. 1978).

20. Lewis F. Powell, dissenting, Amendments to the Federal Rules of Civil Procedure, 48 L.W. 4500 (1980).

21. Arthur Liman, "The Quantum of Discovery vs. The Quality of Justice: More Is Less," 4 *Litigation* 9 (1977). See also Francis R. Kirkham, "Complex Civil Litigation—Have Good Intentions Gone Awry?" 70 *F.R.D.* 199, 1976; William H. Erickson, "The Pound Conference Recommendations: A Blueprint for the Justice System in the Twenty-First Century," 76 *F.R.D.* 277, 288, (1978); "The Costly Paper Chase Clogging the Courts," *Business Week*, June 23, 1980, p. 134.

22. Amendments to the Federal Rules of Civil Procedure, 48 L.W. 4497 (1980).

23. See, for example, Graley v. Satayatham, 74 Ohio Op. 2d 316, 343 N.E. 2d 832 (Ohio C.P. 1976).

24. See Letter, *New York Times*, June 19, 1980, p. A22.

25. Peter H. Schuck, "The Graying of Civil Rights Law: The Age Discrimination Act of 1975," 89 *Yale L. J.* 27 (1979). The quoted sections are at pp. 93, 82, 91–92, 93.

26. For a contemporary analysis, see John Hart Ely, *Democracy and Distrust: A Theory of Judicial Review* (Cambridge: Harvard University Press, 1980).

27. Leonard W. Levy, *Judgments* (Chicago: Quadrangle Books, 1972), pp. 54, 56.

28. Paul D. Carrington, "Ceremony and Realism: Demise of Appellate Procedure," 66 *A.B.A.J.* 860, 861 (1980).

29. Morton Mintz and Jerry S. Cohen, *Power, Inc.* (New York: Viking, 1976), pp. 585, 579.

30. John H. Barton, "Beyond the Legal Explosion," 27 *Stan. L. Rev.* 567, 582 (1975).

31. Sherlock v. Stillwater Clinic, 260 N.W.2d 169 (Minn. 1977).

32. Justice Rehnquist's address is excerpted in *National Law Journal*, July 28, 1980, pp. 15–16.

Acknowledgments

I have profited from discussions with many people, lawyers and litigants, who have experienced lawsuits firsthand. In particular, I am grateful to the following for their willingness to sit for interviews or to answer what to them must have seemed my thick-headed queries: Lori B. Andrews, Sheila Birnbaum, Thomas Ehrlich, Anita Johnson, Earl Johnson, Jr., Angus Macbeth, Victor E. Schwartz, Dr. Julius Shulman, and Aaron D. Twerski. I record special debts to Martin Kessler of Basic Books, who can prod gently and coax literary form from an author contemplating too many roads on the map; and to Ruth Gales for her splendid copy editing. Thanks also to Nancy Brooke Freeman, who always managed to secure elusive bits of information through the telephone and who typed manuscript drafts tirelessly, speedily, and usually even cheerfully. Once again Susan and the children (who helped with the index) bore it all stoically, though Jessica and Seth carried on a fierce debate over the virtues and vices of a typewriter's clacking on school nights.

Index of Cases

Index